# JOHN McLAUGHLIN

# JOHN McLAUGHLIN

## From Miles and Mahavishnu to The 4th Dimension

## MATT PHILLIPS

ROWMAN & LITTLEFIELD
*Lanham • Boulder • New York • London*

Published by Rowman & Littlefield
An imprint of The Rowman & Littlefield Publishing Group, Inc.
4501 Forbes Boulevard, Suite 200, Lanham, Maryland 20706
www.rowman.com

86-90 Paul Street, London EC2A 4NE

British Library Cataloguing in Publication Information Available

**Library of Congress Cataloging-in-Publication Data**

Names: Phillips, Matt, 1972- author.
Title: John McLaughlin : from Miles and Mahavishnu to the 4th Dimension / Matt Phillips.
Description: Lanham : Rowman & Littlefield, 2023. | Includes bibliographical references and index.
Identifiers: LCCN 2023017859 (print) | LCCN 2023017860 (ebook) | ISBN 9781538170946 (cloth) | ISBN 9781538170953 (epub)
Subjects: LCSH: McLaughlin, John, 1942- | Mahavishnu Orchestra. | Shakti (Musical group) | Guitarists—Biography. | Jazz musicians—Biography. | McLaughlin, John, 1942—Criticism and interpretation. | Jazz-rock (Music)—History and criticism.
Classification: LCC ML419.M36 P55 2023 (print) | LCC ML419.M36 (ebook) | DDC 787.87/165092 [B]—dc23/eng/20230419
LC record available at https://lccn.loc.gov/2023017859
LC ebook record available at https://lccn.loc.gov/2023017860

# CONTENTS

# INTRODUCTION

*"The key to understanding JM: he serves Music.
This is what confers upon John his authority, power and
stature as a musician.*

*All else follows from this: technique, vocabulary, musicianship.*

*A leading player of his generation? Certainly.*
The *leading player of his generation? Probably."*

—Robert Fripp
Chiswick, London
Thursday, February 9, 2023

## TUESDAY, FEBRUARY 18, 1969: COLUMBIA STUDIOS B, 30TH STREET, NEW YORK CITY

John McLaughlin walked into Columbia Studios at around 10 a.m. on only his second full day in New York City. As the twenty-seven-year-old English guitarist arrived in the performance area, world-famous Miles Davis and a selection of other all-time-great jazz and fusion players (Herbie Hancock, Joe Zawinul, Chick Corea, Wayne Shorter, Tony Williams) were listening to a rough, home-recorded demo of Zawinul's composition *In A Silent Way*, originally written in 1967. There was a brief greeting from Miles, a brief setup of John's Gibson Hummingbird guitar and amp, and the session got underway. John's life would never be the same again.

He was given a photostat of the piano part, featuring lots of chords. On the first rundown of the tune, Shorter and Miles shared the melody, John and the three keyboard players took care of the harmony, while Williams laid down his version of a bossa-nova beat. Afterward, Miles requested an instant playback from producer Teo Macero, as was his wont. He wasn't happy with what he heard, to say the least. His solution was very swift and also very characteristic, as John remembered:

> He turned to me and said 'Play it on the guitar'. I asked: 'Do you want the melody and chords?' He said: 'Yeah.' I said it's going to take a minute for me to put the two parts together. And he said: 'Is that a fact?' And I was already nervous . . . I was sweating, my clothes were wet . . . I couldn't do it with the piano part. And so here he's waiting for me to do something. And he says: 'Play it like you don't know how to play the guitar.' I mean, what does that mean? That's right out of Zen book, isn't it? Anyway, I knew I had to do something in 10 minutes. So I just threw all the chords out. I put it in E—because anybody knows how to play E on the guitar. No tempo, no chords—and I just played the melody like that. The red light was on by the time I started. I heard Wayne come in, and Miles came in, and we got to the end. And Miles loved it! And I was in shock because he was able to pull something out of me that I didn't know I was capable of doing. I didn't even know what I was playing and he loved it so much he put it at the opening and closing of side one.[1]

*In A Silent Way* was certainly a trial by fire for the young guitarist, but John had earned his shot at the big time. As Steve Martin once said, "Good luck is preparation meeting opportunity." John's NYC sojourn was the catalyst, after a decade of slogging around the British and European jazz, R'n'B, and pop circuits, for one of the most remarkable career turnarounds in modern music, and the beginning of his global fame as a thoroughbred guitarist, composer, bandleader, and conceptualist of the 1970s and beyond.

In the hierarchy of British "jazz" musicians, John arguably holds an unassailable position at the very top. After all, he has mastered several forms of music, influenced legions of guitarists, and carved out one of the most critic-proof careers in music, constantly sidestepping expectations. He has earned respect and plaudits from fans, writers, and musicians all over the world, from Munich to Mumbai. While certainly not the first musician to blend Western and Eastern music, he undoubtedly brought that fusion to a wider audience than ever before, also bringing an intense philosophical curiosity and rigorous discipline to bear on both his life and art. But these explorations have produced anything but a po-faced, "academic" assimilation of cultures; conversely, they have generally been light on their feet, stimulating, sometimes humorous, often explosive, occasionally infuriating, but always relatively accessible.

While possessing a phenomenal technique and seemingly endless ability to develop new ideas and maximize his raw talent, John's music has never depended on mere technical excellence at the expense of emotion. Even his very occasional artistic failures contain rich pickings for research and development. He has also paved the way for countless musicians seeking to fuse jazz, rock, and other esoteric influences, while—it has to be said—spawning many inferior imitators, who generally drew on only the most combustive elements of his music while scrimping on the harmonic sophistication.

Of course, there's some serendipity to all this trailblazing—the guitar was arguably *the* instrument of the 1950s and 1960s, and John made it his business to fully explore its harmonic and technical potential. He took up the guitar at a time when thousands of other young people were doing the same, influenced by the blues and skiffle booms of the mid-to-late 1950s and, later, the Beat revolution (though John was generally fairly scathing about the latter "scene," despite occasionally playing sessions for some of the key pop artists of the day, as we'll see later).

Purely from a guitar standpoint, it's instructive to compare John's career to some near-contemporaries whose formative years also took place during the British baby boom: Jimmy Page, Eric Clapton, Albert Lee, Pete Townshend, Andy Summers, Keith Richards, Ronnie Wood, and Peter Green. It's pretty clear that—a passion for the blues aside—John has little in common with these players. His career has been hugely eclectic in comparison. The only British guitarists of a similar vintage who would seem to approach his worldview are Jeff Beck (named by John in 2015 as his all-time favourite "progressive" musician[2]) and fellow Yorkshireman Allan Holdsworth. John peppered interviews with compliments about both players, and occasionally singled out Clapton, Tal Farlow, Bill Frisell, Django Reinhardt, Jimi Hendrix, John Scofield, and Scott Henderson for praise too. But he has generally been less enamored with guitarists than with saxophonists and pianists (and, after all, his first musical instrument was the piano). The knock-on effect of these non-guitar influences was a harmonically rich soundworld from a very early age, a world away from the three-chord trick.

Indeed, it might not be hyperbole to claim that John pursued music theory with such a rigorous discipline to "inoculate" himself against the type of future that might have awaited a typical young man of his generation, geography, and "class." He might easily have worked down a pit or in a factory (in his early days of gigging, he did, indeed, work an impressive variety of jobs to pay the rent).

And "pop" stardom was not on the agenda. Late in his career, John was openly scathing of such artists ("They've been playing the same stuff since the '60s, out of tune and out of time" was his verdict on The Rolling Stones in 2013[3]), though he enjoyed The Beatles' later work and some mid-1980s stars such as Prince and Billy Idol.

Perhaps most importantly, particularly influenced by Hendrix, Miles, Gil Evans, and John Coltrane, he placed the guitar at the center of an entirely new context, a mixture of jazz, rock, blues, classical, and ethnic musics, foregrounding improvisation and uncommon time signatures. Though other guitarists of a similar ilk were important in the 1960s and 1970s (a list that would have to include Bill Connors, Al Di Meola, Allan Holdsworth, Carols Santana, Steve Khan, Larry Coryell, John Abercrombie, Terje Rypdal, Raymond Gomez, and Jeff Beck), none could match John for compositional flair, unabashed expression, and sheer willpower, no doubt aided immeasurably by his choice of superstar, virtuosic sidemen (and, notably, sidewomen), particularly Jan Hammer on keyboards, L. Shankar on violin, Jaco Pastorius on bass, and drummers Billy Cobham and Narada Michael Walden, all of whom shared a special musical bond with John in the 1970s. This trend continued through the 1980s and 1990s, less so in the decades since.

John also seems like the perpetual seeker with a Zen-like "beginner's mind," someone who never presumes to "know it all." When we listen to his albums or watch him playing live, we hear a great improviser who is trying to communicate and develop new ideas in real time. He opened up on this subject to fellow guitarist Robert Fripp in a revealing 1982 interview from *Musician* magazine:[4]

> It's so hard because you're always looking for colors, for new scales, new chords, new ways to say what you feel . . . Idealistically, music should take what it wants so we should . . . allow it to be. That's difficult because it's a paradox. You have to know everything, then you have to forget it all. Learning is relatively easy. It's difficult to recommend how to get out of the way. That's what I'm learning how to do myself.

John's (and jazz/rock's) detractors have often cited his technical brilliance at the expense of emotional substance. Patently, this is poppycock. His solos on record are seldom perfect, nor would that ever be his goal. Compare any of his guitar statements on, say, *Apocalypse*, to any albums by Yngwie Malmsteen or Steve Vai, and you'll hear brave failures, even the occasional bum note, which, for a lesser guitarist, would necessitate a retake. Heavily influenced by Coltrane and Hendrix, he's more interested in spontaneity, the cry from the heart. Accordingly, he produces solos that consistently evoke the sound of surprise. More instructive than the "too many notes" debate may be Frank Zappa's Hendrix-referencing quote from a *Guitar Player* magazine interview in 1976, when he mentioned that he admired John's ability to use his guitar like a "machine gun."[5] Indeed, John's lead playing generally foregrounds a very hard, non-*legato* attack, with almost every note picked rather than "hammered-on," a legacy of his interest in both Big Bill Broonzy and Coltrane. Just as importantly, John also foregrounded his influences from Black music, blues, and jazz. Even when the music got "technical," as in some of the most extreme Mahavishnu excursions, there was always feeling and "groove." As his friend and collaborator Carlos Santana told Walter Kolosky in *Power, Passion & Beauty:* "If John didn't have the love he had for Black music, I wouldn't have cared for it. He would have sounded just like a heavy metal fast guy . . . I could hear Muddy Waters and all the rest in the music. Mahavishnu (John) just played it in seven!"[6]

Zappa and Coltrane may be apt comparisons with John in another key respect. Apart from them, Santana, and Fripp, it's hard to think of another major artist who has been embraced by such a wide variety of music enthusiasts, equally feted by progressive rock, jazz, fusion, and even classical fans. As such, John's followers have gotten used to surprises. This was a particular pleasure during the late 1980s and 1990s when he jumped from a raucous, techno-fusion reboot of The Mahavishnu Orchestra to an epic orchestral work inspired by the Mediterranean Sea, to a mostly acoustic, world-influenced chamber-jazz/rock group, to a turbo-charged Hammond Organ trio. Even when he seems to settle into a familiar style, such as the run of "classic fusion" albums during the 2000s and 2010s, he always throws in a curveball to challenge himself and his audience, such as 2019's striking one-off *Is That So?* And one hardly needs to look any further than 1974's *Apocalypse* and 2003's *Thieves And Poets* for evidence of a remarkably sophisticated expansion of the standard jazz or jazz/rock repertoire, moving into the realms of through-composed, symphonic music.

Reading most music writers on his work, you could be forgiven for thinking that John's musical potency ended in 1975; this writer begs to differ, and indeed would put the best of his 1980s and 1990s output on a par with anything from the 1970s. But then I'm prejudiced: one of the first gigs I ever attended was John's revamped Mahavishnu Orchestra at London's Hammersmith Odeon on July 12, 1984. Though fairly ignorant of his music at the time, I was a nascent drummer and huge Cobham fan (courtesy of a BBC drum clinic aired in March 1983). But a sign on the Hammersmith box-office door read, "Billy Cobham will not be appearing," and I was crestfallen. From memory, I turned to my dad—already a follower of John's music, mainly by dint of the Miles connection—and impetuously said, "Shall we just go home?" I'm glad he persuaded me otherwise; the excellent Danny Gottlieb filled in on drums (in controversial circumstances, of which more later), it was very loud, John played searing lead guitar sporting black shirt and black headband, and the crowd dug it.

It was the beginning of a love affair with the Yorkshireman's music. Across over forty official studio and live albums, encompassing solo, Mahavishnu Orchestra, Shakti, and co-headlining group projects, John's work has consistently enthralled and surprised, and this book will explore all of it. It's an attempt to bring together all the different strands of this great artist's recorded history. It's not a biography, nor a guitar inventory, nor an exhaustive survey of his 1960s session work, or an in-depth look at The Mahavishnu Orchestra—for those, Colin Harper's excellent *Bathed In Lightning/Glimpses From Then*, Walter Kolosky's *Power, Passion And Beauty*, and Johann Haidenbauer's online discography are heartily recommended, and all have been extremely helpful in the writing of this book. Rather, while investigating the session and Mahavishnu years, I'll focus mainly on his (somewhat neglected) later years as a solo artist, taking the approach of legendary A&R officer Seymour Stein, as outlined in his enjoyable memoir *Siren Song*. Stein worked in a branch of the industry usually known as Artist and Repertoire, but he preferred to think of it simply as People and Music. Those are the key elements of this book, written from the perspective of a fan and musician. As well as trying to explore and hopefully illuminate John's challenging, often majestic work, it'll also look at the lives and careers of the stellar musicians who shared stages and studios with him between 1969 and 2020.

# 1

# THE EARLY YEARS (1942–1968)

Like many Londoners, or at least those fortunate enough to have the financial wherewithal, John McLaughlin's parents moved up north when the Blitz began in earnest. As German bombs battered the capital, they took their four children and settled in Kirk Sandall, a small village in the borough of Doncaster, South Yorkshire. Fortunately, McLaughlin Sr. quickly found some engineering work in the area.

John was born in Kirk Sandall on January 4, 1942. He had three elder brothers—Robert, born in 1933; David, born in 1934; and Alan, born in 1936—and one sister, Florence, born in 1940. Robert, David, and Alan were all music fans, amateur musicians, and confirmed Francophiles, teaching John basic French from the age of three and later passing on their love of Gallic cinema. They were also naturally curious, somewhat philosophical young people; in February 2022, John recalled listening to his elder brothers' deliberations: "They used to discuss the existence of God. And the jury was always out. What that did for me was to encourage me to think for myself."[1]

John traces his first signs of loving music to hearing the final movement of Beethoven's *Ninth Symphony* on a 78 record at around seven years old: "It made my hair stand on end and gave me goosebumps. That was the first indication of what music could do to someone."[2] Also at the age of seven, John's parents separated, and his father essentially disappeared from his life at this point. John's mother took her sons and daughter to live with their grandmother in Monkseaton, a small village by the North Sea, about ten miles from Newcastle-upon-Tyne and near the Scottish border. Thankfully the new house came with a piano—John's sister was learning the instrument during this period, and at the age of nine John started taking lessons too (at his request), which he contin-ued to do for about three years, even though he was not a fan of his overstrict teacher, once describing her as a "dragon"[3]—she would smack his fingers with a ruler if he played a bum note. But all kinds of music fascinated him: "Every summer, the Scottish bagpipe bands used to come. Sometimes they had six or seven bagpipes, with three or four drummers . . . They had a big effect on me."[4] He had also been taught some violin by his mother, but he didn't take to the instrument.

## JOHN'S FIRST GUITAR

When John was around eleven, his brother Alan brought a classical (nylon-stringed) guitar into the house, "an old banger,"[5] according to John. His elder brothers were all becoming big fans of the blues and roots music in general, all of it rubbing off on John. Alan tried to sing some blues and folk songs but got "bored" with the guitar, passing it on to his younger brother David. David too quickly went off the instrument, but when he showed John a D chord, it was a musical epiphany for the younger brother. "I played the strings and a thrill went through my body."[6] He subsequently slept with the guitar every night.

John's siblings were apparently very supportive of his music from this mo-ment on: "My brothers saw right away what happened to me, and they said, 'OK, we've got to take care of our younger brother, because he's in love.'"[7] The piano was all but forgotten now, but the basic principles of that instrument would certainly come in handy later on as a composing tool (and frequently distinguish his compositions from other more "guitaristic" writers).

John became enamored with Mississippi Delta blues players Muddy Waters, Big Bill Broonzy, Leadbelly, and Sonny Terry, all of whom he'd heard on his brothers' gramophone. He loved the sound of the bottleneck, though initially he didn't have a clue what created it, and he developed a penchant for the har-monica, too. It's worth noting this was somewhat out of step with other music-loving British youth of the mid-1950s, who were more likely to be digging trad jazz or skiffle.

Then John's musical boundaries expanded even more with the discovery of Flamenco—particular early passions were guitarists Laurendo Almeida, Carlos Montoya, and guitarist/lutenist Narciso Yepes (who also pioneered a ten-string, nylon-string acoustic guitar, perhaps an inspiration for John during the Shakti era). He was also a big fan of classical maestro Julian Bream, frequently picked up via BBC radio broadcasts. At fourteen, John heard the Belgium-born,

Romani-French guitarist Django Reinhardt and was amazed; he quickly developed a feel for the type of linear, melodic lead playing that Reinhardt made famous, and he also adored the sound of Stephane Grappelli's violin.

At fifteen, John began guitar lessons and received a lot of encouragement from his school music teacher, who encouraged him to play little concerts in front of his class with whichever fellow students he could round up to accompany him. There was also a music club where he could listen to the hip jazz sounds of the day, Oscar Peterson's trio records, and Verve Records founder Norman Granz's *Jazz At The Philharmonic* albums featuring the likes of Lester Young, Charlie Parker, Ella Fitzgerald, and Dizzy Gillespie. In 1956, John heard the music of Tal Farlow coming out of a shop in Newcastle—the American guitarist became another new hero. John was struck by the originality of his harmonic concept, the richness of his chords, and the fluidity of his lines. As he told *Down Beat*'s Bud Koral in February 1973, "He was a great source of inspiration to me. I'm grateful to him and continue to learn from his work. His conception is so contemporary and he has incredible facility and a highly inventive approach to harmony."

During this time, John was playing in a skiffle band alongside his sister on vocals and a school friend Peter Simpson on double bass. He also started a melodic modern jazz quartet modeled on London pianist George Shearing's group. John developed a rich appreciation of East and West Coast schools, naturally preferring the former's grittier, more R'n'B-based roots, gravitating toward the music of Miles Davis, Cannonball Adderley, Charles Mingus, John Coltrane, Eric Dolphy, Thelonious Monk, and Sonny Rollins. But at the same time, classical music was looming large: "Bartok was stupendous; Anton Webern is to me a musician who realised the music of the spheres; Stravinsky is another one."[8] Meanwhile the BBC was broadcasting archivist Alan Lomax's Mississippi Delta Blues and *Temple Music* from South India, huge sources of intrigue and feeling.

## AWAKENING THE SPIRITUAL LIFE

John was also taking an interest in some of the deeper mysteries of life during his early teens. His mother was a confirmed agnostic (as were his siblings), very much against organized religion, but he recalled her taking him to the window one evening and pointing out the planet Mars, and also passing on Ray Bradbury's book *The Martian Chronicles*. John immediately became a huge sci-fi fan and regularly paid tribute to his mother in later life as a regular source of encouragement, support, and intellectual stimulation.

But the guitar was John's main passion. So enamored was he with the instrument, he started working in a repair shop at around sixteen years of age. He also did various other jobs during this time, including driving and farming, and traveled to London to play with a trad jazz band called Professors Of Ragtime. He was growing up fast and felt very strongly that he had to stand on his own two feet. "I left home when I was 15 or 16 and never went back."[9] He met his first proper partner, Margaret Ellen Grey, around this time; they had their first child in 1959 and married a year later.

Saxophone hero John Coltrane's seminal *Giant Steps* album had been released in 1960, becoming an instant favorite in the McLaughlin household. He also became fascinated by the 1960 album *Live In Stockholm*, credited to Miles Davis and John Coltrane, particularly a March 22 interview with the latter by Swedish journalist Carl-Erik Lindgren, who claimed some listeners perceived him as an "unbeautiful" player, to which Coltrane incredulously wondered if that was just another word for "angry." But that Swedish correspondent wasn't alone—legendary jazz critic Whitney Balliett's review of *Giant Steps* in *The New Yorker* proclaimed: "Coltrane's tone is harsh, flat, querulous, and at times almost vindictive . . . His tone is bleaker than need be."[10] Philip Larkin also didn't hold back during his introduction to *All What Jazz*:

> With John Coltrane, metallic and passionless nullity gave way to exercises in gigantic absurdity . . . extended investigations of oriental tedium, long-winded and portentous demonstrations of religiosity. It was with Coltrane, too, that jazz started to be ugly on purpose; his nasty tone would become more and more exacerbated until he was fairly screeching at you like a pair of demonically-possessed bagpipes.

## MOVING TO LONDON

In early 1960, John had moved his young family down south to the London suburbs—103 Buckland Way in Cheam, to be precise, an area possibly familiar to fans of BBC comedy classic *Hancock's Half Hour*—to look for work. He took a position at Selmer's music instrument shop on the Charing Cross Road, right in the center of town, and also one at its more guitar-focused sister premises, Lew Davies, at the junction of Tottenham Court Road and Denmark Street. John was getting a reputation as the top guitar repairman about town, and also very gently blowing people away with his dazzling technique. One visitor to Selmer's was future country-rock axe hero Albert Lee: "Everybody was in great admiration for his playing. I wouldn't say he was gregarious—a very quiet and gentle soul, really."[11] This is borne out by various musicians who remember him as a very shy, understated performer/person in his formative years. As future Soft Machine/Nucleus drummer John Marshall once noted, "He was there but not there."[12] A contributing factor, of course, was that John was already very much a family man, with a lot of responsibilities; his second daughter, Jacqueline, was born on April 2, 1961.

John was now picking up all kinds of gigs at the original Ronnie Scott's club (aka The Old Place) on Gerrard Street, The Flamingo on Wardour Street, and various other London pubs, and he would occasionally tour the country playing at US air force bases. He joined Georgie Fame and The Blue Flames around this time, enjoying a virtual residency at The Flamingo between June 1962 and January 1965. For jazz and blues/R'n'B musicians, this was the center of the universe as far as London clubs went. But many players also reported a distinct pecking order decreed by the club's management. In the BBC documentary *Jazz Britannia*, trumpeter Ian Carr recalled the two Gunnell brothers who owned the club—Rik and John—running down the road and screaming at him, "Jazz is dead! Jazz is dead!" (presumably in a rather drunken stupor) as he left the venue one night. On the other hand, Fame remembered being forbidden to use the Flamingo house piano for his mainly R'n'B-based music. Non-jazzers were expected to hire their own upright pianos. Fame saw which way the wind was blowing, got himself a Hammond organ, and the rest is history. (It's worth noting that this attitude was occasionally reversed—British keyboardist Django Bates fled the Royal College Of Music in the early 1980s after only two weeks when he saw a sign affixed to a piano that read: "Not to be used for the playing of jazz music.")

As well as The Flamingo, there were other regular gigs for John and The Blue Flames: an infamously rough Carnaby Street club called The Roaring 20s, the Eel Pie Island Club in Twickenham (famous for its role in the development of The Rolling Stones and Yardbirds later in the decade), The Scene on Great Windmill Street, Bag O' Nails on Kingly Street, and Klooks Kleek in West Hampstead's Railway Hotel, not far from Decca's recording studios. It was an exhausting schedule, though, with ten gigs a week not an uncommon occurrence. But contemporaries of John remember him as an exceptionally disciplined musician. Although drugs were fairly prevalent on the club scene, especially pills and marijuana, music was very much John's focus during this time.

# ENTER BOND, BRUCE, BAKER, KORNER, AND AUGER

As John's workload increased, he struck up a great musical and personal relationship with organist Brian Auger and also began playing with British blues pioneer Alexis Korner, often appearing onstage alongside bassist Jack Bruce, drummer Ginger Baker (with his homemade Plexiglas drums), and saxist Dick Heckstall-Smith. Bruce and Baker also joined John in The Blue Flames between February and April 1963, and all three of them swiftly gravitated toward The Graham Bond Quartet. This Hammond organist, alto saxist, singer, and composer was an extremely influential figure in John's life. In Ian Carr's book *Music Outside*, drummer and John's friend Jon Hiseman pushed Bond's musical credentials: "Graham was a crusader, a pathfinder . . . The bridge between improvised music and pop music was the blues . . . Graham Bond was one of the pioneers of that. Without him, there wouldn't have been bands like Yes and Cream and Hendrix." Bond's discussions with John were somewhat revelatory:

> He opened up my eyes to a side of myself I was unaware of. I started thinking about possibilities for myself, what my own potential was. He showed me this book about the Tarot . . . I became aware of man's inner faculties and capabilities and latent talents. I wanted to know more about it so I read more and more . . . I tried to relate it to music, only I had great difficulty . . . I started reading these books of a more esoteric nature and going to the Theosophical Society. It was through reading that I came into contact with the Indian philosophy. I also started to do some yoga exercises . . . breathing exercises and trying to do something about my body. In fact, just the process of concentrated relaxation is a very dynamic act.[13]

Bond also passed a book on to John—*The Third Eye* by Lobsang Rampa, published in 1956—that would soon become one of the guitarist's favorites.

It seems that John's first-ever studio recording took place on February 20, 1963, when The Blue Flames recorded "I Saw Her Standing There" (first seeing the light of day on the 2002 Duffy Power anthology *Leapers & Sleepers*). In April, The Graham Bond Quartet played their first gigs at Klooks Kleek, augmented by Heckstall-Smith on saxes, later immortalized on the *Solid Bond* album (which also featured John's first writing credit on "The Grass Is Greener"). But both Baker and Bruce also attest to John's nervousness onstage around this period. For whatever reason, his time with the band was fairly short. He later claimed he left due to the group's lack of success, saying: "We couldn't get any money. People just didn't like what we were doing. They weren't ready for it yet."[14] But Baker had a different take on John's departure—he claims he was sick of John's complaining, finally shouting: "Why don't you fuck off then?" Either way, John fucked off, replaced by Heckstall-Smith. But (much) later, Baker was contrite: "We lost a great guitar player and I lost a good friend," he wrote in his memoir, *Hellraiser*.

The year 1964 brought John regular R'n'B gigs at The Pigalle, just off Piccadilly Circus. By the end of the year, he also had a new baby son to take care of. It was a time of great hardship, with a lot of family responsibilities. Things then got even worse when suddenly he was living alone, separated from his wife. But, conversely, his musical life was looking up: he met bassist Rick Laird while playing some gigs at Ronnie's—Laird was the house bassist, backing superstar American visitors like Freddie Hubbard and Ben Webster. Then John and Laird started working with Auger in a tough R'n'B band. John reported feeling more "connected" to his instrument, his research and study finally paying off:

> One night we were playing, and suddenly the spirit entered into me. I was playing but it was no longer me playing. It was coming through me in a never-ending stream, and it was just delight, fulfilment and joy. I became aware that this thing was a permanent state if one could just reach it.[15]

John became interested in the quest to find that spiritual state in music, also observing it in other performers: "From the point of view of going to concerts myself, if a musician is struggling that night and he's fighting and he doesn't have his shit together, that fact that he's fighting is something beautiful to behold, because it's a human being fighting with his feelings."[16]

## TEACHING GUITAR AND HEARING
## A LOVE SUPREME

John found time to give future Led Zeppelin guitarist Jimmy Page some guitar lessons while working in Selmer's during 1964. Talking to *Guitar Player*'s Steve Rosen in July 1977, Page remembered: "(John) always had that technique right from when I first knew him when he was working in a guitar shop. I would say he was the best jazz guitarist in England then, in the traditional mode of Johnny Smith and Tal Farlow; a combination of those two is exactly what he sounded like."[17]

But outside his Blue Flames "day job," John's first recording as a session player seems to have been on a track called "365 Rolling Stones," credited to

The Andrew Oldham Orchestra and written by future Stones manager Oldham with arranger Mike Leander. It was released by Decca in April 1964. It was not the most auspicious start to his freelance recording career, however, mainly strumming E and A chords. Other tracks from these sessions were collected on the *Metamorphosis* compilation, credited to The Rolling Stones and released in 1975, also featuring drummers Alan White (later of The Plastic Ono Band and Yes) and Clem Cattini, plus Page on guitar and his future Led Zeppelin colleague John Paul Jones on bass. It started a period of regular work for John at the Decca Studios, including a Dionne Warwick session led by Burt Bacharach in November 1964. He also worked on Bacharach's score for the feature film *What's New Pussycat* in early 1965.

On the jazz side, John also began to play with drummer John Stevens, sometimes alongside Laird, in a very free quartet that often played at the Bull's Head in Barnes, by the Thames River in Southwest London. He was perfectly primed for the release of John Coltrane's *A Love Supreme* around this time—it was an absolute revelation: "It had a tremendous influence on me musically and spiritually. I will always read that back cover. It's a statement by a great, noble human being."

The album also made it abundantly clear—as he had hinted for a few years— that Coltrane was more than a little interested in Indian music, and that its influence was seeping into his own compositions. He had been corresponding with sitar master Ravi Shankar as early as 1961, and in 1963 he told esteemed Norwegian jazz writer Randi Hultin: "I've been interested in Ravi Shankar a long time, and I hope that I'll meet him one day."[18] The two did finally meet during November 1965 in New York City. According to J. C. Thomas's *Chasin' The Trane*, they had dinner together, Coltrane choosing a vegetable cutlet and Shankar ordering chicken, for which he apologized to the saxophonist: "I like chicken when I am on a rigorous touring schedule. It helps me keep up my strength." The next day, they had a long talk, with Shankar explaining many of the tenets of Indian music, and then the sitarist attended a Coltrane concert at the Village Gate later that evening. Shankar is quoted as saying: "The music was fantastic. I was much impressed, but one thing distressed me. There was a turbulence in the music that gave me a negative feeling at times but I could not quite put my finger on the trouble."

Apart from an interest in Indian music, Coltrane and McLaughlin also shared an interest in esoterica—Sonny Rollins reportedly turned Coltrane on to Paramahansa Yogananda's *Autobiography Of A Yogi*, Bill Evans recommended him Krishnamurti's *Commentaries On Living*, and visitors to Coltrane's home would have noticed books about Egyptology, Scientology, and Greek philosophy.

His spiritual life might have been expanding rapidly, but back in London, John was still occasionally working at Selmer's in 1965, selling the Who's Pete Townshend his first amp: "It was a Fender Pro. He and I often talked about Indian mysticism, but I didn't meditate."[10] But Townshend also testified to John's natural benevolence in an interview with *Guitar Player*'s Matt Resnicoff in October 1989:

> He was always generous and particular in his recommendations to me even when he was a guitar salesman at Selmer. His playing even then was inspirational, and his willingness to listen and appreciate my own basic rhythmic style gave me a lot of confidence.

## SWINGING LONDON: BOWIE, DONOVAN, TOM JONES, AND PETULA CLARK

London had seriously started swinging in 1965, but for John it was all work, work, work—and musically, not a particularly fulfilling time: "By the time the Beatles came out I was a jazz snob. I was struggling because I couldn't find any guitar player that really spoke to me. The only people who spoke to me were Miles, Trane and Bill Evans and their drummers."[20] (John did, however become a major Beatles fan later, with the releases of *Revolver* and *Sgt. Pepper's*.)

He was picking up a lot of work on the session scene but struggling to come up with a guitar concept that could match Coltrane's. What he did know was that his jazz had to have feeling and soul: "You take the R&B out of jazz, you don't have any jazz. That's why I love Mingus and Monk, because you could feel the blues so deeply in their music."[21]

On February 25, 1965, John played guitar on an album called *British Percussion*, credited to Le London All Stars and recorded at Pye Studios. It featured the cream of the session crop playing psychedelic rock and jazz-tinged R'n'B, designed to show off the pleasures of stereophonic sound. But it was another disappointment—unfortunately, John was reduced to playing fairly humdrum rhythm guitar while Page took all the fuzz-toned solos, and his credit on the sleeve read "Johnnie Mac Cloughlin" upon the album's release in September.

A slightly more rewarding project saw him join Herbie Goins and the Night-Timers, a soul/blues band, alongside organist Mike Carr, brother of trumpeter/composer Ian. John co-wrote "Cruisin'" for their Norman Smith–produced album *No.1 In Your Heart*, recorded at Abbey Road Studios. The title track was released as a single in July 1966, with "Cruisin'" as the B-side. Another single was also issued featuring John, "The Music Played On/Yield Not To Temptation." He was essentially playing James Brown licks in that band, no hardship for him: "I love funk music. I remember seeing Sly & the Family Stone in '69 and I was in ecstasy."[22]

John continued to be in demand as a session player throughout 1966, as live dates with the Blue Flames and Night-Timers wound down. "There You Go" by Duffy Power, recorded in the summer of 1966, is a good portrait of John's musical mood at the time—its potent chordal work and rock-hard attack elevate a fairly standard blues/R'n'B strut. In December 1966, John played sessions at Decca Studios with singer Tom Jones and also recorded "Mellow Yellow" with Donovan, with John Paul Jones as musical director and Paul McCartney on backing vocals, a top-ten single in the UK and the United States.

But though John's playing was still turning heads everywhere, he felt he was treading water. The session scene was also fraught with uncertainty and nerves—many were afflicted with Red Light Fever (a fear of going into "record" mode). Some, like Big Jim Sullivan, took up meditation and yoga to calm themselves. Laird jumped ship and went to study at the legendary Berklee College of Music in Boston, lamenting the loss of the London live scene. Drug use was also becoming more prevalent, though it's important to note that LSD and acid were not illegal in the UK (though marijuana was) until much later, in 1970. "Everybody was tripping," says John. "I was into it, totally. We were all looking for an experience of liberation, for pure, total satisfaction with existence, that can only be obtained from inside."[23] John's use of the drug was very short-lived, though: "After six or seven trips, I got the message. I knew what I had to do. The world was not gonna change but *I* was gonna change. And I changed."[24]

This change was apparent to musicians around him—drummer Jon Hiseman, who replaced Ginger Baker in both The Graham Bond Organization and Georgie Fame's post–Blue Flames band, remembers: "He was the first person I met who was trying to find an inner something. He was trying to love everybody."[25] John's meditation classes had begun in earnest around the spring of 1967, and he was still regularly attending the Theosophical Society. He had developed an interest in Ramana Maharshi, a Hindu sage who had died in 1950, and the British philosopher Douglas Harding. He also entered a new phase in his personal life, moving to leafy Belsize Park in north London with his new wife, Marlene, in tow.

Meanwhile, John reluctantly played out the last gasp of his London studio session career. He worked on two dreary singles by Biddu, "Daughter Of Love" and "Look Out, Here I Come" alongside Page and Jones, and two David Bowie singles during September 1967, "Karma Man" and "Let Me Sleep Beside You," later released on the *World Of David Bowie* album. John would also perform with Bowie on a John Peel BBC *Top Gear* session on May 13, 1968 (alongside keyboard player/future *Grange Hill/Countdown* British TV theme composer Alan Hawkshaw and session bassist Herbie Flowers), possibly the last session he ever did.

## EMERGENCY!: JOHN QUITS THE POP SCENE

By the autumn of 1967, John was seriously in turmoil and made the decision to end his studio career after eighteen months of solid work. He failed to turn up for a session at Decca Studios at the very last minute, literally turning his car around and driving off in the other direction. But as a consequence, he was quickly hard up again, having to sell his 1960 L4C guitar with its Charlie Christian pickup. "I was back to my poverty-stricken days but at least happy not having to go and deal with Tom Jones and Petula Clark. Not that I don't like them personally but it's different when you're in a session doing their music."[26] This was a huge decision, though, one to which many session fixers didn't take kindly. But John was adamant. He might also have been influenced by the news of John Coltrane's death on July 17, 1967.

Though he was still recording with Georgie Fame—on the *Knock On Wood* and *Three Faces Of Fame* albums—John was gravitating more and more toward jazz, where he could explore his instrumental palette to its full spectrum. On September 18, 1967, he appeared with bassist Danny Thompson's trio, alongside multi-reedist Tony Roberts, for a BBC *Jazz Club* concert, released on CD in 2003 as *Live 1967*, featuring standards including Coltrane's "Naima," Miles's "All Blues," and Dave Brubeck's "In Your Own Sweet Way." It's an essential artefact of where John's head and heart were at the time, showcasing clean, undistorted, flowing bebop lines, but with trademark close-interval voicings and use of open strings. This band also played an early version of John's composition "Plectrum Spectrum," later to feature on his solo debut *Extrapolation*.

Then, via a gig with pianist Gordon Beck, John began to play with Tony Oxley, the formidable house drummer at Ronnie Scott's (renamed The Old Place as it played out its last eighteen months of existence). The gifted, though troubled Beck (Ian Carr reported that "he seems to be in a constant state of despair about the selfishness and depravity of human nature, the sickness of the consumer society, the frailty of the whole economic structure of the West" in *Music Outside*, though he also conceded that "as soon as he starts to play the piano, he gives the lie to his own gloom, because his playing is full of joy") recorded the classic album *Experiments With Pops* at London's Lansdowne Studios in December 1967 alongside John and Oxley, a record still seen as a totem of British jazz at the time of writing. Released in April 1968 on Marmalade Records (of which much more later), a subsidiary of Polydor, it's another key exhibit of John's playing during this period, showcasing fiery single-note lines and authentic comping on tunes such as Jimmy Webb's "Up, Up And Away" and even The Who's "I Can See For Miles." John joined Beck's trio for a series of pub gigs around London to support the album.

John was moving ever further into the jazz world at the outset of 1968. He enjoyed a healthy working relationship with Canadian ex-pat trumpeter/flugelhorn player Kenny Wheeler, whose concept album, *Windmill Tilter*—a riff on Cervantes's Don Quixote story—is another pillar of British jazz. John Dankworth, whose Orchestra shared a credit on the album, had also employed Wheeler extensively on his own concept albums of the 1960s (*What The Dickens*, *Zodiac Variations*). In his liner notes for *Windmill Tilter*, Dankworth singled out John's playing, describing him very shrewdly as "an inscrutable genius who could deserve an LP of his own." Despite that, John's soloing was limited to fairly short features on three numbers, ensemble comping mainly being the order of the day among a nineteen-piece band, including bassist Dave Holland. Apart from the occasional nod to the Oliver Nelson school of "outside" blues, the album had an unmistakably British hue.

## TOWARD *EXTRAPOLATION*: ENTER GUNTER HAMPEL AND JOHN SURMAN

John was spending more and more time at The Old Place in early 1968. He performed there with pianist and fellow Yorkshireman Howard Riley on January 21, reportedly telling Riley that his dream was to play with Miles Davis. Riley claims he loaned John the £100 he needed to get on a plane to New York City there and then.

The Old Place was also where John's first, short-lived headlining "band," featuring multi-reedist John Surman, bassist Holland, and Oxley, would begin to meet for occasional rehearsals in early 1968. Surman was a recent arrival in London, settling in the capital in 1962 after growing up in Devon. He then spent three years at the London College of Music studying clarinet, then a further year at London University doing a Diploma in Education. His own quartet had been operating around town by 1966, and he had been picking up work with composer Mike Westbrook's band. John and Surman had also played together on Georgie Fame's "Try My World" in the summer of 1967.

As Surman and John's orbits converged, slowly but surely John was focusing on his own compositions. To some extent, these were informed by his favorite avant-garde sounds from across the pond, the "fire music" of Albert Ayler, Pharoah Sanders, and Don Cherry. Meanwhile The Old Place finally closed its doors on May 25, 1968, with Ronnie permanently moving to new premises on Frith Street, where it resides right up to the time of this writing. John moved with his wife and son from Belsize Park to Ealing, into a block of flats under drummer/Little Theatre Club (another key hangout for jazzers) co-founder John Stevens and his wife, Anne.

But the opening of the new Ronnie's and John's relocation precipitated another period of personal and professional turmoil, culminating in divorce from his second wife. In an echo of Sonny Rollins's famous sojourn on the Williamsburg between 1959 and 1961, which led to the album *The Bridge*, John disappeared up north to Whitley Bay during the early summer of 1968 to work on his guitar technique and recharge his batteries. "One day, I said to myself: I cannot do this any more. I got into my car and just drove and didn't stop until I got to northern England and I stayed with my mother. It was a question of sanity for me."[27]

By late July, John was rejuvenated and back in London, moving in with Holland and working with the Chris McGregor Group at Ronnie's. Drummer Jack DeJohnette was also appearing there with piano legend Bill Evans. John jammed with Holland and DeJohnette during a few afternoons at the club. Miles Davis stopped by to hear Holland playing with vocalist Elaine Delmar, and John was introduced to Miles—an event that would have huge reverberations. By August 1968, Holland had moved to New York to join up with Miles's band, debuting with the quintet at Count Basie's Lounge in Harlem after no rehearsal. "Of course we were all proud when Dave was leaving for New York to play with Miles," John remembered in 1982. "Imagine, an Englishman to play with Miles—it was unheard of at that time. A real coup!"[28]

Meanwhile, Surman was making an enormous impact on the international jazz scene. His performance with Mike Westbrook led to him being voted the best soloist of the 1968 Montreux Jazz Festival, and he was also carving out a niche for himself by focusing mainly on the baritone sax. For his part, John guested on five tracks of Jack Bruce's *Things We Like* album for Polydor, alongside Hiseman and Heckstall-Smith, particularly tearing it up on the funky jazz/R'n'B of "Sam Enchanted Dick." (In his liner notes to the 2003 remaster, Bruce claims he only invited John to play on the album so that the guitarist could earn some money to get over to New York to play with Tony Williams.) Heckstall-Smith also proved something of a confidante to John around this time, as both had recently separated from their wives.

John left London again in the autumn of 1968, traveling to Brussels to work with Gunter Hampel, a German multi-instrumentalist who had recently embraced spiritual jazz in a big way and whose debut international release—*Music From Europe*—had received a rave *Down Beat* review in 1966. They played live on and off throughout 1968 under the banner Time Is Now, often with John's friend Laurie Allan in the drum chair, including a memorable September 29 gig in Essen, Germany, supporting Frank Zappa and The Mothers Of Invention. Another key concert with Hampel occurred in early November at the three-day Total Music festival in Berlin alongside The Spontaneous Music Ensemble. Pharoah Sanders and guitarist Sonny Sharrock joined John onstage for a memorably raucous performance.

Back in London, John briefly formed a trio with Hiseman and bassist Binky McKenzie as a testing ground for his own material, though it was over by the time Hiseman and Heckstall-Smith formed jazz/rock/prog supergroup Colosseum in October 1968. Then, in early November, John received a phone call from Tony Williams in Baltimore—where the drummer was performing with Miles—about forming a new band. Williams explained that Holland had played him a recording of one of John and the bassist's jam sessions at Ronnie Scott's earlier in the year. This, of course, was music to John's ears. But since Williams didn't have any concrete recording or gigging plans, John stayed in London for the time being, occasionally traveling to Europe to play with Hampel.

Then, suddenly, it was January 1969. The stars were aligning for John, and it would be a year of immense upheaval but also great professional development. The first task was to record a debut solo album.

**2**

# 1969–1970

*Extrapolation*, Miles, and Lifetime

John McLaughlin: Acoustic and electric guitar, composer
Tony Oxley: drums
John Surman: Baritone and soprano saxophone
Brian Odgers: Bass
Produced by Giorgio Gomelsky
Recorded at Advision Studios, London, on January 18, 1969

The summer of 1968 was a pivotal time for John, both personally and professionally; he met and fell in love with Catherine Eve Wright via their mutual friend Pete Brown, the lyricist and poet who had written lyrics for Cream's hits "I Feel Free" and "White Room," and then came the opportunity to record his debut solo album.

*Extrapolation* was essentially the brainchild of Giorgio Gomelsky, manager of The Brian Auger Trinity and co-owner of the Station Hotel and Crawdaddy in Richmond, south-west London. Both venues had been crucial stomping grounds for The Rolling Stones and Yardbirds, the latter another band Gromelsky had managed earlier in the 1960s. He started his own progressive imprint, Marmalade—a subsidiary of Polydor—in 1967, and asked Auger for advice on whom he should record for his new label. Auger immediately suggested John: "At the time, I thought he was the best jazz guitar player in Europe and on a par with the Americans. The other guy I recommended was John Surman."[1] Luckily, John was already rehearsing with Surman, but now John had to fill out the rest of the quartet. He had hoped Dave Holland would join them on bass, but John, Holland, Surman, and drummer Tony Oxley only managed one gig at London's 100 Club in late summer 1968 before Holland had left for New York to play with Miles. So, the very dependable Brian Odgers—a regular on the London scene—came on board.

John's choice of drummer seemed shrewd and very *au currant*—in the December 1968 edition of *Melody Maker*, none other than Billy Cobham passed comment on Ronnie Scott's house skinsman Oxley (Cobham had been playing at the club with American pianist Horace Silver): "I think he's one of the best drummers I've ever seen."[2] McLaughlin had tried out various contenders before settling on Oxley, who later proclaimed he had mixed feelings about the *Extrapolation* session, doubting its solid jazz credentials and professing complete ignorance as to why anyone would like it. For his part, John looked back on Oxley's contribution during a 2008 interview with mixed emotions: "He was totally influenced by Tony Williams. He stole everything from Tony, except being Tony himself." But in the same interview he did later concede that Oxley "had wonderful colors."[3] To be fair, on the evidence of *Extrapolation*, both Williams and Elvin Jones are Oxley's touchstones rather than simply the former, hardly outrageous choices since they were by far the most influential jazz drummers of the mid-to-late 1960s.

There were only a few rehearsals for *Extrapolation*—one in the basement of Ronnie's, and several other duo sessions with pianist Bob Cornford, who had played with John on Kenny Wheeler's *Windmill Tilter*. The album was taken up exclusively with John's original compositions, material that challenged Surman in particular: "It was full of monsterly difficult time-signature things. I was still in the stage where a waltz was as tough of a time signature as I got! He was a very ahead-of-it performer."[4]

Gomelsky's choice of studio was Advision, one of the key rock and pop recording venues in central London, situated on Gosfield Street in Fitzrovia and previously used by The Move, T-Rex, The Who, and Yardbirds. In 1982, John claimed that *Extrapolation* was recorded in "two or three afternoons,"[5] but the album sleeve pinpoints its recording date as January 18, 1969. Gomelsky is credited as producer, but Auger is convinced he had no creative or technical input.

The title track retains a Dolphy-esque, quirky charm, John clearly reveling in showcasing Surman's rum, bold baritone sound. At 0:51, the guitarist serves notice of his incredibly advanced rhythmic vocabulary, playing triplets with unpredictable emphases. He has never before sounded so "free," so avant-garde, even throwing in some Sharrock-like squalls here and there during his brief solo. "It's Funny" is a medium-slow waltz with Surman switching to soprano, Oxley delighting in occasionally doubling up the time, and John making the most of his open strings, also adding a little "dirt" to his sound during the solo. The first few notes of "It's Funny" were sampled by hip-hop pioneer Madlib on his posthumously released track "Real Days."

"Arjen's Bag" is in 11/8 and was later reformatted by John for his composition "Follow Your Heart." It was named for Arjen Gorter, the Dutch bassist who worked alongside John in Gunter Hampel's band. Surman summons some fire for his baritone solo, and there's the first sign of reverb both on the saxophone and guitar, possibly added via the Advision echo chamber. "Arjen's Bag" was later covered by Soft Machine on their 1974 album *Seven*, appearing as "Day's Eye," but for reasons unknown not credited to John. "Arjen's Bag" segues straight into "Pete The Poet," a fast waltz named for the aforementioned Pete Brown. Oxley cleverly parrots John's phrase at 1:36 and then subverts the time into 4/4. At 2:19, we hear the first evidence of another of John's future trademarks—triplet-flavored, hammered-on/pulled-off chord clusters—before Oxley's very Elvin Jones–like solo with a lot of reverb added to his snare drum.

"This Is for Us to Share," dedicated to Eve, sees John playing an acoustic nylon-string guitar for the intro before switching to electric and using the sorts of maj-9th chords that will reverberate through his career. It's the least successful track on the album, with a rather unfocused, rubato feel and unsubtle Oxley performance.

"Spectrum" is a fast, bebop-tinged tune pitched somewhere between Charlie Parker and Coltrane's soundworlds. Surman attacks with some gritty lines while John delivers some amazingly deft muted lines during his solo, with a touch of Tal Farlow in the descending sixteenth notes. "Spectrum" was also performed on the Lifetime album *Emergency!*, credited to one A. Hall, a John pseudonym. Its original title was "Spectrum/Plectrum"—BBC archives reveal a performance of that name with the Danny Thompson Trio. Another seamless segue leads into "Binky's Beam," named for gifted London bassist Michael Keith Winston "Binky" McKenzie, who had befriended John during a Duffy Power session ("Just Stay Blue") in 1967. In the immediate aftermath of John's tribute recording, Binky McKenzie's life took on a tragic hue—in July 1971, he killed his mother, father, and brother-in-law and seriously injured his sister. He was convicted of three counts of manslaughter, and one of diminished responsibility, and detained at Broadmoor Prison in 1972, where he resides up to the time of this writing. "Binky's Beam" is a vehicle for John's arpeggiated chords, a slow tune in 9/8 later sped up to create "Celestial Terrestrial Commuters" on the Mahavishnu Orchestra's *Birds Of Fire* album.

The ballad "Really You Know" seems influenced by Thelonious Monk's composition style in general and "Round Midnight" in particular. From a guitar standpoint, John again leans toward Farlow with his clean, speedy lines. "Two For Two" (the title presumably a riff on the Youmans/Caesar standard "Tea For Two") kicks off with a scarily fast head, followed by a demonstration of John's violent chord style on twelve-string semi-acoustic. "Peace Piece" rounds off the album in brief but subtle fashion. John explores modes and single-note lines on unaccompanied gut-string acoustic, his bottom E string tuned down to a D, to create what is essentially a *raga*.

*Extrapolation*'s rushed preparation and recording hasn't stopped it from gaining a fabled reputation in the years since its release. "One of the finest jazz records ever made in Europe. Essential and timeless" was Brian Morton and Richard Cook's verdict in *The Penguin Guide To Jazz On CD*. Indeed, it retains a magical atmosphere; courtesy of Advision house engineer Eddy Offord, it's beautifully recorded (one can hear all the overtones of Oxley's ride cymbal) and features some flowing, inspired performances. Solos are generally brief and right to the point. John's compositions foreground melodic heads that merely suggest a "flavour" for the subsequent improvizations. Several tracks segue without a break, giving the feel of a song cycle, though this may have been necessitated by the brief recording time given to the album.

The title is interesting, too—in what sense is it an extrapolation? Presumably it's an extrapolation of John's somewhat limited pre-1969 recording history, a long-overdue personal statement with the emphasis clearly on jazz rather than rock or pop. Certainly his "searching" guitar sound/style was hitting a nerve with musicians and listeners alike—writer Chip Stern summed up this very well in a recent YouTube comment: "I was looking for someone who embodied what I was hearing from the likes of Monk and Eric Dolphy and Don Cherry on the guitar, and, in retracing his steps and my own, I still get that same buzz of something . . . NEW."[6]

But *Extrapolation* only got a very limited release in the UK and Europe. In 1972, it was issued for the first time in the United States following the success of The Mahavishnu Orchestra's debut album, reaching No.152 on the *Billboard* chart. It was certainly a springboard for Surman and Oxley, though—the latter subsequently became one of the stars of the 1969 Montreux Jazz Festival, playing as part of Alan Skidmore's ensemble that also featured Wheeler on flugelhorn and John Taylor on piano. Oxley walked away with a Best Drummer award. (Skidmore also won Best Musician, and his ensemble got a critics' award for Best Group.)

Both Surman and Oxley would then subsequently play on Skidmore's acclaimed 1970 debut album, *Once Upon A Time*. (Skidmore, too, sensed Oxley's conflicted attitude to playing "straight" jazz, saying in August 2022: "Tony

Oxley's love was avant-garde, free music, but he was one of the greatest time players that I've ever played with. I'm not so sure you can play outside until you can play inside."[7])

## DESTINATION NEW YORK: TONY WILLIAMS'S LIFETIME AND MILES'S *IN A SILENT WAY*

There wasn't much time for John to dwell on the achievement of recording his first solo album (indeed, he has very rarely looked back on it in any detail) because in late January 1969 he finally got the call from Tony Williams: the drummer had secured an audition with Columbia Records, and he wanted John and organist Larry Young in his new band. It was time for John to get over to New York. Dave Holland got wind of Williams's proposal and rang John to give him some advice: "I've only got two words . . . Be strong."[8]

John arrived alone at JFK Airport on February 16, 1969 (not February 3, as some reports claim)—Eve would join him later—and hotfooted it straight to the Club Baron on Lenox Avenue in Harlem, where Williams was playing a residency with Miles. One can only imagine the excitement and nervousness pulsing through the twenty-seven-year-old John's body. That very evening, he jammed with Williams and Young—the beginning of Lifetime. John met Miles for the second time, too, and he recalled the trumpeter making quite an entrance:

> I was standing at the bar the first night. The door opens and Miles walks in, and he had on this big black cape, and he was so handsome and just . . . what an aura he had. And he saw me and, as he walked past me, he brushed me with his cape, and he said 'Johhhhhn'—and he walked on. That blew my mind because he knew my name.[9]

Chick Corea was also in the club that night, as John recalled: "I was sitting at the bar . . . and after the first set Chick came over to me and said, 'Hey man, how ya doing? I hear you're comin' to join Tony, man. That's cool, wow.' I hadn't even had the chance to say hello to him, and he was so gracious and friendly."[10]

As well as Miles and Corea, guitarist Larry Coryell and the entire Cannonball Adderley band were also present, including Joe Zawinul. Coryell struck up an immediate friendship with John, offering him his near-empty West 73rd Street apartment until he got on his feet, as Coryell was in the process of moving out to Rockland County. (Coryell's first album, *Lady Coryell*, recorded in 1968, was partially recorded with John Coltrane's fabled bass-and-drums duo: Jimmy Garrison and Elvin Jones.)

So, John's first day in New York City had been a revelation. The second wasn't uneventful, either. On February 17, 1969, Lifetime made a demo/audition recording for Columbia Records, under the watchful eye of Al Kooper. Kooper had famously played piano and Hammond organ on many of Bob Dylan's 1960s sides. But to John's intense chagrin, the demo tape was rejected. Fortunately, this was just a minor inconvenience—presently, an unexpected offer came from Miles himself to attend the *In A Silent Way* recording session, as John recalled:

> On my second day in New York, Tony had to go to Miles's house to pick up some money. So I went along. Miles said to me, 'Why don't you bring your guitar tomorrow?' Tony wasn't terribly happy about that, because suddenly there was a little competition between Miles and Tony. For me, of course, it was the ultimate.[11]

The *In A Silent Way* session was set for February 18, 1969. This was it—the pressure was on. But John was ready. "I was in a situation that was do or die, and I didn't want to die! I'd already started meditating and practicing yoga before I arrived in New York, and more than likely I would have been nervous wreck without it."[12] But things got even more complicated when, according to Columbia/Legacy Reissue manager Bob Belden, Williams was apparently very irritated to see both McLaughlin and Young (though there's no evidence that Young performed on the album) present at the session. According to Belden, Williams "freaked out."[13] Belden also reports that Williams was resentful that it had been Jack DeJohnette, not him, who had got the call from Miles for the session that had produced the track "Directions" in November the previous year. According to Belden, these factors hastened Williams's split from Miles and may also have explained why his drumming is so restrained on *In A Silent Way*.

But another interesting take on the Miles/Williams schism emerged in 2019 courtesy of a *JazzTimes* article.[14] Trumpeter and close friend of both Williams and Miles Wallace Roney claimed that Miles had heard Lifetime and approached Williams, saying: "I want your band." Williams replied that if Miles named it "Miles Davis Presents The Tony Williams Lifetime," he had a deal. Miles refused. Roney also claims Williams said very pointedly, "I'll never play with you again," to Miles at the end of the *In A Silent Way* session.

However, the release of Columbia's *The Complete In A Silent Way Sessions* in 2010 may shed some more light on the issue, featuring as it does the very first rehearsal take of "In A Silent Way." It's a soft bossa-nova, a rhythm stipulated on Zawinul's original lead sheet, and Williams faithfully interprets it as such. So it's possible that he may simply have carried over this relaxed attitude to the rest of the album session, rather than withholding his best playing as a rebuke to Miles.

Whatever the reasons behind Williams's split from Miles, John's *In A Silent Way* experience was life-changing. During his contribution to "Shhh/Peaceful," John showcased a couple of melodic/rhythmic devices that were rapidly becoming trademarks as his solo style continued to flower: at 11:13, he starts a melodic idea on the second sixteenth note. Then, at 12:20, he achieves drone-like effects with the use of open strings.

After the session, for which John was paid the union scale rate of $86.67, Herbie Hancock reported that the guitarist approached him and asked, "Was that any good, what we did? I mean, what did we do?" Hancock replied: "Welcome to a Miles Davis session. Your guess is as good as mine. I have no idea, but somehow when the records come out, they end up sounding good."[15] Legendary rock critic Lester Bangs agreed—he wrote a famously glowing review of *In A Silent Way* in *Rolling Stone* magazine. It would go on to sell around ninety thousand copies on its initial release and is often cited as the first jazz/rock album of any consequence.

A by-product of *In A Silent Way*'s success is that Miles asked John to join his full-time touring group. It seemed a dream come true, but there was only one answer in John's mind: "Imagine—I had to turn down Miles! I had compositions. And I realized with Tony I would have more of a chance to play them than with Miles."[16] This certainly didn't affect Miles's friendship with John—in fact, it possibly even garnered John even more respect from the superstar. John summed up their relationship during those early years in New York:

> He took care of me, almost like a godfather. I'd be around his house and he'd say: 'Are you eating?' and he wouldn't wait for a reply and stick a hundred dollar bill in my pocket to make sure that I ate. And all the time he stuffed money in my pocket just to make sure I could pay my rent. Of course, when I worked with him I got paid. But when I played with Tony we made $20 a night, max.[17]

Of course, it's possible that John, in his own typically modest way, had failed to see just what a positive effect he had on people—even Miles—and what all the spiritual work he had done on himself gave his "karma" and presence. Miles certainly seemed to recognize something special about John from the beginning, and not just musically: "He's got two sides to him, a lotta sides, actually. I know how soft John is, or can be. That's the way he plays when he's with me. That's what I like about him," Miles told writer Stephen Davis in a famous March 21, 1973, interview published in *The Real Paper*.

## HENDRIX AND *EMERGENCY!*

With his dream trio in place, Williams had high hopes for Lifetime, both commercially and artistically. He explained his philosophy of the band to fellow drummer and journalist Arthur Taylor in the latter's classic book, *Notes And Tones*:

> It's all kinds of influences. I'm not that snobbish to rule out any influence. If people think you're playing rock or trying to play rock or trying to make money, that's their problem. I use electric instruments because it's there; it's another sound. After playing with . . . Wayne, I can't play with any horn player right now. After playing with Miles there aren't any trumpet players for me to listen to . . . so I go somewhere else for something else . . . It's just stimulation for me.

John was all-in with Lifetime, too, but despite an increasingly busy live schedule around New York and the Metropolitan area, he still found time to make other sessions: on March 25, 1969, he jammed with Jimi Hendrix at the Record Plant in New York. They met via Hendrix's drummer Mitch Mitchell, a major Lifetime fan and former member of Georgie Fame & The Blue Flames (he replaced Charlie Watts in the drum chair). Mitchell invited John to the Record Plant after watching Lifetime play at the Village Vanguard. Buddy Miles played drums, Young manned the organ and Dave Holland the electric bass, and there were numerous other guitarists and keyboard players reportedly hanging around too.

Thirty minutes of the jam—during which John played a Gibson Hummingbird—have appeared on the *Hell's Session* bootleg. Despite producer Alan Douglas's claim to its greatness, and Hendrix's apparent enjoyment (he later told journalist Roy Carr in September 1970: "I think I enjoyed that jam much more than John—he's so critical about his own playing. Perhaps one day we'll have to go back and see if there's anything worth putting out. I dunno, I don't think so!"), it's hardly an inspired recording. There are wonderful moments from both players, but it sounds like music best suited to the dirty movies being shown on Times Square, just a "funky" jam in C that speeds up drastically.

John himself later dismissed the recording: "This is what I refused them permission to put out, because what I heard was just three or four minutes of some playing that was really not happening."[18] However, there were no hard feelings: Hendrix later reunited with John after his January 28, 1970, Madison Square Garden gig, again at the invitation of Mitchell, and the two guitarists remained on good terms until Jimi's death in September of that year.

John also made sure that Miles was acquainted with Hendrix, taking the trumpeter to see the D.A. Pennebaker's documentary *Monterey Pop* at a cinema in Greenwich Village in March 1969. John reported that Miles was completely transfixed by Hendrix's screen appearance, intoning: "Damn, Jimi! Damn!" John completed the story to *Jazzwise* magazine's Stuart Nicholson in November 2003: "And when Jimi burned his guitar at the end, Miles just flipped out . . . And while the guitar's burning, it's feeding back and . . . wild sounds are coming out of it. That's was Miles' introduction to Jimi."

Also in March 1969, *Melody Maker* magazine voted John the number-two guitarist in the world, behind Kenny Burrell. His fame and reputation were building. In May, Lifetime signed a record deal with Polydor and speedily recorded their double album *Emergency!* (named—rather ungallantly—by Williams because he considered it to be an "emergency" that he leave Miles's band and explore his own musical direction) between May 26–28 at New York's Olmstead Studios. John contributed the compositions "Where" and "Spectrum" (later to morph into "Awakening" on *The Inner Mountain Flame*, and a tune that made esteemed critic Gary Giddins's list of "key post-war jazz tracks" in the *Village Voice*),[19] and co-wrote "Via De Spectrum Road" with Williams, complete with ponderous lyrics.

Despite the strangeness of Lifetime's music, there's evidence that Williams really believed that, given the right kind of exposure, the band could be a commercial concern. Even if that proved to be a false dawn, musicians of all stripes were taking note. Superstar guitarist/vocalist George Benson recalled first seeing Lifetime play live in his 2012 autobiography:

> John had just come over from England and word on the street was that he was the fastest guitar player in the world. The first time I met John was at a club in Harlem in 1969, with the Tony Williams Lifetime. They were loud, man, loud and out there—a mixture of jazz, rock, avant-garde and noise. Were they a good band? Heck, yeah. Would I have been able to play their sort of music? Heck, no.

Benson also revealed that he had played duet with John at the Lincoln Center soon after this first meeting, and that it was "the first night of a lifelong friendship."

## SUMMER 1969/LIFETIME LIVE/ENTER ZAKIR HUSSAIN

John spent the summer of 1969 in New York, gigging fairly infrequently with Lifetime, recording with Miles and also regularly attending The Sufi Center, very much continuing to explore the spiritual realm. But at the same time, he was seeing the very real effects of jazz's downturn in its homeland. He arrived for a Lifetime gig at the Club Baron in Harlem in early August 1969, and he was amazed to see a disastrously misspelt sign outside: "We pull up outside the club and they've got something like 'Now Appearing—The Tommy Willis Lifestory.' I was shocked beyond belief."[20]

Other jazz legends were struggling during this period too. In *The Real Frank Zappa Book*, Zappa describes watching Duke Ellington beg for a ten-dollar advance from an assistant of promoter George Wein before a concert in South Carolina. (Zappa also reports that he swiftly broke up his ten-piece "rock" band as a result.)

The Lifetime gig was also presenting other challenges for John: He was initially reading from charts when playing live with the band, a holdover from his London studio days. Initially it was required due to the complexity of the material, but John vowed that he would never again read from sheet music onstage, and he has stuck to his word.

Then there was the band's sheer, terrifying volume. Hancock remembers seeing Lifetime at Ungano's in New York around the summer of 1969: "It was the loudest stuff I've ever heard in my life. A lot of people couldn't take the volume. They got up and left. I also knew that if I stayed I would pay the price in later years with my hearing."[21] He stayed, anyway. For his part, John was blown away by Williams's rhythm concepts, and his insistence that everyone in the band must keep good time, not just the drummer: "The way he felt time was wonderful. His groove was just amazing, but he had a sense of dynamics that was revolutionary. And he taught me a lot about phrasing. He wouldn't end a phrase than ended on the '1.' It might end on the '2&' or the 1&.'"[22]

During a run of Club Baron gigs in early August 1969, Miles asked John to take part in the *Bitches Brew* sessions, between August 19–21, kicking off just after the end of the Woodstock Festival. Reportedly Miles insisted on John being right next to him in the studio, leading to some "bleed" between the tracks and problems when the material was edited extremely extensively by Macero between September 22 and October 24.

On September 19, John appeared with Lifetime at the Monterey Jazz Festival alongside Thelonious Monk, Sly & The Family Stone, Miles, and Roberta Flack. Then, in November, they supported The Who at the Boston Tea Party. During this period, John also took part in recording sessions for two key late-1960s jazz albums: Wayne Shorter's *Super Nova* for Blue Note and Miroslav Vitous's *Infinite Search*. Both were the result of the "workshop jam" scene in New York—John had become almost the house guitarist alongside Shorter, Vitous, and the likes of Joe Zawinul, Airto Moreira, and Billy Cobham.

As 1969 came to a close, John reflected on a watershed year in his life and music. He had met and worked with two of his greatest heroes: Miles and Tony Williams. "They must have known how much I revered them both, and I guess that helped the vibe. When my plane landed in the snow in New York back in February 1969, I could have kissed the hallowed ground!"[23]

But he had done a lot of work on himself, too, and he was prepared. He had also never been healthier, having given up cigarettes and become a vegetarian. The year 1970 was to offer even more musical and spiritual challenges as his US-based solo career began in earnest.

**3**

# 1970–1973

## From *Devotion* to *Between Nothingness & Eternity*

### DEVOTION (1970)

Jerry Goodman: Vocals
Buddy Miles: Percussion, drums
John McLaughlin: Guitar, composer
Larry Young: Organ, percussion, keyboards, electric piano
Billy Rich: Bass
Produced by Stefan Bright and Alan Douglas
Recorded at The Record Plant, New York City, February 1970
Released September 1970

John's first interview with the British music press appeared in January 1970, when journalist Richard Williams spoke to all three members of Lifetime for *Melody Maker*. John painted a picture of frantic live playing in the US clubs, mentioning the Village Vanguard, Village Gate, and Electric Circus in New York; Both/And and Fillmore West in San Francisco; and Shelly's Manne-Hole in Los Angeles. This survey of venues also suggests that Lifetime was doing a better job than Miles at inveigling themselves with both jazz and rock audiences. At any rate, both acts shared bills frequently during his time; Lifetime guested with Miles's band on February 20 at the Hill Auditorium, Ann Arbor, Michigan, receiving a rapturous review in *Down Beat* magazine. John also found himself playing on no less than thirteen out of the fourteen Miles studio sessions that took place during the first six months of 1970.

Meanwhile, John met a very influential figure at The Sufi Center: Hazrat Inayat Khan, a mystic and author of *The Mysticism Of Sound: Music, The Power Of The Word, And Cosmic Language*, whose message that life, music, and spiritual aspiration were one and the same was a key tenet for John.

In the midst of this dramatic spiritual development and busy period of live playing, John was offered two thousand dollars to make two solo albums for Jimi Hendrix's mentor/manager, Alan Douglas. (Miles also reported in his *Autobiography* that Douglas had also tried to match Miles with Hendrix in the studio, "but the money wasn't right or we were too busy to get it together." Miles also reports that he and Hendrix "had played a lot with each other at my house, just jamming.") John signed up, pleading a much-needed cash injection.

The first album in the Douglas deal, *Devotion*, was recorded in February 1970 at the Record Plant in New York, just before John became a disciple of Sri Chinmoy. It featured frequent Hendrix collaborators Billy Rich on bass and Buddy Miles on drums, both Douglas recommendations and involved with John's jam with Hendrix a year earlier. Accordingly, *Devotion* was a lot closer to psychedelic rock than jazz or jazz/rock; Douglas later claimed "it was meant to bring . . . R&B and jazz together. John had a certain sequencing and cross-fading planned but it never worked out that way. We tried, but it was very difficult to mix."[1]

A decade on from its recording, John looked back on *Devotion* with a lot of bad feeling, putting much of the blame at Douglas's door:

> A terrible experience. After I recorded it, I went on tour with Tony Williams, and when I came back, he (Douglas) had finished the album, mixed it, cut this out and that, and there were parts in it which I didn't recognise any more as part of our music. I was in total shock.[2]

While this may be true, John generally strives in vain for a meaningful, personal electric guitar tone and compositional approach on *Devotion*. He is not helped by some very of-their-time echo and flanging effects, seemingly random edits, and substandard bass performances from Rich.

"Siren," "Don't Let The Dragon Eat Your Mother," and "Purpose Of When" are three of the least edifying tracks in John's catalog, featuring strange echo, wah-wah, and flanging effects; out-of-tune bass; unsubtle use of feedback; queasy Hammond/electric piano parts; and leaden drums, despite John's spirited soloing. It really does sound like music for a particularly bad trip.

"Marbles," "Dragon Song," and the title track are slightly better, with a little more light and shade, but the still suffer from ill-advised post-production effects and underwhelming instrumental performances. (The former, though, was covered successfully by Carlos Santana and Buddy Miles on their 1972 album *Live!*) These days, *Devotion* is probably only of interest to John completists, though one can hear echoes of future——far superior—material here and there, with early nods to "Resolution," "One Word," and "Follow Your Heart."

The album's already-underwhelming reputation hasn't benefited from sloppy reissues with dodgy cover art (one mid-1980s version features John "as he might look in a funhouse mirror," as reported by writer Howard Mandel in his *Future Jazz* book), incorrectly named titles, and lack of recording information. All in all, *Devotion* seems to be an album that John probably wishes would just disappear from his catalog.

## WHERE FORTUNE SMILES (1970)

Karl Berger: Vibraphone
Dave Holland: Bass
John McLaughlin: Guitar
John Surman: Saxophone
Stu Martin: Drums
Recorded at Apostolic Studios, New York City, late May 1970
Produced by McLaughlin, Surman, Berger, Martin, and Holland

After recording *Devotion*, John was straight back into the studio to work on the second Lifetime album, *Turn It Over*, this time alongside his old friend Jack Bruce on bass. Bruce had been playing with Larry Coryell in the Jack Bruce & Friends band, which toured the United States between January 30 and March 1, 1970. John was Coryell's guest at the first night of the band's Fillmore East concerts, and John took the chance to ask Bruce to come and meet Tony Williams, who, of course, had been a huge Cream fan. Bruce was immediately invited to join Lifetime—he leapt at the chance.

For his part, Coryell in turn speedily requested that John be involved in his third solo album for Vanguard Records, recorded in late March. *Spaces* featured the Coryell/McLaughlin guitar frontline plus Miroslav Vitous on bass, Chick Corea playing keyboards on one track, and Billy Cobham on drums. However, it wasn't at all easy for Coryell to get all the musicians together in one room—all but Vitous were often otherwise engaged with Miles recording sessions. But the effort paid off—although not immediately a success on its initial release, *Spaces* sold very well when reissued a few years later, reportedly around 250,000 copies worldwide. The most memorable track is probably "Rene's Theme," an acoustic duet featuring John playing a Gibson lent to him by the Lovin' Spoonful's John Sebastian.

But *Spaces* would become hugely important to John for another reason. After one session, the producer Danny Weiss informed John—knowing McLaughlin was a yoga aficionado—that he was going up to Connecticut for a Sri Chinmoy meeting. John had heard about Chinmoy and was keen to meet him, so Weiss, John, and Coryell drove upstate. (Coryell reports in his book *Improvisation* that he was destined to be a "dabbler" in the Chinmoy sect, and thus was never given his "spiritual name": "Guru said I needed to put in more time to prove myself as a good disciple—I think he said a year—before he would give me my name. . . . Well, I never got it. I left or lost interest or something. . . . My pursuit of Guru's goal of realisation was hampered by my drug and sex karma. . . .") But it was to be a life-changing meeting for John, as he recalled in 1982:

> I arrived one evening at a meditation . . . and he invited questions. So I said, "What's the relationship between music and spirituality?" and he said, "Well, it's not really a question of what you do. It's what you are or how you are that's important because you can be making the most beautiful music sweeping the road, if you're doing it in a harmonious way, in a beautiful way." It sounds so simple, of course, but it was everything I wanted to hear and I felt I should stay with him, which I did for five years.[3]

At Chinmoy's urging, John was all-in from very early on, telling interviewer Dave Reitman in August 1970: "He said, 'I'm making you disciples.' It was as simple as that . . . We had nothing to do with it. He said, 'Do you want to come?' There's only one thing you can say and that's 'Yes.'"[4] He also gave John a new spiritual name: Mahavishnu. "Mahavishnu is an Indian god; Maha the Creator, and Vishnu the Preserver," was how John explained the name to *Guitar Player* magazine.[5]

Sri Chinmoy was born Chinmoy Kumar Ghose in Bengal, India, in 1931. At fourteen, he reportedly received a direct order from the Supreme to go to New York, which he eventually did in 1964. He obtained a green card and became a meditation guru who prohibited alcohol, caffeine, smoking, drugs, TV, radio, newspapers, meat, dancing, and pets—at least that was the decree for most followers. But as the first "celebrity" disciple, John was reportedly given a lot more freedom than most (shades of George Orwell's *Animal Farm*: "All animals are equal. But some animals are more equal than others . . ."), followed in fairly short order by Carlos Santana (another Coryell connection), both seen as special by the guru, not to mention a superb advert for attracting disciples.

Alongside this spiritual conversion of in the spring of 1970, John was very busy playing with Miles in the studio too: on February 6, 1970, he had recorded "Gemini/Double Image." later to appear on *Live/Evil*. On February 27, there was a version of "Willie Nelson"; on March 3, "Go Ahead John." Finally, on April 7, 1970, most of *A Tribute To Jack Johnson* was recorded, including the majority of the electrifying "Right Off" and probably most of "Yesternow" (which included an edited-in section of "Willie Nelson"). John himself noticed a change in his playing during this latter session: "I had just become a disciple when that was recorded. You might say I was just born."[6] John elaborated on how the majestic "Right Off" came about:

> The bulk of that record came out of some jamming we did in the studio. There was Herbie playing the most horrible Farfisa organ and Michael Henderson on bass, Billy Cobham on drums. We were all in the studio, just waiting for Miles. He was talking to Teo Macero in another room and that went on for 10–15 minutes, and I got bored. I started to play a boogie in E, just to have some fun, that's all. I was playing those funny kind of chords that later I used to more advantage in "Dance of Maya", kind of angular chords but all really related to the blues. That's what "Dance of Maya" is, a blues in E, really, with some funny angular chords. And I was really hitting the strings hard, just going for it. Billy picked it up, Michael picked it up and in a couple of minutes we were gone. So finally the door opened and Miles ran in with his trumpet. The (recording) light was on and he just played for about 20 minutes, which I had never seen him do before. It was a situation where he just walked in and everything was happening already. And he played so fine. It was so spontaneous, such a great moment. That whole record was.[7]

Cobham, for his part, had an interesting alternative/revealing take on how "Right Off" came about, telling Tingen in *Miles Beyond*: "All of a sudden McLaughlin got this shuffled groove happening while trying to get (recording) levels. It was really very infectious and Michael Henderson started playing it with John. Miles told us not to play because the studio technicians were still getting a balance. Anyone who knows McLaughlin knows that if you say 'No', he'll keep on doing it. So he kept playing, and we all joined in, and the groove got more and more infectious."

But there is also an interesting selection of what-ifs around the *Jack Johnson* sessions—for his part, Cobham claims the core *Jack Johnson* band met at Miles's house before the "Right Off" session: "Something came out on a piece of paper that kind of vaguely resembled a scale, and that was the tune."[8] Bassist Michael Henderson disputes this, once reporting that "Buddy Miles actually was supposed to be doing the session but he didn't show up."[9] If Henderson is right, it's interesting to consider that John and Cobham might never have hit it off so well at that famous session, and the Mahavishnu Orchestra we know and love might have taken a vastly different form.

Whatever the genesis of the piece, "Right Off" is certainly one of the most extraordinary performances of John's career, aided by Teo Macero's novel use of stereo echo. *Bitches Brew* was also finally released in April 1970, becoming an immediate runaway success for Miles, and a big boon for John, though Lifetime was still his main priority. On the evening of April 7, straight after the "Right Off" session, the new four-piece band, now featuring Bruce on bass, made its debut at Slug's in Manhattan's Lower East Side, infamous less than a year later for being the site of trumpet master Lee Morgan's murder at the hands of his estranged wife. Bruce soon found he shared John's outlook regarding Lifetime: he loved the music, but the money was seriously tight.

On May 19, 1970, John recorded "Honky Tonk" with Miles, Keith Jarrett, Michael Henderson, and Herbie Hancock, later to appear on *Get Up With It*. Soon after, John was reunited socially with John Surman and Dave Holland. Surman was in New York for just two weeks, playing in drummer Stu Martin's band. Martin was a child prodigy, a professional big-band musician by the age of just sixteen who had played with Count Basie, Quincy Jones, Maynard Ferguson, and Duke Ellington in the 1960s. John, Holland, Surman, and Martin pledged to quickly gather to record something. The result was the album *When Fortune Smiles* (co-headlined by John and Surman, though mysteriously it's credited to "Various Artists" on streaming platforms at the time of this writing). The line-up was completed by German vibes player Karl Berger, a recommendation from Holland who had made a name for himself playing in Don Cherry's band. Berger had also recorded two solo albums for independent European labels before relocating to Woodstock, New York State.

John suggested recording *When Fortune Smiles* at the small Apostolic Studios at 53 East 10th Street in Greenwich Village, reportedly the United States' first twelve-track studio and recently used by Frank Zappa and the Grateful Dead. The album was recorded in one evening at breakneck pace and intense volume—the two relatively serene duets were apparently reactions to neighbors complaining about the noise. Surman then took the tapes back to the UK, where they were remixed and sequenced by producer Peter Eden, and eventually released by Dawn Records. John's three compositions are credited to "Chinmoy Music" and demonstrate an interest in unabashed avant-garde music, from Sun Ra to Cherry.

Though it received little attention upon its release, *When Fortune Smiles* is beautifully recorded with excellent instrument separation and superb performances from Holland and Surman, but it is nonetheless somewhat of a curio and hardly a "lost classic." However, it's an important album and a fascinating document of John's work under the influence of Chinmoy, and he sounds completely liberated and uncommonly playful—at times, even humorous. It was also a very important springboard for Surman—he embarked on his prodigious solo career, first in a band called SOS alongside Alan Skidmore and Mike Osborne, and then for the increasingly influential German-based ECM Records.

John's sound is immediately recognizable, and it's striking how much more assured he sounds here than he does on *Devotion*. But if his electric guitar tone is not yet fully realized, his technical facility certainly is, demonstrating a barrage of string bends and highly original tension/release patterns. On the title track, John explores the same chords later used to greater effect on The Mahavishnu Orchestra's "A Lotus On Irish Streams" and "Thousand Island Park." On "New Place, Old Place," John experiments with some abstract, dissonant textures later put to more effective use on 1978's "Phenomenon: Compulsion."

## MY GOAL'S BEYOND (1971)

John McLaughlin: Acoustic guitar
Jerry Goodman: Violin
Dave Liebman: Tenor and soprano sax, flute
Charlie Haden: Bass
Billy Cobham: Drums
Airto Moreira: Percussion
Badal Roy: Tablas
Eve McLaughlin (alias Mahalakshmi): Tambura
Recorded in New York City, March 1971
Produced by John McLaughlin
Released August 1971

In the immediate aftermath of *When Fortune Smiles*, John continued playing live with Lifetime, supporting rock acts such as Mountain across the United States and also doing occasional club headliners throughout May and June 1970. On May 21, 1970, he recorded "Konda" with Miles, later released on the 1981 compilation album *Directions*, his last Miles studio session for almost two years.

Then, on July 1, John headed to Rudy Van Gelder's famous studio in Englewood Cliffs, New Jersey, to guest on *The Joe Farrell Quartet* for Creed Taylor's CTI Records, contributing "Follow Your Heart." It was later released as a single spread over two sides (and later played live by The Mahavishnu Orchestra in 1973). Texas blues/rock band ZZ Top later appropriated some of its chords for their 1977 track "Manic Mechanic." Esteemed British poet and occasional jazz critic Philip Larkin reviewed *The Joe Farrell Quartet* (briefly) for the *Daily Telegraph*'s September 18, 1971, issue: "Of all the various modes of modern non-jazz, this sugar-fairy kind seems to me the oddest, but no one could call it unpleasant."[10]

John then played with Lifetime at the Newport Jazz Festival on July 11, 1970, following a set by Gary Burton's famous, if short-lived group featuring Keith Jarrett on piano. John was delighted to meet his hero, Tal Farlow, at the festival, and he also ran into his old friend and colleague Ian Carr. Carr had enjoyed some Stateside success with his band, Nucleus, winning first prize in the International Jazz Festival at Montreux and playing at the Village Gate in NYC. But, in his book *Music Outside*, Carr described his painful jolt of reality as he returned to England after Newport:

> It seemed we could do no wrong in America. A day or so later we were in a jumbo jet flying back to London . . . back to the anonymity of Britain. It was like returning from a forest full of wild beasts where one could never be certain who was the hunter or who or what was being hunted, to a small landscape garden with some plastic gnomes in it. For two months after our return, nothing interesting happened—no press coverage, no work, nothing.

John had seemingly escaped all this. Lifetime continued to play live regularly through the summer of 1970, doing a run of thirteen gigs at Ungano's through July and August. Lifetime also recorded a stand-alone UK single in July, "One Word," backed with "Two Worlds," both featuring Bruce's debut on vocals. It was closely followed by the second Lifetime album, *Turn It Over*. It featured a lot more singing from Williams (disastrously on "This Night This Song" and the ill-judged Jobim cover "Once I Loved"), plus John's strange, scary whispering on "A Famous Blues," the psychedelic raveup "Right On," and Coltrane cover "Big Nick."

Again, with a less-than-forgiving sound quality and lots of edgy microtones courtesy of John's string-bending, Young's scarifying Hammond, Bruce's less-than-perfect fretless bass intonation, and Williams's tentative vocals, *Turn It*

*Over* was a very difficult listen. Unsurprisingly, the most successful tracks were the trio of instrumentals: "Allah Be Praised," "Vuelta Abajo," and "Big Nick."

Alongside a couple of underperforming studio albums, the band now had to contend with management problems, too—Williams complained there weren't enough gigs, and also that Polydor Records wasn't distributing their records adequately in the United States. And despite his love of the band, lack of money was still a perennial problem for John. Miles finally gave him some advice: go and see Nat Weiss. He was Miles's business advisor, The Beatles' legal representative in the States during the Brian Epstein era, and also confidante to James Taylor, Bonnie Raitt, and Cat Stevens. John immediately signed with Weiss, leading to some bad vibes with the Lifetime management: "They were very abusive to me," reported John, after he had succeeded in holding out from signing any contracts with them.[11]

Lifetime toured the UK during the autumn of 1970, including memorable gigs at Ronnie Scott's, the Marquee (Richard Williams from thebluemoment.com: "When a friend asked me this week to name the most memorable gig I've ever attended, I could answer him in a heartbeat: the Tony Williams Lifetime at the Marquee on October 6, 1970. Nothing has ever felt more like the future exploding in the audience's ears"), Speakeasy, and Fairfield Halls in Croydon on November 29. The next day, McLaughlin was married to Eve at the Chelsea Registry Office. Lifetime stayed on for a gig at Chelsea College on December 5, and then returned to New York.

Two days later, John and Bruce were at RCA Studios recording "Rawalpindi Blues" for Carla Bley's *Escalator Over The Hill* album. He also guested with Miles's band at the Cellar Door club in Washington on December 19, 1970, the final night of a weeklong residency. Extracts of the gig were issued on Davis's *Live-Evil* album. Bandmate Jarrett was less than ecstatic about the results, however: "John McLaughlin just happened to be in town. He just sat in, and the band sound wasn't the same because there was now a different voice. CBS did such a terrible job of recording I couldn't believe it—if I didn't recognize the notes I wouldn't have recognized the sound."[12]

It was a musically fertile, yet intense period for John. Accordingly, he and his new wife were very much following the spiritual path, looking for stability in a somewhat volatile America. It helped that they were living in the relatively benign environs of Rockland County, and more spiritual sustenance came from a series of devotional acoustic concerts played by John, Eve, and Larry Coryell at the *Love And Serve* restaurant, run by Chinmoy disciples, opposite Westport County train station. Occasionally they would also perform at the Cami Hall on

57th Street, across the road from Carnegie Hall. In 2014, John looked back on his initiation into the heart of the Chinmoy culture:

> Sri Chinmoy was a very intense meditator. Frankly, as the only way to some kind of self-knowledge is through meditation, I began to learn much about myself and my inner life. Personally, I am convinced that everything we do in life is based on our inner existence. This includes music.[13]

Lifetime had essentially split up by December 1970. John couldn't afford to stay in the band, finding that he was spending his own money to keep it afloat. (Bruce reported doing the same.) John and Eve moved into the top three floors of a 160th Street townhouse in Queens. One floor was rented out to Chinmoy disciples, one became a music rehearsal room/home studio (including a yellow Gretsch drumkit, inspired by Williams), and one housed the McLaughlins. They were very much part of the Chinmoy community, part-owning a vegetarian restaurant (the Annam Brahma on 164th Street, still standing at the time of this writing) and frequenting the health-food shops and *Smile Of The Beyond* restaurant (soon to inspire the title of one of McLaughlin's finest compositions) nearby. John and Eve were happily settled in a bustling area of musicians, disciples, and artists.

Musically, though, John still felt very much still like a sideman through this period, despite new management and his extrication from Lifetime (who carried on with new guitarist, Ted Dunbar). He considered finally joining Miles's touring band after yet another invitation in December 1970, but again declined. However, Miles still wanted John around to play as many live dates as possible. One of these was particularly life-changing—a gig at Lennie's On The Turnpike in Boston in early March 1971. It had been a terrible concert. The two sat in silence together for a while in the band room. John made a weary apology to Miles for his lackluster performance. Miles turned and said, "John, it's time you formed your own band." This was a revelation, but also an important decree from the master. "I didn't think I was ready at the time. But . . . when somebody like Miles says that to you, it really hits you."[14] John also reported that Chinmoy had said something similar to him during this period.

John had made tentative moves to record his third solo album the previous August, recording some skeleton tracks with Isaac Hayes's rhythm section, but nothing came of them. *My Goal's Beyond* was John's first—albeit fairly tentative—step to constructing a viable solo career, recorded in late March 1971. It was the second album in that very dodgy deal he made in haste with Alan Douglas, much to new manager Nat Weiss's chagrin. It was the first album that bore the moniker "Mahavishnu" next to his name and also his most "Indian-sound-ing" album to date. And though there certainly was a precedent for the fusion of jazz, rock, folk, and Eastern music showcased on *My Goal's Beyond*, particularly in British music (such as Joe Harriott's *Indo-Jazz Suite* from 1966), in the age of Led Zeppelin, The Who, and Sly & The Family Stone, it was certainly a brave choice for a guitarist to record a meditative, all-acoustic album. And it proved to be highly influential, arguably ushering in a new vogue for unplugged guitar in jazz as demonstrated by players such as Ralph Towner, Steve Khan, John Abercrombie, Bill Connors, Philip Catherine and, of course, Coryell.

John used an Ovation acoustic guitar exclusively on the album: "That was the best acoustic I could find. I never liked a Martin sound; it's great, but it was a folk guitar. And I liked the Hummingbird, but what I liked about the Ovation was its projection. Plus, you ever throw an Ovation on the ground? It bounces back up. It's really hard to break."[15]

John also yearned for the sound of the violin, harking back to his mother's influence and also that of Stéphane Grappelli, a huge favorite in his forma-tive years. Jerry Goodman had the goods. He was a Chicago native, born on March 16, 1949, classically trained, and with quite a musical pedigree—both parents were members of the Chicago Symphony. Goodman's playing with San Francisco–based rock band The Flock had caught John's ear, particularly on their 1970 album, *Dinosaur Swamps*. Goodman mainly showcased a fusion of rock and blues, but his look was proto-Grunge, with torn T-shirts and jeans (later, John correctly surmised that Goodman would be a good onstage foil for his own clean-cut image in the Mahavishnu Orchestra). But the *My Goal's Beyond* album session, initially, was just that for Goodman—a session. John covered his plane ticket from San Francisco; he played the music, got paid, and went home, not realizing there would soon be a lot more to come from John.

Billy Cobham was John's choice of drummer for *My Goal's Beyond*, even if his contributions were fairly minimal. He was born William Emanuel Cobham in Colon, Panama on May 16, 1944. He and his family moved to Bedford-Stuyvesant in Brooklyn when he was eight, and he became besotted by two things: baseball and music. He had been inspired by a cousin in Panama who made timbales, congas, and steel drums, and percussion and the drum kit be-came his passion. The family moved to Jamaica, Queens, when Cobham was thirteen, and he started doing drum corps at school and also sitting in on jazz gigs with his piano-playing father. He attended the School of Performing Arts in NYC, where he learned classical music and played percussion at children's concerts with the Philharmonic. But he also attended the army, moonlight-ing with the likes of pianist Billy Taylor during his time off. As he turned professional, making record dates principally with Creed Taylor's CTI (George Benson, Deodata, Freddie Hubbard, Stanley Turrentine) and Atlantic (Donny Hathaway, Les McCann, Mose Allison), versatility was paramount:

> I always wanted to be a studio musician. Playing with Aretha Franklin, Roberta Flack, the Stax soul thing was as normal to me as playing with Tito Puente or Miles Davis. The point was to be versatile. The idea that you could back up Frank Sinatra and three hours later you'd be playing with James Brown before going on to do a Latin session in the evening—that for me was the ultimate.[16]

Before joining John in The Mahavishnu Orchestra, the nearest Cobham had come to a band was Dreams, a unit he co-founded in 1969 with bassist Doug Lubahn and keyboardist Jeff Kent, later to feature legendary players the Brecker Brothers on horns, guitarist John Abercrombie, and bassist Will Lee. But Dreams folded after two albums, the second of which was produced by Steve Cropper of Booker T and the M. G.'s. Cobham's initiation into Miles's world came via a recommendation from fellow drummer Jack DeJohnette. They—and John—had played together during the various jam sessions popping up all over New York, often involving Chick Corea, Miroslav Vitous, bassist Walter Booker, percussionist Airto Moreira, Wayne Shorter, Joe Zawinul (Cobham almost joined Zawinul and Shorter's Weather Report before Alphonse Mouzon got the nod) and Larry Coryell. Cobham remembers thinking nothing of hawking his kit around New York City on the bus—"I could carry my bass drum and two tom-toms and everything inside each other...... It cost me 25 cents to go across town and do something."[17] The jam scene and John's association with Cobham from the Miles sessions (Cobham played on seven between November 19, 1969, and May 19, 1970) led to the call for *My Goal's Beyond*.

The intermittently interesting lead track "Peace One" is pure Coltrane, showcasing Charlie Haden's ostinato in D Dorian with a somewhat austere 6/4 feel. John, Goodman, and Liebman solo expressively, but Cobham's drums are so far back in the mix they're almost indistinguishable. On "Peace Two," John's acoustic guitar sounds at times uncannily like a sitar. Every solo is in a different mode of G (a trick rock guitarist Steve Vai borrowed for his 1990 track "The Riddle"), but there's a ponderous, undercooked quality to the piece. John's take on Charles Mingus's "Goodbye Pork Pie Hat" remains a groundbreaking, influential reading, while Dave Herman's composition "Something Spiritual"— sometimes mislabeled as "Something Special" on rereleases—was originally performed on Lifetime's *Emergency!*, but is here a simple acoustic workout with cymbal washes by Cobham and some Reinhardt-like flourishes by John.

More successful is the mini trilogy of "Hearts and Flowers," "Phillip Lane," and "Waltz For Bill Evans," full of harmonic intrigue and subtle dynamic shifts. "Follow Your Heart" showcases John's novel use of open strings, while "Song for My Mother" inserts disquieting cymbal crashes and bells alongside some striking sixteenth notes by John—a bizarre tribute, indeed. The closing "Blue In Green" sees John overdubbing his twelve-string acoustic to winning effect, detuning his low E strings down to G—a highly original reading of the Miles/ Bill Evans standard.

As with *Devotion*, it's hard to separate *My Goal's Beyond* (whose many reissues have often been incorrectly labeled, maybe because the title is so obtuse— in what sense is John's goal "beyond"? Should there even be an apostrophe? There wasn't for the 1982 reissue on Elektra/Musician, nor for the 1987 Rykodisc CD/cassette version) from the musical/cultural era that spawned it, but is it a viable "jazz" album over fifty years on? Sadly, it now seems very much a psychedelic trinket, albeit with some novel approaches to the acoustic guitar and undoubtedly a large subsequent influence on contemporary musicians. But it garnered some spectacular reviews and certainly remains a favorite for many of John's fans who came of age in the *Sgt. Pepper's* era but were maybe put off by the bombast and sheer volume of The Mahavishnu Orchestra.

## *THE INNER MOUNTING FLAME* (1971)

John McLaughlin: Guitar
Jan Hammer: Piano and keyboards
Jerry Goodman: Violin
Rick Laird: Bass
Billy Cobham: Drums
Produced by John McLaughlin
Recorded August 14, 1971, at Columbia Studios, New York City
Released November 3, 1971

The year 1971 had begun with Miles's decree that John should form his own band. Meanwhile *Bitches Brew*—prominently featuring John and including a composition bearing his name—was selling very well. New York was buzzing with music and John was right in the middle of everything. The contrast with the early-1970s British jazz scene John had left behind couldn't have been starker. Ian Carr's book *Music Outside* painted a grim picture (perhaps with unfortunate shades of the British government's attitudes to "artists" during the COVID-19 pandemic in 2020):

> (Esteemed British jazz pianist) Stan Tracey rang me up and asked me to go to a meeting he was organising to discuss the situation of jazz music and jazz musicians in Britain. During the course of the conversation, I asked him how he was doing himself and he replied: "Terribly! I've been on the dole (unemployment benefit) so long that they want to retrain me for other work!" Suppose, for instance, that Harold Pinter or the painter Richard Hamilton were on the dole and being pressured to train as a clerk or bus conductor.

(The only positive outcome of that state of affairs seems to be that the Musicians' Action Group *was* formed after that initial meeting.) However, it was a chastening fact that two of the great British players of the 1960s jazz scene—saxophonist Joe Harriott and drummer Phil Seamen—both died during 1972 in their early forties (and sax legend Tubby Hayes a year later, at the age of just thirty-eight). As Carr said, "For the heroic few who do continue to be totally committed to the music after they have reached their forties, there is often a terrible price to pay." Surman also went to ground during early 1972, after four years of nonstop travel, retiring to the Kent countryside to focus on composing.

By contrast, John was completely subsumed by the American scene. He had to form his own touring band, and quick. He was developing his own compositions, exploring odd-time signatures in great depth, more evidence of his naturally inquisitive mind. In 2008, he reminisced about the *modus operandi* behind some of these experiments: "If you get people to play in different degrees—like a 10/4 with a 20/8, but subdivided differently, which came from the first Mahavishnu Orchestra—it'll work only if you're in the pocket. To improvise on that—it really puts your foot on your behind! The whole thing works in cycles."[18] This focus on compound time signatures reflected his study of Indian music. He also revealed that many of his composing ideas came from practice routines: "I . . . use a cassette player, and write down random sets of chords, then play them rhythmically—6/8, 4/8, 3/8, 7/8, 5/8, 9/8, 11/8, 13/8, 21/8, anything you want. Just write out some sequences and improvise through them."[19]

John's first choice for the Mahavishnu drum chair was always Cobham. The drummer was working with Quincy Jones on *The Anderson Tapes* soundtrack when he got John's call. They found time to jam extensively at Megaphone, a SoHo rehearsal space, playing from 10 a.m. to 6 p.m. for several days, and the rapport was instant. Cobham remembered the intensity of those early duet sessions:

We went up to this loft and started practicing. I had no idea it was for anything, I just wanted to play. John presented themes and we would play and solo around them with the whole objective being to interact and not just to play time. It gave me a lot of freedom. He would play a theme and I would listen and think how I was going to play it . . . there was no talking. He had a notebook and he would find a theme in it . . . and the next thing we had something. It was just about the language of playing the music. It was never about how many beats were in the bar, it was all about how to develop a foundation rhythmically.[20]

In response to John's penchant for odd-time signatures, Cobham developed a rather novel approach: "To me, the groove was always 4/4 plus the rest of whatever was left over and, as long as you remembered how much that was, it was fine. I would always be surprised: 'Wow! Was that in 11? You mean we don't play anything in 4/4?'"[21] Cobham also saw some benefit in remembering his roots when playing with Mahavishnu: "If you come out of a Latin family, which I do, you are playing timbales at the drum set and I was doing that. It wasn't about being the first or blowing anyone anyway, it was about playing what was correct in order to make the music happen."[22] But as well as expanding/developing Cobham's rhythm conception, John was also adamant that Cobham expand his kit:

Within about six months, I started to speak to Billy about getting double bass drums. He said, "Come on, no way." I said, "Billy, go for it. With double bass drums you're going to destroy." It took me about four months to convince him, but he finally did it.[23]

Cobham put together his new Fibes Plexiglass double-bass drum set at Frank Ippolito's Professional Percussion Center at Eighth Avenue and Fifth Street in New York City. But meanwhile the energy/volume levels being demanded of him were initially a great challenge: "The music was taxing on me because I didn't know how to approach it. . . . I used to put all my energies into it and I'd come away huffing and puffing and, really, it would frighten me. . . . Then, all of a sudden, I began to learn how to pace myself. It was either that or die."[24] But John knew this guitar/drums foundation was absolutely crucial to the success of the new band, and the dynamic matchup reminded many of Jimi Hendrix's kinship with Mitch Mitchell. It was also clear—and vital to John's plans—that Cobham was a top-notch groove player, just as comfortable laying it down with Curtis Mayfield and Roy Ayers as he was tearing it up with Horace Silver or Freddie Hubbard.

Amid all this excitement, out of the blue John received a call from Miroslav Vitous about joining Weather Report alongside Joe Zawinul, Wayne Shorter, and Alphonse Mouzon. John was both flattered and delighted but had to decline—he was under orders from Miles. John then asked Vitous if he could recommend a keyboard player. Vitous immediately mentioned his fellow Czechoslovakian Jan Hammer, who was in California backing jazz vocal legend Sarah Vaughan. Vitous and his drummer brother, Alan, had played with Hammer during their teenage years.

Born in Prague on April 17, 1948, Hammer had a rich musical pedigree: his mother, noted jazz singer Vlasta Pruchova, had encouraged his piano playing from a very early age, and he had his own trio at high school before earning a place at Prague's Academy Of Musical Arts. Upon the Soviet Union's invasion of Czechoslovakia, Hammer moved to America to study music at the Berklee School in Boston, leading to the Vaughan gig courtesy of her bassist, Gene Perla. Suddenly he was on *The Tonight Show Starring Johnny Carson*. He moved into a loft on the Lower East Side with Perla and found himself right in the heart of the New York scene. He was invited to an audition/jam with Miles, but Keith Jarrett got the gig. Hammer remembers the first time he played with John, Cobham, and Goodman at his loft, when The Mahavishnu Orchestra really began in earnest. Hammer immediately felt a kinship with Cobham: "I was able to click with (him) right away. It was amazing how we could lock rhythmically. That was one of the major parts of how that band clicked."[25]

Goodman was amazed at the musicianship on show from everyone, as well as the volume. But as these rehearsals continued and John began to bring in more original music, Goodman was not exactly sure what he could contribute. It was uncharted territory for a classically trained, virtuoso rock violin player not necessarily known for improvising and with limited exposure to odd meters. Goodman was also sight-reading John's handwritten charts at this point. But he soon realized "the melodies were designed to be cues to get in and out of solos"—an interesting revelation that resonates with John's music right up to the time of writing.[26]

Bassist Rick Laird—John's old buddy from the London gigging scene—was the final piece of The Mahavishnu Orchestra puzzle, though he was John's second choice. His first had been Tony Levin (who truly was the "nearly man" of fusion—he was also offered the Weather Report gig after Jaco Pastorius left in 1982). Born on February 5, 1941, Laird grew up in rural Ireland. His mother, Muriel, was a big jazz and classical music fan while his father, Bill, played ukulele. Laird gravitated toward piano music at a young age: Debussy, Rachmaninov, Fats Waller, and Erroll Garner. At sixteen, the family moved to New

Zealand, and he began to play a lot of jazz guitar, gigging regularly. He moved to Sydney, Australia, and had a revelation when hearing Ray Brown on acoustic bass with the Oscar Peterson Trio, and Scott LaFaro with Bill Evans. At eighteen, Laird switched over to the bass full-time and moved to London, where he quickly got the gig as bassist in the Ronnie Scott's house band. He played with all the great visiting players—Ben Webster, Benny Golson, Roland Kirk, Stan Getz et al.—and also performed on the *Alfie* soundtrack with Sonny Rollins. Needing a break from London, he moved to the States to study at Boston's Berklee School in 1966. By 1969, he was working with drum hero Buddy Rich, but he jumped ship while in London during 1971, tired of being constantly fired and rehired by the drummer. Just before getting John's call, Laird was considering leaving music altogether and becoming a carpenter.

Delighted though he was to become part of The Mahavishnu Orchestra, there were issues, firstly with the volume levels—"I used to wear earplugs a lot. Billy was right behind me, and he was phenomenally loud. Jerry's high-pitched violin was very loud. It was very challenging to get a bass sound."[27] Then there were the time signatures—Laird initially found that he had to count everything very deliberately and methodically while playing the tunes. It's also worth noting there was no real roadmap for electric bass in "fusion" music back in 1971. Players such as Monk Montgomery, Jack Casady, Billy Cox, Phil Lesh, Jack Bruce, and Noel Redding were important early pioneers, and Dave Holland had begun to plug in with Miles, most notably at the Isle Of Wight Festival gig the previous August. But before the emergence of Stanley Clarke, Alphonso Johnson, Jaco, and Jeff Berlin as bona-fide jazz/rock bass masters, Laird's lot was a fairly lonely one (though it's worth watching his stellar "One Word" solo from the 1973 ABC TV performance on YouTube, where he stakes out similar ground to that which Clarke would soon occupy). Hammer, though, immediately acknowledged the bassist's role: "The band really needed a fulcrum. And Rick became that fulcrum. It was a total stroke of fortune that he ended up being in that band."[28]

The band was in place. John couldn't believe his luck that—initially at least—all five members seemed to be on the same page: "ESP happens in this band. It's a solid physical fact. We are not separate. . . . If love is there, anything is possible."[29] He was willing to push the late-1960s ideals of peace, love, and understanding to the ultimate degree (though no Mahavishnu band members have ever reported being pressured about joining the Chinmoy cult or being ostracized by John for their lack of "belief"). As far as the band name is concerned, Nat Weiss was apparently a little puzzled by the moniker, asking Kit Lambert for his opinion. The Who's manager heartily endorsed it, presumably enjoying the the novelty factor.

Weiss also took John to see Clive Davis for a meeting about signing the band to Columbia Records. Davis was the newly installed executive charged with turning the rock and jazz divisions of the company into moneymaking concerns, instead of the financial dead-ends they had been between 1960 and 1966—with the exceptions of Miles, Dave Brubeck, and Vladimir Horovitz. Davis had been a lawyer at Columbia, but he was appointed vice president and general manager in 1966, and a year later was named president. By most accounts, a visit to the Monterey Pop Festival of the summer of 1967, featuring Hendrix, the Grateful Dead, Janis Joplin (with the Big Brother Holding Company), and Jefferson Airplane, was a revelation to Davis. According to David Hepworth in his book *A Fabulous Creation*, "He returned an apparently changed man, suddenly affecting Nehru jackets and flashing the sign of peace." If you were being a little more cynical, you might say that he saw a huge, hitherto-untapped market of young rock fans, and dollar signs flashed before his eyes. (Neil Young: "Maybe it just goes back to when the freeway was crammed on the way to Woodstock. It was in the newspaper, and the guys that read *The Wall Street Journal* said: 'Wow, look at that market!' And the rest is history. . . ."[30])

On the jazz side, Davis figured prominently in shaping Miles and Herbie Hancock's careers. Despite that, a shrewd marketing ploy—which would soon augment The Mahavishnu Orchestra's debut release—removed the "J" word completely, preferring the term "Progressive," while also complimenting the audience: "Today's music audience is more sophisticated and better educated than ever before. . . . They are demanding higher and higher standards of musicianship and artistic excellence."[31]

Davis possibly thought of John's music essentially as "rock rhythms with jazz solos." There were many contemporaneous examples of this approach, courtesy of the Doors, Cream, Chicago, and Blood Sweat & Tears, while Steely Dan was about to hit it big with two long "jazz" solos (somewhat edited for the single version) on "Do It Again."

What's certain is that John made quite an impression on Davis during their first meeting in early 1971 at the Columbia corporate headquarters—nicknamed Black Rock—at 51 West 52nd Street in midtown Manhattan. John recalled that Davis asked him, "What kind of music are you going to be doing?" John answered, "It's very difficult to put a name to it, but I know it's going to be great." Davis thought for a second and said, "You know, I like the way you talk. Let's sign!"[32] It was another Miles-like first impression. But Clive Davis probably sensed that signing The Mahavishnu Orchestra was simply great timing—Hendrix had gone, rock was stagnating, and the long-playing album was all the rage. The result was that John's music—which could not depend on radio airplay alone—would be promoted by Columbia alongside long-established commercial acts,

The Mahavishnu Orchestra's first gig was at Greenwich Village's Gaslight Au-Go-Go club on July 21, 1971, supporting blues legend John Lee Hooker. John played a black Gibson Les Paul Custom, Hammer an electric piano with a ring modulator, and Laird a Fender Jazz bass. The show was accompanied by a huge industry buzz. But on that first night, many little things went wrong—Cobham had problems with an errant bass-drum pedal, John broke a string, and Hammer's keyboard rig inexplicably gave up the ghost—but still the impact was indelible. Hammer reports: "I remember, after the first tune, people didn't clap. There was a stunned silence for quite a while. It was the most unusual reaction I've ever heard. They were shocked!"[33]

The band was initially booked for a week but then kept on for three more. A month later, on August 14, 1971, *The Inner Mounting Flame* was recorded in Studio B on the second floor of 49 East 52nd Street in one day. Despite Columbia's marketing clout, this was a jazz budget and timescale, not rock (Simon & Garfunkel's Columbia album *Bridge Over Troubled Water*, released in January 1970, reportedly took three months to record). But it shows just how prepared the band was and how useful their jazz "hit it from bar one" backgrounds were. Still, volume levels were an immediate issue—some reports suggest the session's first engineer walked out, frustrated by his inability to prevent separate tracks from bleeding into each other. Safe pair of hands and in-house engineer Don Puluse came in at short notice, capturing everything live in a long session between 10 a.m. and midnight. There was only one overdub—an extraordinary aspect of this groundbreaking recording.

*The Inner Mounting Flame* developed many of John's previously touched-upon musical interests, but now with improved intensity and increased virtuosity. His approach to broken chords was influenced both by The Beatles and Thelonious Monk. Elsewhere there were odd meters, compound rhythms, a use of dissonance, and a huge dynamic range.

Upon its December 1971 release, true to Clive Davis's word, the album was on show alongside all the big "pop" acts of the day, and consequently reportedly sold twenty thousand in its first three weeks, hitting #89 on the Billboard pop charts and #11 in Jazz. Columbia accounted it as selling fifty thousand copies in its first two months. (Weather Report's debut album sales during the same time period were estimated at around forty thousand.) *The Inner Mounting Flame* was nominated for a Best Pop Instrumental Grammy at the 1973 awards

and named Jazz Album of the Year, Pop Album of the Year, and Rock/Pop/
Blues Album of the Year in *Down Beat* magazine—a triumph and a sure sign the
pure jazz critics were onside, at least for the time being. It also made #11 in *The
Village Voice*'s influential Pazz & Jop Critics Poll.

The album was supported by a long tour, first around New York and the
Metropolitan area and then elsewhere in the United States, with Elliot Sears and
Anthony Barone coming onboard as joint road managers. The first gig outside
New York was at Milwaukee's Marquette University in late August 1971, at
the outset of which Cobham broke his bass-drum skin during the set-opening
"Meeting Of The Spirits." Then there were college dates all over the Northeast
supporting rock acts like Yes, Santana, The Eagles, and ELP. John, wearing
a white *kurta* (a traditional long shirt often worn in India, Afghanistan, and
Pakistan), would ask for a period of silence at the beginning of each gig. Aside
from this undoubtedly well-intentioned, spiritually motivated move, it was also
undoubtedly a great "gimmick" to achieve silence in a noisy concert hall or club
and then explode into "Meeting Of The Spirits."

There has been some interesting discourse about the role of silence in music
and culture. Singer/songwriter Mark Hollis of British avant-pop pioneers Talk
Talk had his own take: "I like silence. If you're going to break into it, just try and
have a reason for doing it." In Studs Terkel's book *And They All Sang*, concert
pianist and author Alfred Brendel states: "Silence, I think, is the basis of music.
All important music incorporates silence. There is a connection between silence
and good music." During their June 1974 American concerts, King Crimson,
led by Robert Fripp, often arrived onstage to the quiet, meditative strains of "No
Pussyfooting" before the audience was rudely interrupted by Fripp's deafening
opening chords to "Larks' Tongues In Aspic Part II." (As Crimson drummer
Bill Bruford once noted, an audience particularly notices two things—when a
musician starts playing and when he/she stops.) Spiritual leader and writer Eck-
hart Tolle requests a period of silence at the beginning of his meetings. Laird for
one was delighted that audiences were generally receptive to John's request for
quiet, and it reaffirmed his faith in the band:

> We've experienced audiences that were like a bunch of wild animals and after five
> minutes, not even a sound! They wait the whole time. That's really encouraging
> to see people do this, giving our music respect and a lot of listening. That's really
> beautiful. It's more than we ever expected, believe me. But we all, I think, knew
> at the beginning what we were doing. Getting out on a journey like this was not a
> gig. I cannot treat this as a gig as I have for 10 or 12 years. This is an experience.
> It's like a mission.[34]

There followed some more New York dates (during which John started playing his double-neck Gibson EDS-1275, one six-string electric and one semi-acoustic twelve-string), including a famous support slot at the Carnegie Hall on December 29, 1971, with the folk/rock group It's A Beautiful Day. The band recruited many new fans at this gig, including seventeen-year-old future Weather Report/Maynard Ferguson/Kate Bush drummer Peter Erskine, who attended with his friend, the pianist Alan Pasqua: "We drove from my parents' house near Atlantic City. . . . It was a mind-blowing experience for us and everyone who was there too. Afterwards, Alan and I drove all night from Manhattan to Bloomington, Indiana, turning to each other in the van and shouting, 'I can't believe we just saw that!' for almost the entire trip."[35]

Then, throughout the early months of 1972, Mahavishnu was sometimes supported by New York-based, neo-Stones riffmasters Aerosmith. Their drummer, Joey Kramer, was amazed by Cobham: "He was so good I could not really believe I was playing the same instrument as he was."[36] John and the band then supported ELP at San Francisco's Winterland in March, a concert that stunned Carlos Santana: "They just destroyed it! The music was very challenging, like Coltrane before he left this earth."[37] This was a new period of enlightenment for Santana, a rock superstar at the time but increasingly unhappy. He turned to music for healing: "I was fasting and listening to John McLaughlin, John Coltrane, Martin Luther King, Mahalia Jackson and reading books about Paramahansaa Yogananda. . . . My soul was aspiring for guidance."[38]

On April 3, The Mahavishnu Orchestra journeyed to Puerto Rico to play the Mar Y Sol Pop Festival alongside Rod Stewart, ELP, The Allman Brothers, Billy Joel, BB King, and Alice Cooper. (A version of "The Noonward Race" was later issued on the compilation album *Mar Y Sol.*) On April 21, Mahavishnu supported Procol Harum and Jack Bruce's new trio in Cleveland, Ohio, recorded by Columbia for a potential live album. On May 6, before a Miami University gig, Cobham was delivered his new Fibes Plexiglas kit, the one he had picked out at Professional Percussion. Larry Coryell and his new jazz/rock band, Eleventh House, opened the show, and one stunned attendee was future guitar star Pat Metheny (alongside future Metheny Band associates Lyle Mays and Danny Gottlieb), during his first year living in the area after moving from Missouri: "We were watching three people (Cobham, McLaughlin, and Hammer) completely and forever reinvent the meaning of their instruments in jazz."[39] Future guitar star Steve Morse also attended the concert.

Nat Weiss was keeping the Orchestra as busy as possible, relying on word of mouth, as the Columbia marketing machine had not yet fully got behind the band as a live entity. The band reportedly shared a lot of interests on tour—a love of *Monty Python's Flying Circus*, Indian classical music, and Bartok. They were certainly getting a reputation as a very hard act to follow, a headliner's nightmare. Frank Zappa allegedly refused to let them open for him, while Mott The Hoople complained they were getting frequently upstaged. Consequently, as the influential summer of 1972 US sojourn developed, Mahavishnu quickly became top of many bills, often supported by Yes. But on the other hand, the newfound success brought some issues. According to Kolosky in *Power, Passion*, factions developed when John and Cobham started traveling in one car and Goodman, Laird, and Hammer in another. Then concert promoters regularly billed the band as "John McLaughlin & The Mahavishnu Orchestra," when, according to Barone, contractually they were supposed to simply be named The Mahavishnu Orchestra. Then there was the fact that Columbia's Clive Davis–endorsed deal was purely with John, not the rest of the band. These aspects would slowly begin to fester, though by most accounts they didn't affect their first year of live performances.

On July 6, 1972, Mahavishnu appeared at the Newport Jazz Festival, transplanted temporarily to Carnegie Hall in the heart of New York. They arrived onstage at 5 p.m., after a set by the Count Basie Orchestra. Esteemed jazz critic Whitney Balliett reported on the concert in his book *New York Notes*: "It operated at well above the 100-decibel level, and it was curious to hear improvisation so highly magnified. It was like walking through a garden full of Maillol nudes." According to Kolosky, the audience also fled in droves. The band then moved to Europe, and on August 25, headlined the BBC *In Concert* programme, a broadcast from the corporation's Wood Lane studio in West London. It blew the minds of a generation of British viewers, including a young Mark King, later to become famous bassist/vocalist with the band Level 42. Looking back in 1991, he remembered:

> The best thing that happened to me was switching over a television channel when I was about thirteen years old and tuning into an *In Concert* with the Mahavishnu Orchestra. Suddenly there was a guy on this double-necked guitar, another guy with a Perspex drum kit, two bass drums . . . and this psychopathic looking guy on a Fender Rhodes with the top torn off it; and this freaky violinist as well. It was fantastic! I just sat there gobsmacked![40]

King wasn't the only one freaking out: the white-coated BBC engineers were reportedly terrified of the volume levels, frequently running out into the performance area, frantically brandishing sound meters.

## Meeting of the Spirits    6:52

John explained the title: "We are here and functioning in the physical human flesh and blood. But if you cut me open are you going to find me anywhere? Of course not. You can't cut up a flower and find it. You can't cut open a human being and find him or her. We are all invisible. So this group of people coming together to form a band is a meeting of the spirits. Every time music is made, there is a meeting of the spirits. Every time people meet, it is a meeting of the spirits." [41] The tune is in 6/4 time, but the feel is twelve eighth notes in the grouping of five/five/two. This was the real beginning of John's investigation of guitar arpeggios, played in a combination of Phrygian and pentatonic modes. "Meeting Of The Spirits" was sampled by hip-hop band Jurassic 5 on "Lesson 6 (The Lecture)" in 1997.

## Dawn    5:10

"Dawn" is in 7/4 time, split into two sections of different tempi. It features John's first stunning solo of the album on a drastically overdriven Les Paul, Hammer digs in with some funky Rhodes vamping (but the track fades just as he begins his solo), and Goodman's violin is put through a Leslie speaker. Jeff Beck paid tribute to a recurring riff (first heard at 2:34) on his track "Sling Shot" from the 1989 album *Jeff Beck's Guitar Shop With Tony Hymas And Terry Bozzio*.

## The Noonward Race    6:28

Based around a G9 chord, the opening section refers occasionally to the funky riff from Miles's "Right Off" from the *A Tribute To Jack Johnson* album. Goodman's solo is again played through a Leslie speaker, while Hammer employs a ring modulator, a trick that Chick Corea also often used when performing with Miles during this era. It's a furious, exhausting performance from all the players.

## A Lotus On Irish Streams    5:39

Here is a wholly unexpected detour into acoustic, pastoral music (some have even described it as "New Age"). It's a hugely influential and much-loved track, featuring superb piano accompaniment by Hammer. His rippling interjection at 1:30 is the one and only overdub of the album. John's nuanced acoustic playing demonstrates a marked improvement from the *My Goal's Beyond* era.

## Vital Transformation   6:16

This was reportedly the first tune played by live by The Mahavishnu Orchestra on July 21, 1971. It's mainly in 9/8, with a strong Latin influence courtesy of Cobham's groove, arguably rooted in timbale technique. (Sheila E, also a percussion/drum-kit double threat of Latin heritage, has based her jazz/rock drumming around this style, particularly audible on the Prince track "Dance On.") There's a strange/abrupt tape edit at 0:13, and then the first melodic riff appears in a minor pentatonic mode. Hammer's gritty comping in the right speaker is a delight to hear. John and Hammer solo effectively over Laird's F# vamp.

## The Dance Of Maya   7:17

This hugely influential, epochal composition features two rhythms that juxtapose and then seem to "join up" with each other. John reportedly thought of the tune as being in 10/4, subdivided 3-4-3. However, Laird was convinced it was in thirteen. Cobham enters at 0:54 with the half-time groove that had drummers running to their rehearsal rooms. The blues sections certainly have more than a hint of Jimi Hendrix's "Still Raining, Still Dreaming" from his 1968 album, *Electric Ladyland*, about them. John himself located the harmonic DNA of the track in his earlier experiments on "Right Off" from Miles's *Jack Johnson*. Guitar master George Benson failed to identify John or the Orchestra when asked about the track in a May 1978 *Down Beat* Blindfold Test, first curiously mentioning that it reminded him of both Allan Holdsworth and Hiram Bullock, then giving his mark out of five: "I'm not really into that kind of thing, but it got very interesting at the end when they cross-connected the melody. They had a line going at these two difficult tempos. Nice. I mean, it was interesting but not my kind of thing because I'm not really into distortion. It's a two-star situation."[42]

## You Know, You Know   5:07

The perennially popular, much-covered "You Know, You Know" is in a heavily disguised 4/4. Goodman's violin intro is delightfully mellow (later augmented by a little wah-wah pedal), and Hammer plays a superb Rhodes solo. "You Know, You Know" was sampled by British artist David Sylvian for the 1999 track "I Surrender" from his *Dead Bees On A Cake* album. (The spiritual animus behind John's Mahavishnu Orchestra would not have been lost on Sylvian—he, too, had a guru, Shree Maa.) "You Know, You Know" is a great favorite of hip-hop producers—it was sampled by Mos Def for "Kalifornia," Massive Attack for "One Love," and Jill Scott for "The Real Thing." It was chosen by neo-soul star D'Angelo as one of his favorite-ever tracks during his Radio Hour.[43]

### Awakening   3:32

"Awakening" strikes like a panther and doesn't let up for its full duration. In the published score, John writes that solos should be performed in a key that reflects each player's astrological sign. Much later, John alluded to the fact that this was quite a common feature of the original Mahavishnu Orchestra's music: "What I found with the Tarot and Egyptian solutions is the 12 signs of the Zodiac have the 12 tones of the scale assigned to each of the astrological sign. With Mahavishnu, this fascinated me because it related music to our particular star sign. Whether or not you believe in astrology, it's really interesting to hear in a musical way one's personal astrological harmony in harmonic terms. I integrated these elements into Mahavishnu and I put all the solos in their particular sun sign, which is a combination of sun sign and moon sign."[44] During "Awakening," Goodman solos in A. Hammer solos in C#. John is ushered toward Eb by Laird. Cobham's solo is a mini masterpiece. What a way to close one of the most remarkable debut albums in music history.

## BIRDS OF FIRE (1973)

Jerry Goodman: Violin
Jan Hammer: Piano, electric piano, Moog
John McLaughlin: Electric guitar
Rick Laird: Electric bass
Billy Cobham: Drums
Recorded at Trident Studios, London, and Electric Lady Studios, New York City, September and October 1972
Produced by John McLaughlin
Released January 1973

During 1972, The Mahavishnu Orchestra had played around two hundred one-nighters. That would increase to about 250 in the following year; fairly relentless, but demand just wasn't letting up. These were long, exhausting gigs, especially for Cobham, but the drummer revealed that John advised him to pace himself for the sometimes-three-hour headliners: "He helped me to focus and control the tempo of my breathing. . . . He told me to just play within myself, breathe normally and relax with every stroke so that the drum did not play me but . . . the other way around."[45] Cobham's lot was also improved immeasurably by the band's new and improved live sound, courtesy of legendary English engineer and monitor mixer Stuart "Dinky" Dawson, which meant the band could hear each other onstage a lot more effectively, and it was a far more pleasant experience for audiences, too.

But as the Mahavishnu moved into their second full year, with a hit debut album under their belts, tensions were becoming evident, chiefly based around songwriter credits—Hammer and Goodman in particular wanted their input to be recognized to a greater extent, believing their melodic contributions went beyond just arrangement ideas and into the realm of composition. Laird, for his part, was more concerned that his own tunes were not even being considered for recording. Of course, these were first-world problems, a direct result of the band's sudden, immense popularity—no one fights for 1 percent of nothing. But John's somewhat laissez-faire attitude to writer credits—or, to be less kind, his refusal to discuss the issue—may be best summarized by his comments about the genesis of Miles Davis's "Right Off":

> Why even bother to discuss who wrote what? What happened with all the musicians who played with Miles in the studio was strictly Miles' doing. Let's make that perfectly clear. Miles' records were always quite carefully directed by him, orchestrated in a way that was not quite obvious. Because he had that thing, that ability to be able to make musicians play in a way that they would not normally think of. He certainly did it to me. So it was absolutely Miles' vision. I think we have to put the credit on Miles. We all had ideas. Everybody would come up with things . . . a riff or a motif. But they were all really in function of Miles and his music. We were only concerned with what we could do to contribute to what he was playing. And I think everybody more or less had that same idea. So it's a kind of useless question: who wrote what? Because the concept and the way the music grew and was recorded was truly, absolutely Miles. And I think that was true even in the latter days, when he got more into funk and hip-hop.[46]

Meanwhile *Down Beat* ran its first "Jazz-Rock" cover story in November 1972, strongly featuring the Mahavishnu Orchestra, but Columbia's marketing vice president Bruce Lundvall was still trying to avoid the J-word altogether when promoting them. One piece of ad copy, also featuring Weather Report and Miles, read: "The Progressives: Yesterday And Tomorrow." The era of the fusion supergroup was hitting its peak, and musical communities would contrast and compare Return To Forever and Mahavishnu, especially the relative merits of respective drummers Lenny White and Cobham. The fact that they were both openhanded (leading with the left hand but playing right-handed kits) only added to the competition. White himself tried to characterize the relationship between the two bands, looking back in 2008:

> I've been told that the difference between Mahavishnu and Return To Forever is that we were approachable and played music to the people, related to the people, and we even spoke to the audience through the mic. Stanley, Chick and I all came from jazz. . . . We phrased like we would in a jazz band. With Mahavishnu, there were great compositions, but it wasn't set up like a jazz band in terms of phrasing or form.[47]

The irony that Corea's Return To Forever began as a fairly light, "pastoral" jazz band with Latin influences, but then transformed into a powerful, guitar-oriented jazz/rock unit around early 1973, didn't escape John, but he felt no animus toward his friend. Quite the opposite, in fact, as he reported in 2021: "I remember Chick Corea coming to see us at the Felt Forum where we were opening for this English rock band Gentle Giant. Afterwards Chick came backstage and said, 'Man, that was amazing. I'm going to form a band just like that.' Stanley Clarke was there at the time too. . . . Chick always said that Return To Forever were Son of Mahavishnu. I was immensely proud that he would say such a thing."[48]

But John had a different concept in mind for the second Mahavishnu album, *Birds Of Fire*. He wanted a warmer, more nuanced sound this time, with deeper grooves and a slicker production, and he believed English recording engineer Ken Scott was the man for the job. Scott already had a rich pedigree by the summer of 1972—he cut his teeth as a house engineer at London's Abbey Road Studios on The Beatles' *Hard Day's Night* album, and later on epochal tracks "I Am The Walrus," "Hello Goodbye," and "Hey Jude," as well as John Lennon's "Give Peace A Chance" single and George Harrison's *All Things Must Pass* triple album. He also co-produced David Bowie's *Hunky Dory* and *Ziggy Stardust And The Spiders From Mars*, both recorded at Trident Studios in London's Soho, on St. Anne's Court just off Wardour Street.

Scott's first exposure to The Mahavishnu Orchestra had occurred when Elton John and his producer, Gus Dudgeon, were playing *The Inner Mounting Flame* at the Château d'Hérouville in Val d'Oise, France, in January 1972, during the recording of Elton's *Honky Chateau*. Scott was unimpressed with John's music at the time, saying to Kolosky: "I just thought it was a bunch of drugged-out jazzers each playing in a separate room. . . . It sounded like rubbish to me."[49] Six weeks later, though, John phoned Scott out of the blue to offer him the engineering gig on *Birds Of Fire*. Scott quickly re-listened to the album and of course was "blown away," suddenly eager to get involved. The band speedily convened at Trident to record most of *Birds Of Fire* at the end of August 1972. Much of the material was road-tested, so they were, as usual, extremely well prepared.

Cobham's kit was initially too big for the Trident drum booth, so he was put in the main studio with a lot of baffles around him. Cobham muffled his snare drum by placing a wallet on the batter head. There were other equipment modifications: Hammer added the Mini Moog to his arsenal, his phrasing hugely influenced by a South Indian *vina* master called S. Balachander, via a recommendation from John. (Hammer later pointed to his own 1975 piece "The Animals" as the ultimate expression of this approach.) Indeed, an Indian influence was permeating the whole band, John increasingly bending strings during his solos to add spice and color (also very much in evidence during his extraordinary playing on Miles's *On The Corner*, recorded in June and July 1972).

As for *Birds Of Fire*'s title, it was clearly a nod to Stravinsky's *Firebird Suite*. John was in good company, as Alice Coltrane told writer J.C. Thomas in the book *Chasin' The Trane*: "John (Coltrane) never spoke more highly of any classical composer than Stravinsky. Once, when we were visiting his mother, he brought out a record and said, 'I think I've found my universal musician.' Then he played *Firebird Suite*."

The band took a break from recording *Birds Of Fire* to play two key concerts. On August 23, 1972, they appeared at Chateauvallon in France alongside Tony Williams's short-lived trio with bassist Stanley Clarke and violinist Jean-Luc Ponty (Clarke later recorded a very Mahavishnu-like, Williams-dedicated piece "Chateauvallon 1972" for his 2006 album, *The Toys Of Men*), and then South London's Crystal Palace Garden Party on September 2, during which a radio broadcast from the notorious 1972 Munich Olympic Games was blasted out through the PA in the middle of a John solo, loudly transmitting the swimming results. (Crystal Palace hosted a renowned Olympic-sized pool.)

The band then traveled over to the Bee Gees' Criteria Studios in Miami to attempt to finish off *Birds Of Fire*. But John was dismayed to find it a very characterless, dead-sounding space, okay for acts like Fleetwood Mac and The Eagles, but not for the fireworks of Mahavishnu. So, *Birds Of Fire* was completed somewhat surreptitiously back in New York at Electric Lady (not credited on the album); Columbia had been putting pressure on their artists to record exclusively at the CBS Studios, but John had always favored Jimi Hendrix's old studio, for reasons both musical and sentimental.

Expectations could hardly be higher for the sophomore Mahavishnu Orchestra album as a kind of musical Anglophilia was breaking out all across the United States. Progressive rock was taking hold—King Crimson, ELP, Genesis (who were showing signs of a Phil Collins–inspired Mahavishnu influence on tracks such as "Dancing With The Moonlight Knight" and "The Cinema Show"), and Pink Floyd were selling enormous numbers of albums and concert tickets.

Accordingly, upon its January 1973 release, *Birds Of Fire* reached an impressive #15 on the *Billboard* pop charts, and #20 in the UK. By the end of the year, it was certified Gold alongside Herbie Hancock's *Head Hunters*, Cobham's *Spectrum*, and McLaughlin/Santana's *Love Devotion Surrender* (the latter two of which much more soon). It was nominated for Best Pop Instrumental award at the 1974 Grammys, but it didn't appear in the Jazz category (and, strangely, it wouldn't be until 1980 that a Grammy Jazz Fusion Performance category was added). As well as all members receiving their due in the *Down Beat* player polls, John also got third place in the Pop Musician Of The Year list.

So, the album had obviously an impact way outside jazz or jazz/rock, though it also forced "rivals" like Return To Forever and Weather Report to up the ante—suddenly, with albums *Hymn Of The Seventh Galaxy* (featuring the notably red-blooded guitar sound of Bill Connors) and *Sweetnighter* respectively, they were courting bigger sounds and bigger audiences. Rock bands like Focus and Journey were also hugely influenced by The Mahavishnu Orchestra, as well as other guitarists who would soon make significant statements in jazz and related forms—future ECM stars Ralph Towner and John Abercrombie have both reported playing in Mahavishnu tribute bands during their formative years.

John, Hammer, Cobham, Laird, and Goodman set off on a headlining North American tour from January to May 1973, sometimes in tandem with Frank Zappa's Mothers Of Invention. A notable gig at the Philadelphia Spectrum saw many of the fifteen-thousand-strong audience displaying their lighters in tribute to *The Inner Mounting Flame*. Mothers bassist Tom Fowler reported that Zappa was very influenced by John's use of odd-time signatures and used them more in his music post-1973. Percussionist Ruth Underwood also claims Zappa was taken aback by the Orchestra's power and wanted more of that in his own band, arguably setting in motion the more combustible, rock-influenced Mothers outfits that developed from the middle to late 1970s, particularly influenced by drummers Terry Bozzio and Vinnie Colaiuta. Writer Bill Milkowski witnessed a life-changing Mahavishnu show with Zappa at Milwaukee on May 11, 1973:

I was in no way prepared for what I was about to experience when the Mahavishnu Orchestra took to the stage. . . . The leader was dressed in all white and had a spiritual demeanour about him. He put his hands together in a praying gesture before they lit into their first song and humbly asked for quiet in the auditorium. At that point, some moron in the back row let out with an inebriated, leather-lunged cry: "Boooggieeeeee!!" . . . John delved into some deep waters that night and changed my life in the process.[50]

(Robert Fripp, playing live with King Crimson in America during 1974, re-layed an interesting alternative reaction to this during an interview with *UNCUT* magazine in December 2013: "Someone in the audience shouted 'Boogie!' And I went to the microphone and said, 'We shall *not* boogie . . .'")[51]

In March 1973, the Orchestra stunned a whole generation of American TV viewers when they appeared on the *ABC In Concert* program taped at Banan-afish Gardens in New York. A knockout opening medley of an apocalyptic "Hope" and epic "One Word"—complete with a remarkable Cobham solo that went from deafening to whisper-like—gave notice that this was no ordinary tele-vised gig. (Also caught by the cameras was the striking juxtaposition of boogie-ing teenagers and people apparently running toward the exits!)

Then, on April 29, 1973, Miles; Mahavishnu; Bruce Springsteen; Earth, Wind & Fire; Billy Paul; the Staple Singers; and Loudon Wainwright played to-gether (with Bill Cosby and Richard Pryor emceeing) at the Ahmanson Theater in Los Angeles for a Columbia Records soiree titled "A Week To Remember," a brainchild of Clive Davis. (It was one of his last acts at Columbia—he was fired on May 29 following allegations that his son's bar mitzvah had partly been paid for using Columbia's coffers, to the tune of eighteen thousand dollars. CBS also accused him of wrongfully obtaining around ninety-four thousand dollars over a six-year period, leaving a trail of phony invoices, and also using $53,700 of company funds for renovations to his Central Park West apartment—Davis "disagreed" with the accusations.[52]) For his part, John donated his concert fee to the Ali Akbar School Of Music, where future Shakti bandmate Zakir Hussain was a teacher.

An energized Cobham used a brief break from touring to record his first solo album, *Spectrum*, during May 1973 at Electric Lady, with Ken Scott engineer-ing and Hammer heavily featured on Mini Moog and Rhodes. It took just two days to commit to tape: the first dealt with the "rock" material with the remark-able playing of twenty-one-year-old guitarist Tommy Bolin much in evidence, the second featured Ron Carter on acoustic bass plus a horn ensemble. It was to become a hugely successful release. John's thoughts on *Spectrum* and Bolin are not recorded, but one guitarist from across the pond—Jeff Beck, of which much more soon—was bowled over by both.

Cobham reconvened with the Orchestra in June 1973 for their first and only full UK tour. There were six dates, opening at the Manchester Free Trade Hall. John successfully reduced the promoter's proposed ticket prices for the Newcastle City Hall gig, the day after which he visited his mother in nearby Whitley Bay. It was a much-needed taste of home in preparation for a turbulent period in his life and career.

## Birds of Fire   5:50

Cobham's ominous gongs—with a little phasing courtesy of Ken Scott—usher in a quintessential Mahavishnu joint. The sound is noticeably richer and more nuanced than on *The Inner Mounting Flame*. The tune is in 9/4 time but probably best counted as eighteen, grouped 5/5/5/3. A pentatonic minor blues scale informs the main theme. John's outrageous solo is accompanied by stacked/overdubbed Goodman chords that cross from the left to right channel. Hammer is noticeably low in the mix until his piquant Moog solo. At 3:40, Cobham almost loses his way, but somehow regroups to finish the take. "Birds Of Fire" was nominated for a Grammy for Best Pop Instrumental Performance, losing to Deodato's "Also Sprach Zarathustra," which also featured Cobham on drums.

## Miles Beyond (dedicated to Miles Davis)   4:47

John reported to Kolosky that Miles occasionally came to see The Mahavishnu Orchestra in concert but neglected to pass judgment: "I don't know to this day what he thought about the music or the band. I was just happy to see him and have him in the audience."[53] Laird's bass sound and pocket are deep and soulful. Goodman "picks" his violin, in a remarkable piece of musicianship. John's triplet-inflected solo, doubled by Cobham, is one of the most thrilling moments during The Orchestra's first iteration. The terrific "Miles Beyond" has been sampled by various hip-hop artists, including A Tribe Called Quest on "Same Ol' Thing" (1991).

## Celestial Terrestrial Commuters   2:54

This brief, explosive, and much-covered piece in 19/8 was apparently known by the band as "Binky's" because it was an update of "Binky's Beam" from John's *Extrapolation*. Hammer gets a dirty sound on his Moog, and Laird finds a very logical, simple groove that locks everything together. All in all, "Celestial

Terrestrial Commuters" comes across as a kind of Mahavishnu Greatest Hits, showcasing all the players very well.

### Sapphire Bullets Of Pure Love    0:24

Is it a segment of a jam or a soundcheck? Whatever it is, it's credited to John, a source of great annoyance to the band—understandably, given the fact that some major income could be generated from co-writing a track on a million-selling album. The tune's title was borrowed by quirky pop band They Might Be Giants for a track on their 1990 album, *Flood*.

### Thousand Island Park    3:23

Recorded at CBS Studios so Hammer could make use of its famous Steinway piano, this is a companion piece to "A Lotus On Irish Streams." Laird plays acoustic bass for the first and only time on a Mahavishnu Orchestra record. The title comes from an area of New York State beloved of Chinmoy devotees.

### Hope    1:59

This stunning—though strangely curtailed—piece in 7/8 looks forward to the larger ensemble style of *Visions Of Emerald Beyond*, as do its escalating chords. Goodman double-tracks his violin, and Hammer plays a Moog modified to sound like a harpsichord, possibly influenced by tracks such as The Beatles' "Because" and Hendrix's "Burning Of The Midnight Lamp." The menacing chords and odd harmonic movement sit in stark contrast to the composition's title. Return To Forever drummer Lenny White spoke about "Hope" during his *Down Beat* Blindfold Test of May 1978:

> I've always liked Mahavishnu. When he first came out on the scene, he (John) had something new. And when Billy Cobham played with that group, it was really great. All those guys were great. On this tune, which was in an odd-time signature, the drummer basically played in and around the theme. A lot of times when guys play odd-time signatures like this, they jerk. But this flowed well. The sound on this cut was very full. It was probably more than Jerry Goodman on violin there. They probably overdubbed several times. Whether they did or not, it was hot. I liked it and would like to have heard more. I'd give this one three stars. For me, three is really good. Five has to be a classic.

## One Word   9:57

Arguably, this is the ultimate Mahavishnu piece. Laird contributes a memorable, melodic solo, underpinned by John's twelve-string comping in the right speaker, Goodman's funky wah-wah on the left, and Hammer's drone synth. Cobham's groove has been appropriated by everyone from Harvey Mason to Dennis Chambers. Then there are traded solos of ever-decreasing durations—four/two/one/half a bar. It was a variation on the old call-and-response sections on R'n'B records, and it had become a feature of John's music, especially in concert. Cobham takes over with one of the greatest of all recorded drum solos. At 6:54, he plays timbale-like rhythms on his snare over a bass-drum clave, reinforcing the ever-present Latin influence in his playing.

## Sanctuary   5:05

Again, the title seems bittersweet/ironic—sanctuary from what/whom? From everyday life? The music's unresolved harmony and unsettling mood suggest it's not going to be easy to find. The composition opens with a very slow swing groove in 9/4 time, Hammer's Moog sounding uncannily like a flute. "Sanctuary" features over the end credits of Atom Egoyan's 2005 film *Where The Truth Lies*.

## Open Country Joy   3:56

John's D/C/G twelve-string chords and the cheery groove seem almost a pastiche after the previous nightmarish vision. But then there's a pause and a breakout of funky 4/4 with hysterical John, Goodman, and Hammer solos. At 2:28, Ken Scott comes into his own with a remarkable tape edit, the band shifting down into the "hippie" section again (Cobham going miraculously from sticks to brushes). The tune closes out with Goodman's country licks. All in all, it's a curious but likeable piece.

## Resolution   2:09

This extraordinary album closed with a composition originally played by Lifetime (and sung by Jack Bruce) on 1970's *Turn It Over* and titled "One Word." A, B, Bb-min7, and Eb chords are played over a Bb pedal point. This stacking of triads and the ascending melody again look forward to the *Visions Of The Emerald Beyond* sound. And again, the title seems ironic—the track never finds resolution.

# *LOVE DEVOTION SURRENDER* (1973)

John McLaughlin: Guitar, piano
Carlos Santana: Guitar
Khalid Yasin (Larry Young): Organ
Doug Rauch: Bass
Billy Cobham, Don Alias, Jan Hammer, Mike Shrieve: Drums
Armando Peraza: Congas
Produced by Carlos Santana and John McLaughlin
Recorded October/November 1972 and March 1973, Columbia Studios
Released July 20, 1973

McLaughlin claims the idea of *Love Devotion Surrender*—his collaboration with superstar guitarist Carlos Santana—came to him in a dream: "One night in New York, I dreamt that we were playing together. I called Clive Davis the next day and I said, 'You know, Clive, I had this amazing dream. Me and Carlos were playing.' He said, 'Let's do it, let's do it!'"

Santana was a huge fan of John's playing long before he was invited to do the album. He had first caught Lifetime at Slug's in New York in November 1969, checking them out in between his sets at the nearby Fillmore East, and he later attended all of The Mahavishnu Orchestra's first Bay Area gigs. John and Carlos then became good friends when Santana turned up unannounced backstage after a Mahavishnu gig (supporting ELP) at San Francisco's Winterland in March 1972. Carlos remembered: "When I first talked to John, the first thing I said was 'I love what you played with Wayne (Shorter) on *Super Nova*' and we became friends. We both knew that we adored Wayne and Bill Evans and Coltrane, and that was it."[54] It was a typically left-field observation from Santana, sure to catch John's ear. He was born Carlos Augusto Santana Alves Santana in Autlán de Navarro in Jalisco, Mexico, on July 20, 1947. A move to Tijuana led to young Carlos forming his Blues Band in 1966, harnessing influences from John Lee Hooker and BB King to Mongo Santamaria and Tito Puente, and from there he gravitated quickly toward a record deal with Columbia in late 1968.

Since the mid-1960s, a constant in Santana's life had been his love for the music of John Coltrane. In *Chasin' The Trane*, he said: "I haven't heard anything higher than 'The Father And The Son And The Holy Ghost' from the *Meditations* album. I would often play it at four in the morning, the traditional time for meditation. I could hear God's mind in that music. . . . I hear the Supreme One playing music through John Coltrane's mind." (His neighbors' opinions on those 4 a.m. listening sessions remain unreported.)

In Ashley Kahn's book about Coltrane's epochal 1965 album, *A Love Supreme*, Santana spoke about the first time he heard it: "It really was an assault. It could've been from Mars, as far as I was concerned, or another galaxy. . . . The music didn't fit into the patterns of my brain at that point. It was like someone trying to tell a monkey about spirituality or computers, you know, it just didn't compute." In the same book, John concurred, claiming: "To be honest, I didn't get any of it on the first listening. I actually couldn't even understand what he was playing musically, or what he was feeling emotionally." But it seemed a very logical move to take on Coltrane's music once they had decided to collaborate: "It was, for all intents and purposes, a simple expression of our individual and collective affection and admiration for Coltrane," John told Kahn. "The idea of playing our version of *A Love Supreme* came quite naturally. It seemed to me that one of the wonderful aspects of Coltrane's music is its liberating aspect."

*Love Devotion Surrender* was another speedy recording, with the November 1972 session seeing the whole band recording live together in the largest room of Columbia's East 36th Street studio. John brought Jan Hammer and Billy Cobham along to play drums and percussion, and Khalid Yasin (Larry Young) was added on organ. Carlos brought in his Santana bandmates: Doug Rauch on bass, Armando Peraza on percussion, and Mingo Lewis on congas. Drummer/percussionist Don Alias, best known for his work on Miles's albums *Bitches Brew* and *On The Corner*, also joined the fray.

During these initial sessions, the two guitarists became great friends, and Santana would often stay at John's property in New York. John also took Santana to a weekly Chinmoy meditation meeting at the United Nations building, and the guru blessed him there and then, also giving him the spiritual name Devadip, which loosely translates as "the lamp, light and eye of God." This came at just the right time for Santana, who had been drifting for a while in a spiritually confused state, tiring of the darker side of the music business with attendant drug issues, dodgy managers, cloying fans expecting "the answer," and sometimes unscrupulous accountants and promoters. He was after a new humility, one that would keep him able to continue in the industry, a lifesaving mission. Chinmoy fitted the bill perfectly. (In 2022, he described his faith as a "devotion of humility" and also credited promoter/impresario Bill Graham for giving him a wake-up call as to what may lie ahead if he continued down the "rock star" path.[55])

Buoyed by his new faith, Santana left for a European tour with his band, and the final sessions for *Love Devotion Surrender* took place upon his return to New York in March 1973. The difference in Carlos now was striking—he left the November before wearing jeans and a T-shirt and sporting long, flowing locks, but now he returned in a white suit and with cropped hair, a true Chinmoy disciple. And a musician with an increasingly open mind.

Taken as a whole, *Love Devotion Surrender* was yet another remarkably brave recording from John, again made under "jazz" circumstances, with spontaneity and passion in the front seat, an anathema to the days of Pro Tools and post-production prevalent at the time of this writing. As a result, the album has many flaws—the recording is muddy, there are a myriad of fluffs, and the mix is rather forbidding. And, as both John and Santana play Gibson Les Pauls on the electric tracks, at times their tones are somewhat interchangeable. But *Love Devotion Surrender* is such an uncompromising piece of work that it demands respect, and it also features several quite outrageous bits of musicianship can still enthrall today. But in its own way, it's as difficult to listen to as Albert Ayler's most challenging work, its fusion of jazz, R'n'B, rock, Latin, and gospel radical and fairly unprecedented.

At the time of its release, John was extremely positive about the album and collaboration: "We had a very strong rapport. And neither of us dominates the music. Spiritual harmony creates musical harmony. The result is different from the Mahavishnu Orchestra and different from Santana. I think it's greater than them both."[56]

Columbia also pushed the boat out for the LP, issuing it in a gatefold sleeve, including two pre-irony photos of John, Santana, and Chinmoy, the latter looking like the proud father of his two sons. There was also a transcription of a lecture given by Chinmoy at the American International School in Zurich, Switzerland, on November 27, 1970. It included one telling quote from philosopher and theologian Saint Augustine, which, taken out of context, possibly prompted a few unintended interpretations: "Love and then do what you like."

While John and Santana's collaboration was obviously borne purely out of love and respect—both for Coltrane's music and for each other—it's not difficult to imagine that Carlos's fans were rather more disappointed, or at least puzzled, than John's. Still, *Love Devotion Surrender* found an audience quickly, reaching a very impressive #7 on the UK album charts, #14 in the United States, and quickly becoming a Gold record. John reminisced about the album twenty-eight years after its release, telling Kahn: "I look back on it like I look back on all of my recordings: they're all like paintings, full of faults, but the best we could do at that time."[57] For his part, Santana sensed a wasted opportunity, wishing they could do *Love Devotion Surrender* all over again:

I would do it with a symphony, with real African drummers, Brazilian musicians, with Alice Coltrane, Ali Akbar Khan, Wayne Shorter, Pharoah Sanders, Herbie,

McCoy and everyone in tuxedos. In that way, when people hear it, they'll be dancing in the aisles, laughing and crying at the same time like they have the Holy Spirit in them. Before I leave this planet, that's how I would like to turn on the masses to *A Love Supreme.*[58]

(Santana, when presenting the Record Of The Year Grammy award to U2 in 2001, joked with his co-host, Joni Mitchell—a fellow Coltrane fan—that the winner should be *A Love Supreme.*) In April 1973, John also co-composed and guested on the eleven-minute track "Flame—Sky" from the Santana album *Welcome* (whose title track was a cover of the John Coltrane classic), released on November 9. It was an extension of the *Love Devotion Surrender* sound, a long, meditative, electric track with elements of Latin and modal jazz/rock in 9/8, with a briefly thrilling trading of fours by John and Carlos.

Then, just to reaffirm their musical and spiritual kinship, it was announced that the two guitarists would embark on a US tour through August and September 1973. All the personnel from the album sessions would be retained for the touring band with the exceptions of Alias and Hammer. The New York rehearsals were attended by future Mahavishnu drummer Narada Michael Walden, who "sat cross-legged on the floor right behind Billy Cobham. . . . What a monster! We had never heard the likes of him before."[59] Santana also revealed in 2022 that Chinmoy had "warned him" about Walden, saying there was a guy who played "like a fire hydrant"![60]

Santana was amazed by the power of the music the band played during the tour: "For me, it was almost like being a kid four or five years out of high school and then suddenly driving a twelve-cylinder Maserati."[61] The setlist included "Flame—Sky," an electric duet version of "Meditation" and also a track of unknown origin named "I'm Aware Of You."

Around this time, John and Santana also composed the music for the short film *Awakening*, directed by Anthony Hixon in 1974, subtitled *The Art Of Meditation With Sri Chinmoy And His Disciples.* It was essentially a PR piece, interviewing disciples as they went about their daily life in New York City, showing their meditation classes and a "track and field day," including some extraordinary footage of Chinmoy sprinting, throwing a javelin and a shotput, and blessing some food his disciples had prepared. There's a fascinating moment when an unnamed disciple relays the answer Chinmoy gave to the question as to why he chose America for his base of operations. He said it was due to the "spontaneity, child-like simplicity and openness of Americans." The soundtrack includes an interesting acoustic duet take on "Follow Your Heart," with John taking the lead on twelve-string, while elsewhere Santana briefly appears playing solo acoustic guitar. (John doesn't appear in the film.)

Some bizarre footage has also emerged of John and Santana playing on a float at a Chinmoy street parade in New York on March 8, 1975, before they gave a free concert in Central Park celebrating Chinmoy's ten-thousandth "Jharna-Kala" painting. Jharna-Kala is a Bengali phrase translating as "fountain art." John and Santana sing an original piece of the same name and a guitar improvisation that includes elements from "Flame—Sky" and "Meeting Of The Spirits." Narada Michael Walden also briefly appears playing a marching snare drum and then is seen sitting on the ground, watching the concert and clapping along. Reportedly John and Santana also played "Let Us Go into the House of the Lord" during this concert, but it is not shown.

Santana went on to accompany Alice Coltrane, Dave Holland, Peraza, and Jack DeJohnette on the 1974 album *Illuminations*. He reports he was particularly daunted to play with Coltrane, but she quickly put his mind at rest, telling him: "Walk like a giant because you're one of us."[62] By 1980, Santana was no longer a Chinmoy devotee, but as late as 1995 he was still publicly proclaiming some of his teachings, telling *Guitar Player* magazine: "If you're going to sweep the floor, sweep it better than anybody in town. And if you're going to play the guitar, really, really, really get in it, and don't be jivin.'"[63]

In 2001, musician and producer Bill Laswell—also a controversial interpreter of Miles's 1969-1974 music on the *Panthalassa* set—released a remix album featuring four songs from *Love Devotion Surrender* named *Divine Light: Reconstruction & Mix Translation*, alongside elements from *Illuminations*.

## A Love Supreme  (John Coltrane)  7:48

This is actually a version of "Acknowledgement," the first part of John Coltrane's *A Love Supreme* suite. John's solos—higher in the mix than Santana's—are particularly superb. An alternate, more elaborate take was included on the 2003 reissue featuring no flanger effect on Rauch's bass, a different stereo mix (John on the left, Santana on the right) and a slightly different chord harmony implied by Yasin (Young) on organ.

## Naima  (John Coltrane)  3:09

An unexpected treat, this is a simple acoustic reading of the classic composition from Coltrane's 1959 album, *Giant Steps*, perhaps inspired by "Rene's Theme" on the Larry Coryell album *Spaces*. A superior alternate mix appeared on the

2003 reissue of *Love Devotion Surrender*, with better instrument separation and clearer sound.

## The Life Divine    9:30

This is Cobham's only appearance on the album, but the track's poor recording and muddy mix mean that individual instruments are very hard to pick out. The uncertain vocals and bass again allude to Coltrane's "Acknowledgement." Santana's first solo features Echoplex and wah-wah and is apparently designed to invoke fear and dread—John deliberately goes in the opposite direction. The quadrophonic vinyl release of *Love Surrender Devotion* features a different John solo.

## Let Us Go into the House of the Lord (traditional)    15:45

The title comes from the Bible's Psalm 122:1, spoken by David (interestingly, of course, the name of John's older brother). Spiritual jazz pioneer and Coltrane collaborator Pharoah Sanders performed it on his 1970 album *Deaf Dumb Blind*, with an arrangement by Lonnie Liston Smith. The first half of John and Carlos's version sticks to Smith's *rubato* arrangement, but then—presumably at Santana's urging—a lengthy Latin section is added. Though the track is a fairly exhausting listen and John's guitar is often out of tune, the trading of fours beginning at 11:23 is some of the most exciting playing of both John and Santana's careers.

## Meditation    2:45

The opening sound effect is perhaps a nod to Weather Report's "Milky Way," from their 1970 self-titled debut album. John plays simple piano on this extremely effective, memorable track. At 2:17, he refers to a melodic idea that he will explore more fully a year later on "Power Of Love" from *Apocalypse*.

## THE LOST TRIDENT SESSIONS (RECORDED 1973, RELEASED SEPTEMBER 21, 1999)

John McLaughlin: Six- and twelve-string electric guitar and acoustic guitar
Jerry Goodman: Electric violin, viola, and violow (custom viola with cello strings)

Jan Hammer: Electric piano and synthesizers
Rick Laird: Bass
Billy Cobham: Drums
Produced by The Mahavishnu Orchestra (1999 version produced by Bob Belden)
Recorded at Trident Studios, London, England, June 25–29, 1973

The Mahavishnu Orchestra's summer UK tour of 1973 was a huge success. The final date took place at London's Rainbow Theatre on June 30, and in the run-up to the concert, John took advantage of being in the capital to book some time at Trident. It seemed like the most natural fit; Engineer Ken Scott knew the studio inside and out, having worked there on records like David Bowie's *Hunky Dory*, John Lennon's *Give Peace A Chance*, and George Harrison's *All Things Must Pass*. Though the atmosphere in the band was not exactly convivial, John and Laird in particular were very happy to be back in London, visiting old friends and collaborators during their (infrequent) time off.

But Scott ended up presiding over a rather unsettled group of musicians and a very disparate set of recordings: "John wasn't happy in the slightest. It was the hardest bunch of sessions I have ever gone through."[64] Coming from the man who worked on The Beatles' *White Album*, this is a serious claim. John certainly made no bones about being in a very emotional state during the Trident sessions, allegedly leaving one in tears. He outlined the heart of the problem:

> I can still say music is God . . . the face of God . . . but that's not how everybody sees it. And, of course, what happened in interviews, especially in collective interviews, was that people would ask me questions and I would talk about development and ideals . . . and these questions would be posed to the other musicians and they would say, 'We don't want to feel that way at all, we're not into that.'[65]

One such interview was granted by Hammer to *Crawdaddy* magazine just after the Trident sessions. "The studio is so great, the sound was so incredible, but . . . the band just didn't play well. We can't use any of it because we didn't rehearse." Though it's easy to disagree with Hammer—there's plenty of excellent playing on the album, particularly from Cobham and the keyboardist himself—his mood during the sessions can't have been helped by the fact that he was seriously unwell, requiring throat surgery after the recording. It's also remarkable to consider that Hammer and Goodman were only in their early twenties during this period. Cobham, for his part, was very aware of the nervous tension around the group when listening back on the sessions twenty-five years later: "It is shocking to hear how fast we played many of those compositions."[66]

But were the Trident recordings an attempt by John to mollify the other band members? He certainly included more of their compositions, while providing "Dream," "Trilogy," and "John's Song #2" (the former two were also played live regularly during 1973). The latter, a superbly arranged six minutes of controlled virtuosity, is underpinned by a striking "drone" effect from Hammer's Moog. Laird is a lot higher in the mix than previously and contributes "Steppings Tones," whose title comes from a word game played by the band while on the road. Laird was reportedly very unhappy with this version.

Goodman contributes "I Wonder"—there are rumors that the violinist also played rhythm guitar on this track. John plays one of the most "conventional" electric solos of his career, almost taking it into arena-rock territory. Apparently, a live version of "I Wonder" from Hiroshima, Japan (September 26, 1973, available to hear on YouTube), features Carlos Santana's favorite-ever piece of John's guitar playing: "It is incredibly emotional and moving. It is not notes anymore. It is pure slices of life."[67]

Hammer contributes "Sister Andrea," featuring a knockout Moog solo by the composer with a little help from a ring modulator. He generally expands his arsenal on his album, also playing his Fender Rhodes through a phaser pedal (used to sublime, soulful effect on "Dream").

There were rumors that John gave less than 100-percent effort when performing on others' compositions—completely refuted by Elliott Sears in Kolosky's *Power, Passion*. But the jury's out on whether Laird, Hammer, and Goodman's compositions are really "Mahavishnu tunes," and whether John's heart was ever really in a fully cooperative band effort. Cobham decided to forego submitting compositions for the album, saving them for *Spectrum*, as he reported in the 1999 liner notes:

> I was not comfortable writing for the band. I didn't want to write like John, I wanted to have my own personality come through. And at that point, it would've been painful to be put down, to have a piece of mine rejected. The rest of the guys would fight for the right to express themselves in the band. Meanwhile, I had already decided that this was not the theatre of operations to comfortably present my ideas. So I decided to parallel that by making my own record.

Despite his own compositional contribution, Laird was also ambivalent about the new material on *The Lost Trident Sessions*, also outlined in the liner notes:

One of the drawbacks that I think began to affect us, even at that point, was the fact that we were so busy traveling and it was so exhausting that there was very little time for development of the music . . . for new music. We never rehearsed. Rehearsals never happened. In fact, I don't think we rehearsed at all after the initial two or three months. There just wasn't any time. So I think that affected things pretty badly in terms of musical growth.

John once alluded to the fact that he intended to add strings to the Trident recordings at a later date in New York ("Last year I wanted to record a symphonic album, but it was completely denied me by the group. I thought this was a pity because we could have done something really significant."[68] This is particularly apparent on the more meditative, spacey moments of the album, such as the opening of "Dream" and pastoral sections of "Trilogy," which seem tailor-made for something a little more widescreen. Mike Gibbs also remembers attending Trident with a view to adding orchestral arrangement, but he reports this didn't go down well with the band.

Characteristically, John has generally looked back favorably on the sessions, stating in the 1999 liner notes: "I was very happy, actually, with the lost album. Of course, by the time we finished that recording, there was a lot of dissonance in the band, discontent . . . I have a tendency to forget the bad things. I remember the good things." Twenty-two years later, he shed more light on those issues: "At the end of mixing, everyone seemed happy. A couple of weeks went by, then Jan and Jerry told me they didn't want to release it. They never told me why. As a result, we recorded the Central Park show (as heard on *Between Nothingness And Eternity*) to replace it."[69]

For his part, Elliott Sears was astonished to find that no one working in Sony Records' jazz division during the late 1990s knew they had the tapes in their midst: "When I told the people at Sony that this album existed, they were dumbfounded. They had no idea. How many people do you think who worked at Columbia Records in 1973 are still there today (in 1999)? No-one. People move on, especially executives. So it was forgotten and buried, until I told Bob Belden about it." In November 1998, while working on the *Birds Of Fire* reissue in Sony's Los Angeles vault, Belden came across two unmarked quarter-inch tapes, the fabled two-track mixes of *The Lost Trident Sessions*.

Still, Sony's decision to finally unleash it on the world seemed to pay off when, upon its eventual September 1999 release, *The Lost Trident Sessions* hit #2 on the Billboard Jazz charts. But John was ambivalent about the company's judgment call, telling Anil Prasad:

I didn't authorize them! I don't have any power whatsoever over these people, let's get this clear right away. They do precisely what they want. They don't care what I want or don't want. They are essentially the owner of the tape and I am a secondary consideration. It's as simple as that. . . . But I'm delighted because it's a wonderful recording and they are idiots for losing the tapes and not releasing them a long time ago.[70]

Meanwhile, in the slipstream of recording the lost album, July 1973 began on a slightly more positive note as the *NME* published a glowing survey of John's career so far written by esteemed essayist Ian MacDonald. But there was hardly time for John and the band to catch their breath—the Canadian Mahavishnu Orchestra tour began with a July 13 gig at the Montreal Forum. Then it was back to the States in August for some exhausting one-nighters, followed by a Japanese sojourn throughout September—during which all hell broke loose.

## BETWEEN NOTHINGNESS & ETERNITY (1973)

John McLaughlin: Guitar
Jerry Goodman: Violin
Jan Hammer: Piano, Moog
Rick Laird: Bass
Billy Cobham: Drums
Recorded live on August 18, 1973, in Central Park, New York City
Produced by Murray Krugman and John McLaughlin.
Released November 1973

The Orchestra played two free concerts in New York's Central Park on August 17 and 18, 1973 as part of the Schaefer Music Festival. This was a major musical and cultural event—reportedly they performed to ten thousand people each night. Columbia recorded both shows, but in the end, all the music included on the album *Between Nothingness And Eternity* came from the second night. They played a lot of new material from *The Lost Trident Sessions*, but according to Laird: "It was pretty loose. We were throwing things together backstage that night with no rehearsal."[71]

There were other developments, too—for the first time ever, John made a point of announcing each band member at the start of both gigs. The concerts were also notable for featuring John's famous new twin-neck Double Rainbow guitar, which took luthier Rex Bogue a whole year to design and build. Bogue was already a major fan when he appeared backstage at the Whiskey A-Go-Go on Sunset Boulevard in March 1972 to demonstrate one of his solid-body electrics. John was immediately impressed but asked for a double-neck, one with twelve strings, one with six. He had a few other stipulations too: he wanted "Guru Alo"—roughly translated as "He who leads from darkness into lightness"—inscribed at the base of the fingerboards. According to Bogue, "He also wanted the neck to go to high D instead of C#, and he asked for Gibson-style humbucking pickups."[72] The guitar was completed on July 18, 1973, weighed about thirty pounds, and was sold to John for five thousand dollars. John played it for the first time in concert on July 21 at the Lenox Arts Festival in Massachusetts. The new guitar certainly seems to unleash something—*Between Nothingness & Eternity* features arguably the loudest and fastest electric playing of John's entire career.

Even if some reports state that the sound at the Central Park gigs was far from excellent, Hammer had no complaints about the onstage mix: "It was a fantastic experience. I remember doing the soundcheck with this humungous sound system. . . . I felt all of New York heard me. It was an amazing feeling."[73] However, it's hard to escape the conclusion that the sound on *Between Nothingness & Eternity* is anything but pristine—it suffers from a very muddy mix throughout, though this never derails the mostly spellbinding music.

There were other issues around the Central Park concerts: Cobham revealed that one of his treasured kits was stolen after the second night: "Once we had finished the show, the truck was stolen with the drums in it. We never found the truck or the drums or anything else. That was the smoke grey Fibes kit. I played it twice and then it was gone."[74]

In 2011, Columbia issued *The Complete Columbia Albums Collection*, credited to The Original Mahavishnu Orchestra, which featured other tracks from the two Central Park concerts not included on the original album: "Hope," "Awakening," "You Know, You Know," "One Word" (featuring a superb Laird wah-wah bass solo), "Steppings Tones" (mislabeled as "Stepping Tones"), "Vital Transformation," and "The Dance Of Maya." These are well worth seeking out, especially from a drumming perspective, and it is a shame they weren't originally issued on *Between Nothingness & Eternity*.

The rest of 1973 was destined to be a tumultuous period in the life of Mahavishnu Mark 1. After the Central Park concerts, John and Cobham joined Santana on tour in August and September to support *Love Devotion Surrender* while Goodman, Laird, and Hammer went on holiday in Hawaii. They then all embarked on a long flight to Japan, during which John read an advanced copy of a long band profile for *Crawdaddy* magazine ("Two Sides To Every Satori," November 1973), in which Hammer was less than complimentary about the guitarist, and other members expressed worries about composition credits. John was reportedly very upset (though, according to Kolosky, he has no memory of this flight); the subsequent Tokyo press conference was apparently extremely uncomfortable.

Part of the problem seems to be that John was often confused by his band-mates' apparent indifference to his spiritual belief system, in direct contrast to the openness of journalists and fans: "People were very interested in it. They asked me lots of questions about Sri Chinmoy and all the spiritual things—meditation and India and religion. But of course none of the other musicians went into that."[75] At the outset of the Japanese tour, Hammer and Goodman were reportedly refusing to speak to John. Cobham was inclined to side more with John, wondering why the rest of the band didn't do more sideman work. He also later located something musical in the discord: "John was getting very upset with Jerry and Jan, who emulated him on their instruments, especially Jan. Jan had a better guitar sound on the Moog than John did."[76] Laird hovered between the two factions, sympathetic to John while concerned over royalties and unwilling to relinquish complete control to Chinmoy. (Laird did, however, regularly go to meetings with Sri Swami Satchidananda, later to be immortalized in an Alice Coltrane album and song title.)

Elliott Sears witnessed these *contretemps* first-hand, and he looked back with some regret in the *Lost Trident Sessions* liner notes: "What they should've done was vent their frustrations in a room with the door locked with the five of them together and maybe Nat Weiss as a referee. But they did it in print, which wasn't smart. John read the transcript of the magazine on the airplane on the way to Japan, and he felt like, 'How could you say this about me?' And that was really the beginning of the end."

After the Osaka gig of September 21, 1973, it was crunch time. A distraught John, faced with a band of silent, sullen musicians, played his last card:

> I said, 'Look, why doesn't anyone say one word to me? If you have something on your mind, just say you hate me, just tell me. It's OK. Tell me and things will get better.' But neither of them (Hammer and Goodman) would say a word and Rick Laird told them: 'Why don't you tell him? You are always talking to me when he is not around.' I realized this was the end of the band. It also had to do with success. . . . Success is hard to take.[77]

Back in the States, as touring resumed in October, things didn't improve, though now everyone in the band was receiving an equal share of concert revenues via the newly established Mahavishnu, Inc. And the band was still drawing new converts, such as future Miles/Weather Report/John Scofield/Sting drummer Omar Hakim, who witnessed them at Queens College in Flushing, New York, on October 7, 1973: "It was the loudest thing I'd ever experienced! It was ferocious, a remarkable show. Back then, we had no preconceptions about what to expect."[78] Meanwhile, according to Laird, John and Nat Weiss had agreed to end The Mahavishnu Orchestra at the end of 1973, and Weiss alone—not John—informed the rest of the band. But Hammer insists there was a band meeting with John present, too, during which financial settlements were arranged. (Goodman is on record as saying he doesn't remember this meeting.) For his part, Cobham recalls that John privately told him about the impending split, and that he wanted Cobham to stay on for Mahavishnu Mark 2. But this changed when Cobham became very aware of Narada Michael Walden's presence toward the end of 1973.

Meanwhile the band struggled on, but the pressure began to bear down on Cobham, who had a mini physical and mental breakdown before a show in Atlanta, Georgia, which was subsequently cancelled. They then played on Boxing Day in Florida, then at New York's Avery Fisher Hall on December 27 and the Philharmonic Hall a day later. The original Mahavishnu Orchestra's final gig took place on December 30, 1973, at the Masonic Temple in Detroit, Michigan. Laird was given his longest-ever bass solo during the encore, a stunning version of "One Word." John then ended the concert with the following announcement: "Thank you from all of us. God bless you all. May you have many happy new years."[79]

According to Laird, they didn't say good-bye to each other after the last concert: "I do remember thinking how stupid it was to be ending the band. All we really needed was some time off to recover from the brutal touring schedule and perhaps a little therapy!"[80] Sadly, the kind of group counseling witnessed in the 2004 rockumentary *Metallica: Some Kind Of Monster* was decades away. Hammer had mixed feelings: "I remember being sad at the end . . . I personally felt my contribution to the band was greater than it was given credit."[81] For his part, John looked back only with sadness: "Of all the groups I've been in, this is the one that didn't end well. I probably will regret that to the end of my days."[82]

In the immediate aftermath of the breakup, Cobham continued with his very successful solo career, delivering the #23 *Billboard* pop album *Crosswinds*. Hammer formed a duet with Goodman (who sometimes played guitar as well as violin) to make *Like Children* for Nemperor Records, which featured Laird's

"Steppings Tones." The bassist returned to New York City to carve out a career as a session player. In 1982, he left the music business to become a professional photographer. (Ironically, he credits Billy Cobham as his main inspiration, also a talented and enthusiastic photographer.) He later wrote two bass instruction books and died on July 4, 2021.

### Trilogy: Sunlit Path/La Mere de la Mer/Tomorrow's Story Not The Same    12:16

After Cobham's gong silences the crowd, the opening section is in 7/8. Laird isn't heard properly until 2:20—presumably due to sound problems—and Hammer often sounds like he's playing deliberately "obvious" licks, perhaps his small way of expressing discontent? Cobham taps into his own "Quadrant 4" for a marvelous double-bass shuffle alongside a distinctly Hendrix-like riff. At 10:57, the "Sunlit Path" theme returns, and then there's a wrong-footing riff later quoted by Level 42's Mark King during the band's "88" on their 1985 live album, *A Physical Presence*.

### Sister Andrea (Jan Hammer)    8:45

Hammer's tune—kicking off with a funky vamp in G—is named for his sister back in Prague. Laird gets a full-bodied bass tone, and John plays a hysterical guitar feature over augmented A chords. The composer then sets off on a memorable Moog odyssey, while Cobham—uncharacteristically—speeds up a great deal.

### Dream    21:24

The opening section is in a very slow 15/4. Moving into a brisk 15/16, John fires off a delicious solo with microtonal string bends and a flamenco-like attack. Cobham plays soft sticks around the toms while Hammer experiments with serialism. Laird moves to a wah-wah vamp, and Hammer and John duel in A, followed by some of the most ferocious riffing in the history of the band with a nod to Cream's "Sunshine Of Your Love." John then plays arguably the fastest, loudest solo of his career. It certainly sounds like he's letting off a great deal of steam. Despite the remarkable virtuosity at play, "Dream" is much closer to progressive rock than "fusion."

# 4

# 1974–1979

## From *Apocalpyse* to *Electric Dreams*

### APOCALYPSE (1974)

John McLaughlin: Electric guitars, vocals
Jean-Luc Ponty: Electric violin, electric baritone violin
Gayle Moran: Keyboards, vocals
Ralphe Armstrong: Acoustic bass, electric bass, vocals
Narada Michael Walden: Drums, percussion, vocals
Carol Shive: Violin, vocals
Marsha Westbrook: Biola
Philip Hirschi: Cello, vocals
The London Symphony Orchestra led by Hugh Beau
Michael Tilson Thomas: Piano, conductor
Michael Gibbs: Orchestrator
Recorded at AIR Studios, London, March 9–15, 1974
Produced by George Martin
Released June 1974

It was a huge decision for John to arrest the first iteration of The Mahavishnu Orchestra, affecting agents, managers, lawyers—and musicians. Some estimated that John himself was due to lose around a million dollars in lost touring revenue. But at least on the surface, the schism didn't affect his relationship with Columbia Records.

In early 1974, he was ready to branch out with the second version of The Orchestra. This new band would feature several Chinmoy disciples, one of which was the drumming wunderkind Narada Michael Walden. In February 1973, he was just a scrappy eighteen-year-old kid named Michael Walden, a promising young player based in Canaan, Connecticut. Growing up in Kalamazoo, Michigan, his parents had been fans of jazz and musical theater, and he had taken up the piano and drums at an early age, inspired by Jimi Hendrix, Smokey Robinson, Curtis Mayfield, and The Who. But his hero was drummer Art Blakey, particularly carrying a torch for the Jazz Messenger's playing on guitarist Kenny Burrell's *The Sermon* album. Walden was soon a drum major at high school and became part of the army band.

At the end of 1972, Walden was playing with a Miami-based unit called The New McGuire Sisters alongside talented sixteen-year-old bassist Ralphe Armstrong. Armstrong was already emerging as a highly original player, a double threat on fretless electric and standup acoustic, influenced by Ron Carter, Michael Henderson, and James Jamerson. He had also studied classical bass at Michigan's Interlochen Arts Academy.

Walden had excessively indulged in alcohol and drugs as a youth, but he was yearning to find more stability in his life. Accordingly, he had already visited a Chinmoy Centre in Miami before hearing that The Mahavishnu Orchestra were coming to play in Hartford. He got a ride to the gig, and his life was never the same again. He was already a huge Cobham fan, of course: "He was completely the most awesome drummer in the world. You've never seen or heard anything as powerful or strong. (He was) James Brown funk fused into jazz and fusion so furious, so profound that it would stop anyone."[1] Walden waited around after the concert, and another Chinmoy disciple in the audience introduced Walden to John. Walden gave John his phone number, and John promised to tell Chinmoy about their meeting. Walden got a call from John a week later, urging the drummer to go to a Chinmoy gathering in Norwalk, Connecticut. There, Walden found Chinmoy playing the harmonium, flanked by young men and women. A woman read poems from a book called *The Dance Of Life Part 2*. Walden felt a life-changing surge. After the session, he went upstairs to visit Chinmoy's library of books, and he suddenly came face-to-face with the guru. After telling Walden that John was currently traveling on a plane but was thinking about them, Chinmoy asked Walden: "You would like to be my disciple?" Walden replied: "I think I'm ready." Chinmoy answered: "I accept you within my heart." Walden exploded with "waves of gratitude," and the roots of Mahavishnu Mark II were sown.[2]

Later, in July 1973, after another Mahavishnu concert, John and Walden drove to the drummer's house. They meditated together in Walden's cabin, in the middle of the woods, for twenty minutes, during which Walden was astonished to see John weeping, tears falling down onto the wooden floor. "I had to ask myself: Am I really ready for this? Am I ready to go on this journey?"[3] John, Armstrong, and Walden then jammed on some fast funk, John strangely emotionless. As Walden reported, "I closed my eyes and looked down. . . . As long as I looked in his face, looking at me like that, it was just too tripped out, man. I'm used to a cat showing the agony, showing the pain!"[4]

John went away to Cuba with Chinmoy to meditate during Christmas 1973, and he offered Walden and Armstrong the Mahavishnu Orchestra gig on his return to the United States in January 1974. (Armstrong also claims Jaco Pastorius auditioned after him, and also that he was an unexpected inspiration for Pastorius's famous fretless bass sound: "He came and auditioned after me and John gave me the gig because he loved the sound of the fretless Precision bass. And Jaco got mad and ripped all the frets out of his bass and put epoxy in there!") Armstrong also claims Carlos Santana contacted him during the same week, offering him a gig, too; he wondered if John and Santana had flipped a coin to see who would get Walden and Armstrong. (Walden would later collaborate with Santana, writing the 1979 classic "Song For Devadip" from the *Oneness* album.)

Walden moved his home near a Chinmoy Centre in Norwalk, and he started playing in a band of disciples called Jatra. Chinmoy also gave Walden the name "Narada," disciple to Vishnu (John), a role Walden was very happy to play. Musically, Walden's first port of call was learning to play comfortably in odd meters, though he had done a little of that with The New McGuire Sisters. John coached Walden on playing in seven, nine, eleven, and thirteen, without ever stressing the downbeat (the "one" of the bar). As Walden said, "Mahavishnu is the king of cat and mouse. Don't play the downbeat. In odd meters, that's really rough."[5] (It's interesting to note that neither John nor Walden considered there might be value to the *audience* to hear the "one.") Walden learned to watch John's body language rather than his eyes, to "feel" the bar lines (here there's a striking similarity to how some of Miles's bandmates "read" the trumpeter's body language—saxophone Sonny Fortune reports in Tingen's *Miles Beyond*: "We knew his movements. Everybody watched him. I guess we took it upon ourselves to try and read the small amount of instructions or movements he presented to us. We weren't going to say to him, 'Man, make yourself clear,' because we recognized magic.") John could be a hard taskmaster, though: "You didn't listen very well tonight" was a frequent refrain. But when it worked, he would often say: "You were a tiger tonight." Still, it was an intense school for Walden, and he would record rehearsals on his tape player and listen back endlessly to learn the music—there were no written charts.

Despite any misgivings Walden had about following Cobham onto the Mahavishnu drum chair, it quickly became apparent to everyone that he was a monster player. Guitarist Allan Holdsworth recalled hearing *Apocalypse* and being astonished by the drumming: "Everyone thought, 'Billy Cobham was absolutely unbelievable, how's anybody going to follow that?' Then the new McLaughlin album came out and there was this insane drummer on it. Geez, where did he come from?"[6] Holdsworth later employed Walden for his debut (subsequently disowned) solo album, 1976's *Velvet Darkness*.

For Armstrong's part, the Mahavishnu gig was very hard work but extraordinarily rewarding: "Well, it was a blessing. . . . It was a great thrill. I learned so much about music from him. He was a real disciplinarian with us. He made us play, man. We had rehearsals after the gig. . . . He worked our tongues out!"[7]

The new Mahavishnu lineup was then completed via a variety of sources. Twenty-three-year-old Gayle Moran came in on keyboards and vocals. She was born near Detroit, the daughter of a Christian minister, and had sung at some of the evangelist Billy Graham's shows. She spent eighteen months touring with a production of *Jesus Christ Superstar*, then moved to New York at the recommendation of Chick Corea. She was playing with Walden in the Chinmoy house band Jatra when John recruited her. Moran enjoyed the atmosphere around the new group, but she had some reservations about her own technical prowess: "It was a very warm and friendly band. . . . It was to my advantage that I didn't know much about fusion. I wasn't trying to be like Jan Hammer, though he was very kind, spending some time with me so I could learn a few things . . . I was just into singing and doing what was asked of me."[8]

Violinst Carol Shive—already a big fan of the original Mahavishnu—was recruited from the Honolulu Philharmonic. (She had even played with Elvis Presley on the *Aloha From Hawaii* concert.) She was a Christian who converted to the Chinmoy cult when the guru came to Honolulu. John had also been in the crowd when she played a Bach partita at a Chinmoy Centre in Manhattan. Phil Hirschi came in on cello, a graduate of Yale University where he had studied English literature and played in the orchestra. He was a Chinmoy disciple who lived near John in Queens. Viola player Marsha Westbrook was a non-disciple, a talented New York session player who looked upon her role in the Orchestra merely as a high-quality, well-paid gig. Finally, in late 1973, John upped the ante in terms of a solo foil, bringing in French violin virtuoso Jean-Luc Ponty. He had made his name as a jazz player in the 1960s, before moving to America to play with Frank Zappa. He was planning a solo career when he heard from John.

The core five-piece band (John, Walden, Armstrong, Moran, Luc-Ponty) rehearsed for a month at SIR in New York during early 1974, with James Taylor and Yoko Ono down the corridor. The new Mahavishnu Orchestra's first concert was in Buffalo, New York, on February 21. Violinist/conductor Isaac Stern had been booked to perform a benefit with the Buffalo Philharmonic, but he had to pull out. Michael Tilson Thomas, musical director and guest conductor of the Philharmonic, suggested that John's new band step in, with the symphony orchestra joining them on one section. Tilson Thomas was just twenty-eight years old at the time, a former child prodigy who had met John in 1973 via a contact at Columbia. They hit it off immediately, John realizing that Tilson Thomas loved soul and funk as much as he did Western classical music. During that first gig, the twenty-five-minute performance of "Hymn To Him" floored Walden—he virtually had to be dragged from the stage, he was so high from the music.

The new Orchestra in place, the stage was set for John's most ambitious project yet, a collaboration between "rock" group—albeit of the super-charged, jazz-and-funk-inflected variety—and symphony orchestra. Of course, this basic concept was nothing new. Arguably, it all started with The Beatles' "A Day In The Life," progressing to The Moody Blues' *Days Of Future Passed*, Deep Purple's *Concerto For Group And Orchestra*, The Nice's *Five Bridges Suite*, Pink Floyd's *Atom Heart Mother*, and Zappa's *200 Motels* (Don Sebesky's 1973 album, *Giant Box*, had also featured a segue of Stravinsky's *Firebird Suite* and John's *Birds Of Fire*, with Cobham on drums, Ron Carter on bass, and Airto on percussion). John invited arranger Mike Gibbs to orchestrate *Apocalypse* as a result of hearing his distinctly Gil Evans-esque "Some Echoes, Some Shadows," featuring Jack Bruce, guitarist Ray Russell, and Kenny Wheeler, appearing on Gibbs's 1970 self-titled album.

Gibbs was born in Rhodesia—now Zimbabwe—in 1937. He studied orchestral music and in the late 1950s won a place at the Berklee music school in Boston, where he began a lifelong association with vibraphonist and improvisation teacher Gary Burton. Gibbs also credits Burton as the person who inspired him to start composing, a process culminating in him writing the title track of Stan Getz's 1969 Verve album, *Sweet Rain* (also featuring Chick Corea and Tony Williams). Gibbs studied under Third Stream pioneer/composer Gunter Schuller in New York in the early 1960s, becoming enamored with Oliver Messiaen, Charles Ives, and Krzysztof Penderecki. Gibbs then moved to London, where he met his English wife, Cilla, crossing paths with John while both playing with fellow ex-Berklee graduate Graham Collier and Dankworth on Wheeler's *Windmill Tilter*. He also found work as musical director for the cult BBC comedy

*The Goodies* and recorded the *In The Public Interest* album for Polydor Records alongside Burton.

Gibbs had to move fast once he was informed by John that The London Symphony Orchestra (who completed their work in just five three-hour sessions), producer George Martin (apparently already a big fan of John's work), and engineer Geoff Emerick had been booked for the second week of March 1974 at Martin's AIR Studios just off Oxford Street in central London. Gibbs had just a few weeks to produce his charts. He told Kolosky about his approach to orchestrating the album in the book *Power, Passion and Beauty*: "All of the music's structure was quite established. I didn't need to add any bars. For want of a better description, I would say John gave me an elaborate piano lead sheet and then I orchestrated it."

The band stayed at the Churchill Hotel on Oxford Street during the recording of *Apocalypse*. It was an eye-opener for the young Armstrong, who was on his first-ever trip overseas, and he found himself being taken under Jeff Beck's wing. The guitarist drove Armstrong around town, regularly taking him to the Speakeasy club.

Martin and Emerick initially wanted to set the whole band and orchestra up in the very large Studio 1. But as soon as they heard Walden hit his snare drum, they realized the electric ensemble would have to be split off from the LSO. Martin and Emerick put everyone bar Walden in the control room of Studio 3. Walden set up in a vocal booth, where he had a video link to see Tilson Thomas conducting. However, after the orchestra and band had been catered for, there were only three microphones left to put on Walden's kit: one overhead, one for the snare, and one in the bass drum.

Tilson Thomas apparently walked straight off a plane to the studio session, conducting completely cold, having never seen the music before. He was totally unprepared for the volume of the band, though. The first two recording days were spent getting live takes of the material, and then on the third the orchestra overdubbed, while John and Ponty redid some of their solos. It was the recording debut of John's doubleneck Rex Bogue guitar, and he frequently employed a phaser pedal to augment his basic sound.

The orchestra was reportedly not a happy bunch, though, hardly a surprise if one has read Richard Williams's account of their contribution to Ornette Coleman's *Skies Of America* album[9] or Zappa's various essays on working with large ensembles. Shive remembers Walden having to coach the LSO on how to play in odd-time signatures, and they also objected very much to Shive, Westbrook, and Hischi sitting with them—the orchestra complained to the Musicians Union, and subsequently the three were only allowed to record a brief section on "Smile Of The Beyond." But Hirshi remembered how well John, Armstrong, Walden, Moran, and Martin got on—it helped that the core band were major Beatles fans. Walden also recalled asking Martin to "phase" his cymbals a bit in post-production—Martin refused, saying: "We don't do that anymore!"[10] Martin also befriended the somewhat out-of-sorts Ponty, loving his musicianship, quickly twigging that he wasn't part of the whole Chinmoy "thing" and inviting him round to his house for a slap-up meal. As for Gibbs, Martin was apparently very impressed with his arrangements—Martin employed him in 1994 to arrange four tracks for his *Glory Of Gershwin* tribute album.

John was thrilled with *Apocalypse*. Martin rated it as "one of the best records I've ever made" in his autobiography, *All You Need Is Ears*, and Emerick also later listed it as the project he was most proud of alongside his work on The Beatles songs "Tomorrow Never Knows," "All You Need Is Love," and "Eleanor Rigby."[11] John was in pretty good company.

*Apocalypse* was released at the beginning of June 1974, just as news came through that Graham Bond had died under a tube train at London's Finsbury Park Station—the verdict, at the time of writing, still reads "open." Buoyed by an excellent, striking cover design, the album was another strong seller, reaching #43 on the *Billboard* pop charts.

It was a serious cultural event when the new Mahavishnu Orchestra toured the United States in the summer of 1974, kicking off on May Day in Washington, DC. Trumpeters Bob Knapp and Steve Frankovich joined the ensemble (the former also played some flute and flugelhorn), the latter via a recommendation from Walden. Frankovitch had played with Lionel Hampton and Frankie Valli at just nineteen years old. Eighteen-year-old prodigy and Chinmoy devotee Steven Kindler came in on violin. King Crimson's Bill Bruford remembered sharing the bill with the new Mahavishnu at the Cape Cod Coliseum on June 26, 1974, and being blown away by Walden's drumming: "Damn me if he didn't sound as good as Billy. Back to the woodshed."[12]

Another memorable gig was a free show in Central Park on June 24, 1974. During "Sanctuary," when the music went down to near-silence during a rainstorm, Walden remembers looking up at a mirror above the stage and seeing Chick Corea, Stanley Clarke (who, according to Bob Knapp, had been offered the Mahavishnu gig after the departure of Rick Laird), Lenny White, and Jan Hammer, the kings of mid-1970s fusion, all standing behind him! Though Walden was now a dab hand at playing odd-time signatures, it was also very important for him to keep things "grooving," something he often rammed home to the audience during his solos: "So much of the music was in seven, nine, 11 or 13. Because of all these odd meters, it was very refreshing during my solo to play a simple backbeat. What a concept!"[13]

John was very confident about his new music, especially in the live arena: "This band plays rock, jazz and classical music all merged together in a way that's never been heard before. Sometimes they sound like the old Mahavishnu Orchestra, sometimes they sound like Beethoven."[14] But this was also a hugely demanding live experience, particularly for John, Walden, and Ponty—the latter remembers Walden puffing after gigs as if he had been playing a soccer match. The tour moved to Europe in July, huge outdoor concerts in Barcelona, Madrid, Switzerland (the Montreux Jazz Festival), and France (the Antibes Jazz Festival) commanding massive audiences. Then an estimated eighty thousand watched their performance at Knebworth House near London. Frankovich was fired in Gothenburg, Sweden, after a night of carousing. The tour paused in August, but then carried on in Australasia and the Far East until early December.

Despite its orchestral grandeur and rich harmonic depth, *Apocalypse* has provided rich pickings for hip-hop producers and artists in the 1990s and 2000s, and they have been much-sampled. This was a great testament to the Walden/Armstrong rhythm section's ability to groove strongly even while there was a maelstrom of music whirling around them.

### Power Of Love   4:36

Featuring Tilson Thomas on piano, this effective opener begins with seven descending chords, Walden's assorted bells, and John's plaintive acoustic guitar. The use of French horn and other close-interval brass brings to mind Gil Evans's soundworld. Ponty's phased violin is somewhat of a fly in the ointment, though.

### Vision Is A Naked Sword   14:16

This menacing piece initially in 11/8 was apparently rehearsed with the first Mahavishnu Orchestra but later "rejected" by Jan Hammer, according to Harper in *Bathed In Lightning*. It owes a large debt to "The Dance Of Maya," and is that final (dis)chord a nod to Bernard Herrmann's *Psycho* score?

### Smile Of The Beyond (lyrics by Eve McLaughlin)   7:56

A beautiful piece named after the Queens vegetarian diner opened and run by Chinmoy devotees, still in existence at the time of writing. Moran later claimed she believed her vocal take to be a rough run-through—she was even chewing gum. She was desperate to have another pass at singing it, but Martin was adamant—that was *the* take, and it was magical: "I insisted on going with that performance and never regretted it. The others agreed."[15] She also pleaded with him to submerge her voice deeper into the mix. "This is a first," said Martin. "I've never been asked that before."[16] The fast, "funky" middle section, beginning at 4:00, is almost a major-key version of Miles's "It's About That Time," and it is the only part of the album to feature Shive, Hirschi, and Westbrook. Armstrong plays very much in a James Jamerson style. Gibbs was nominated for a Best Arrangement Accompanying Vocalist Grammy in 1975 for this piece. (Joni Mitchell and Tom Scott won for the former's "Down To You.")

**Wings Of Karma    6:12**

Gibbs should probably have received a co-composer credit on this excellent opening to the original LP's side two—he claims the introduction was completely his confection, heavily influenced by Arnold Schoenberg's piece "Accompaniment To A Film Scene." At 2:10, the band enters in 11/8 time, Armstrong detuning his E string down to a C (possibly taking a cue from Miles bassist Michael Henderson) and John's guitar melody nodding to "Goodbye Pork Pie Hat."

**Hymn To Him    19:23**

This tribute to Chinmoy was the first piece to be rehearsed by Mahavishnu Mark 2. It's a moving, majestic composition, full of intriguing chord harmony, but slightly hampered by a "funky" middle section featuring a hysterical Ponty solo that quickly becomes tiresome. Walden reported that it was tricky following the orchestra during the fast, swirling string parts beginning at 13:30—George Martin reportedly had to come over to his drum booth and slow him down.

## *VISIONS OF THE EMERALD BEYOND* (1975)

John McLaughlin: Six and twelve string guitars, vocals
Jean-Luc Ponty: Electric violin, electric baritone violin
Gayle Moran: Keyboards, vocals
Ralphe Armstrong: Bass guitar, contra bass, vocals
Michael Walden: Drums, percussion, vocals, clavinet
Steve Kindler: First violin, Cadenza in "Pastoral"

## CHAPTER 4

Carol Shive: Second violin, vocals
Phillip Hirschi: Cello
Bob Knapp: Trumpet, flugelhorn, flute, vocals
Russell Tubbs: Alto and soprano sax
Recorded at Electric Lady Studios, New York, December 4-14, 1974
Mixed at Trident Studios, London, December 16-24, 1974
Produced by Ken Scott and Mahavishnu John McLaughlin
Released February 1975

Despite a relatively happy, fruitful 1974, John was starting to feel the pressure after four years of almost nonstop touring and recording. Late in the year, he finally threw in the towel for a while, disappearing to a monastery in the French Alps, where he mucked in with Trappist monks for ten days. This sojourn possibly contributed to John's subsequent leaving of the Chinmoy cult toward the end of 1975.

Returning to New York City, he was quickly back on the treadmill. He guested on two memorable John Coltrane–celebrating tracks ("Song To John" parts 1 and 2) at Electric Lady with Stanley Clarke and Chick Corea for the former's *Journey To Love* album, then recorded the next Mahavishnu Orchestra album in the same studio during December 1974, with Ken Scott onboard as coproducer. Marsha Westbrook had left the band, tired after the long *Apocalypse* tour, while Premik Russell Tubbs, who had played with Walden in Jatra, came in on saxophone. Meanwhile there were reports of some tension between Ponty and Kindler now that they were competing for the position of "lead violinist."

Walden was in seventh heaven recording in Hendrix's studio—he set up his kit "right in the corner where Mitch Mitchell used to be."[17] (He would later set up in exactly the same spot to record "Marching Powder" with Tommy Bolin.) He spent a lot of time with Scott on his drum sound. They experimented with damping techniques and varying the playback speed to give the kit an abnormal "heaviness," a trick regularly used during The Beatles' psychedelic era.

But original material was much more difficult to come by for *Visions*, with some compositions worked up in the studio. Even so, there were rumors that John intended it to be a double album, featuring one Mahavishnu Orchestra record and another featuring pastoral duets with wife, Eve, plus his early, all-acoustic excursions with Anglo-Indian band Shakti. It didn't happen for various reasons, but John was particularly pleased with *Visions*, looking back in the early 1980s: "That record was one of the greatest I ever made."[18] The album certainly has some brilliant moments, but it's hard to escape the conclusion that it's also very inconsistent. Some pieces barely register—particularly the short, controversial solo spots, of which much more later, and the ill-advised voyages into funk.

John mixed *Visions* at Trident Studios, where he also held a press-conference-cum-playback session, leading to a mixed review from *Melody Maker*'s Steve Lake: "Everybody is staggered by the intensity . . . but when all is said and done, are we were really bearing witness to anything of greater import than a latter-day Ten Years After trip?" Bob Palmer posted a sparkling review in *Rolling Stone*, though: "He has never packed this many vivid melodic flourishes and varied instrumental voicings into a single LP. . . . The concluding 'On The Way Home To Earth' features guitar with tonal expanders and sounds like a cross between Led Zeppelin and Sun Ra. . . . The best Mahavishnu Orchestra album since *The Inner Mounting Flame*, and an achievement which most of McLaughlin's competitors, M.O. graduates included, will find it difficult to equal."

Gayle Moran left the band after the recording of *Visions*, unwilling to continue touring. Stu Goldberg came in on keyboards, destined to be a key part of John's musical life for the next five years. He was born on July 10, 1954, in Malden, Massachusetts, but grew up in Seattle. He studied music at the University of Utah and formed his own band featuring brothers Walt and Bruce Fowler, intermittently part of Frank Zappa's groups. Zappa's keyboard player George Duke took a shine to Goldberg, and he urged him to move to the West Coast. Goldberg did so and quickly got gigs in the legendary big bands of Don Ellis and Oliver Nelson. Duke also recommended him to John. Goldberg was just nineteen years old when he got John's call. Suddenly Goldberg was auditioning for John on the Rhodes, Mini Moog, and clavinet in his little Santa Monica studio flat. But John seemed most interested in his library, particularly impressed to see *Autobiography Of A Yogi* by Paramahansa Yogananda. The next day, John's tour manager, Joseph D'Anna, phoned to tell Goldberg to get on a plane to New York for rehearsals at SIR. He was in the band, now featuring a string quartet and solo saxophone. Seven of the nine Mahavishnu Orchestra members were now Chinmoy devotees.

The European tour kicked off at Croydon's Fairfield Halls on January 19, 1975. It was beset by sound problems—"Dinky" Dawson blaming an overuse of Morley effects pedals—but there were some happy times too, John and Ponty sometimes dueting on Django Reinhardt/Stephane Grappelli material while traveling on the tour bus. But the violinist left later in the year, stung by the lack of a credit on "Pegasus" and "Opus 1"—strange, because during an interview a year before, John had alluded to the fact that he had encouraged Ponty to contribute some compositions: "I have invited him to author any piece that he wants to for consideration. He's making his own album, so it's quite possible that he himself is using the material he's written for me."[19] There are also reports that Ponty was feeling some pressure to join the Chinmoy cult.

Bob Knapp also left after the European tour, replaced by saxophonist and New McGuire Sister alumnus Norma Jean Bell. The band was getting funkier. A huge American tour was put together, co-headlining with English guitar hero Jeff Beck. The collaboration was long overdue. Beck had been fascinated by John's music since *My Goal's Beyond*, but he really started to pick up on the jazz/rock sound when Billy Cobham's *Spectrum* was released in October 1973, courtesy of a car ride in drummer Carmine Appice's Pantera: "I thought it was Badfinger, because he was always playing Badfinger. . . . It wasn't. It was *Spectrum*. *Spectrum* changed my whole musical outlook. I thought, 'this is the shit we need'."[20] Beck made it a priority to fuse jazz and rock on his next album. It worked—*Blow By Blow*, released in March 1975, was a huge runaway hit in the States, making the top ten on the pop charts and selling five hundred thousand within three months of release—to Beck's amazement. In a sense, the album was a distillation of The Mahavishnu Orchestra's strengths but delivered in a much more listener-friendly, "funky" package, aided by George Martin's production and string arrangements.

The joint Mahavishnu/Beck US tour ran from April 24 to June 15, 1975, with two weeks off in the middle (May 12–27), during which Kindler guested on *The First Seven Days*, Jan Hammer's debut solo album. The Mahavishnu Orchestra would go on first, with John still asking for a moment of silence, though Kindler reports that audiences seldom complied.

Beck and his band—Max Middleton on keyboards, Wilbur Bascomb on bass and Bernard "Pretty" Purdie on drums—came on after the interval, and they often got a far better reception than The Mahavishhnu Orchestra. Beck thought he knew the reason why: "A lot of girls don't understand it. They don't like screeching, million-note guitar solos. They're impressed for a few minutes; then the next song has that in it, and the next one, and the next. It's much too deep for most people," he reminisced to *Musician* in 1989.[21] But this was an extraordinary tour, numbers-wise —the audiences averaged out at about twelve thousand per show for some of the most advanced jazz/rock playing ever heard.

They played a big gig in Los Angeles on May 30, 1975, soon after which John's Rex Bogue guitar was mysteriously destroyed, splitting right down the middle. John suspected supernatural forces. In "Dinky" Dawson's memoir *Life On The Road*, he intimated to John that it was a sign for him to move on from The Mahavishnu Orchestra. John wryly acknowledged the comment but didn't express an opinion either way.

According to Middleton, John signed off from the US tour with a typically generous gesture, buying Beck—who had struggled with various substandard guitars throughout—a new white Stratocaster. The Mahavishnu Orchestra then continued on with their own European tour during the late summer of 1975.

**Eternity's Breath—Part 1    3:10**

John's volume-pedal swells and Walden's cymbals kick off the album, like the dawning of a new world. Ponty's wah-wah violin—which very much divides opinion—is now a vital part of the Mahavishnu sound. Armstrong detunes his E string down to a C as John's fantastic blues riff explodes out of the speakers. Both parts 1 and 2 of "Eternity's Breath" were inspired by a Chinmoy poem— John expounded on its theme to Kolosky: "Eternity is where we have always belonged and will always belong in our unconscious way. . . . We are breathing in this marvellous gas the earth has made that is life-supporting."[22] "Eternity's Breath—Part 1" was regularly played by NBC's *The Tonight Show* house band (with Kevin Eubanks and Branford Marsalis) between 1992 and 1995 and also by Jeff Beck on the *Live At Ronnie Scott's* DVD and album.

**Eternity's Breath—Part 2    4:50**

The lyrics "Let me fulfil thy will/Not mine but thine" crisscross from right to left speakers. Then there's a stirring 6/8 groove with some majestic Moran chords and superbly played unison violins from Kindler and Ponty. This terrific piece is a highlight of John's 1970s output, despite a few tuning problems.

**Lila's Dance    5:37**

"Lila's Dance" is a popular piece in the slipstream of "The Dance Of Maya" and "Vision Is A Naked Sword" that seems to be in 20/8 (John's guitar arpeggios may be subdivided 5/5/3/1/3/3). John's solo really does sound like what Hendrix might have come up with had he lived a few years longer. Armstrong adds some marvelous Mu-Tron III–assisted notes here and there. The section when John's rhythm guitar returns at 4:16 is a classic Mahavishnu moment.

**Can't Stand Your Funk    2:10**

The funk tunes on *Visions* sadly barely reach beyond novelty factor. This one is based around a Bm7 chord in 10/8 time, and it's not helped by John's reliance on his phaser pedal, nor the unhip horn arrangements. Walden's ingenious groove is by far the best thing about the track.

## Pastoral   3:41

It doesn't matter how many flashy runs the violinists play—they can't make this one-chord piece interesting. The only section of note, beginning at 2:00, sounds uncannily like a Kindler arrangement, similar to his work on Jan Hammer's *The First Seven Days* and beyond. The track ends with Kindler's striking cadenza reminiscent of Ralph Vaughan Williams's *The Lark Ascending*.

## Faith   2:01

In its own modest way, this is an album standout. John's double-tracked twelve-string starts in 6/4 but then moves to a very slow 10/8. The ascending melody and chords are close relatives of "Hope" and "Resolution." Carol Shive laughs at the absurdity of nailing the blazingly fast final motif, all forty-four notes of it.

## Cosmic Strut   (Narada Michael Walden)   3:21

Walden's sophistifunk tune opened the original vinyl side two—it was his first composition for the band and released as a single in early 1975. Kolosky reports that it even appeared on a few jukeboxes in New York's East Village. John's guitar sound at 0:46 was later borrowed—with the aid of Ken Scott—by Jeff Beck on "Too Much To Lose" from his 1980 album, *There And Back*.

## If I Could See   1:17

Moran's beatific—if not perfectly in tune—vocals swirl above Walden's slowed-down Beatles drums and a zany horn arrangement. It's very brief and very strange, but "If I Could See" is another standout.

## Be Happy   3:33

John and Ponty trade sixteens, eights, fours, and then twos over a riff originated from "John's Song #2" from *The Lost Trident Sessions*. The piece is exciting at times but again marred by that ugly phaser pedal.

## Earth Ship    3:43

Walden sings, "Peace in the heart of the lover/Joy in the heart of the giver" over a gentle groove in either 18/4 or 9/8. The rippling violin riff beginning at 0:20 may be inspired by Stanley Clarke's "Yesterday Princess" from his 1974 self-titled album. Moran's Rhodes chords were sampled by British dance act Rae & Christian for their 2000 track, "Not Just Anybody."

## Pegasus    1:48

This was a brief, improvised Ponty solo featuring an Echoplex and phaser pedal. He was appalled at the lack of a composition credit, a matter later settled with John out of court.

## Opus 1    0:25

Kindler's brief improvisation—see above.

## On The Way Home To Earth    4:45

John takes us through the sound barrier—with the aid of an analog frequency shifter—and looks ahead to *Inner Worlds*. Two distinct sections then seem to "meld"—a testament to Ken Scott's technical mastery. John's second solo seems to have been a big influence on Frank Zappa—his 1976 track "The Ocean Is The Ultimate Solution," later appearing on the *Sleep Dirt* album, inhabits a similar sonic space.

## INNER WORLDS (1976)

John McLaughlin: Guitars, 360 systems frequency shifter, guitar synthesizer, backing vocals, E-mu synthesizer/sequencer

Stu Goldberg: Customized Mini-Moog and Steiner-Parker synthesizers, clavinet, organ, piano, backing vocals, Steiner-Parker and string synthesizers

Ralphe Armstrong: Bass, double bass, vocals

Narada Michael Walden: Drums, tympani, congas, gong, bass marimba, shaker, lead vocals, piano, sleigh bells

Recorded at Le Chateau d'Herouville, France, July and August 1975

Produced by John McLaughlin and Dennis Mackay

Released February 1976

After the Jeff Beck tour, John dismantled the large Mahavishnu ensemble. Hirs-chi, Shive, Tubbs, and Bell were let go. John was reportedly very gracious about it, taking the former for dinner at *Annam Bramah*. The band was now down to a four-piece. John was no longer using the name "Mahavishnu" (though he revealed in 2022 that he still loved Chinmoy, and kept in regular contact with many of his disciples[23]), but *Inner Worlds* was credited to John and The Mahav-ishnu Orchestra, two separate entities.

*Inner Worlds* in some ways represented a return to John's "secular" interests. He later characterized his severance from Chinmoy, thus: "I guess the break was a matter of my assuming total responsibility for my own actions."[24] Here there was an interesting parallel to Robert Fripp's debut 1979 solo album, *Exposure*, his return to "normal service" after three years studying with J.G. Bennett, a Guirdjieff protégé, at Sherborne House in Gloucestershire, England.

*Inner Worlds* is an album of contradictions. There are passages of great turbulence and chaos, but also meditative moments. There is a lot of pent-up anger, and an exploration of the sometimes-troublesome inner worlds we all inhabit from time to time. Given the circumstances of John's personal life in the summer of 1975, this is hardly surprising: his wife, Eve, had left him for another guitarist named Doug Quinn. (According to Carol Shive, "There was even some implication of Sri Chinmoy. . . . We realised all spiritual leaders have clay feet," she reported in *Bathed In Lightning*, though the animus behind this comment isn't clear.) John reported to *Jazzwise* magazine in May 2022 that there was another aspect to the breakup, too:

> We all know the pain of sorrow, we all know the loss of loved ones, particularly as you grow older, but to be unceremoniously dumped by one's wife, and she goes off and crashes your new car with her boyfriend—it's a bit strong, isn't it? I can laugh about it now, but it wasn't funny when it happened![25]

John responded by selling his Queens property—there were reports he also smashed up a lot of personal effects, including images of Chinmoy. He subse-quently moved into an Upper West Side apartment. Meanwhile, his great friend and mentor, Miles, was struggling with his own inner worlds, holed up in his West 77th Street townhouse and embarking on his infamous Lost Years. John expressed his feelings to friend and Miles biographer, Ian Carr: "It was very disquieting. I was very worried about him—whether he would live or die—and a lot of people were also. We're all fragile to some extent physically, spiritually, emotionally, and we're all subject to the whims of whatever karma is going to fly unexpectedly into the face. And nobody can escape, including Miles Davis. He's a great man, but he's a man."[26]

*Inner Worlds* was recorded in France at the aforementioned Château d'Hérouville. Londoner Dennis Mackay, who had learned his trade at Trident Studios under Ken Scott's tutelage, was brought in to engineer and co-produce, a very hands-off, technically minded collaborator. Nothing was left to chance this time—Mackay and Walden spent a whole week getting a (very) decent drum sound, and then it took another few days to harness John's new guitar-synth setup. Every string was hooked up to a Mini Moog and then put through a ring modulator; unsurprisingly, there were some serious tuning problems, but John was determined to experiment.

But after this initial bedding-in process, the work was fairly swift; John, Armstrong, Goldberg, and Walden would record several live takes of each tune, and then John would usually redo his solos. According to Goldberg, "He would work hours on them. There was a tremendous striving for perfection."[27] This is an interesting comment, given the fact there's a rough-and-ready quality to John's lead playing on *Inner Worlds*—you'd be very hard-pressed to call it "perfect." But John was eager to give his band a lot more creative and compositional input on this album. For Walden, this was a blast, allowing him to channel all of his influences, from The Beatles to Art Blakey, but he was also noticing a change in John's guitar playing: "For me, all I thought about was Jimi Hendrix. . . . It was demonic and then heavenly. . . . John's playing was completely different on *Inner Worlds*."[28]

Sadly, despite some memorable moments, the album was essentially one step forward and two steps back from *Visions Of The Emerald Beyond*. In the former camp was Walden's fantastic "The Way Of The Pilgrim," named after a book by Tibetan saint Milarepa (a recommendation from John to Walden) and composed on a Fender Rhodes also donated by John. Goldberg's Moog solo generates some serious energy before John's beatific Les Paul feature. Armstrong's "Planetary Citizen" just about works as a cosmic funk track with a much-sampled opening vocal exaltation. (Bristol trip-hop band Massive Attack allegedly used it without permission on their 1991 hit "Unfinished Sympathy.") Years later, Armstrong also heard parts of the song sampled in an Adidas commercial and on the soundtrack of Sharon Stone's 1993 movie, *Sliver*. Armstrong received big out-of-court settlements for both, enabling him to buy a Jaguar, get a son through college, and pay off his mortgage.

"All in the Family," a spiritual jazz blowout in 6/4 with elements of Ravel's "Bolero" and John's own "Earth Ship," works, too, getting by on sheer exuberance and a superb Walden drum performance. Apparently, Goldberg's organ solo was very much an afterthought, overdubbed at London's Abbey Road at John's urging—he had initially recorded a long Rhodes solo on the tracking date. "Miles Out" possibly references Davis's increasingly sketchy mental state, aided by John's mind-bending ring modulator. He was still searching for the guitar equivalent of John Coltrane's multiphonics.

But then there are the misfires: the Walden/John cowrite "In My Life" is soppy and slightly embarrassing, despite John's brilliant twelve-string solo, while "Gita," "River Of My Heart" (apparently a favorite of John's), and "Morning Calls" aren't much better. "Lotus Feet" is an important John composition with a very special mood, but it would be performed a lot more effectively in the future.

All told, *Inner Worlds* took around three weeks to complete—pretty unheard of for a "jazz" album. But it was a fractious period for John and everyone in the studio, emphasized by the fact that one night the entire band and crew had a huge food fight, causing thousands of pounds of damage.

John mixed the album at Trident Studios before the new quartet began a European tour on August 5, 1975, in Copenhagen, Denmark, as part of Miles Copeland's *Star Truckin'* package that also featured Lou Reed, Soft Machine, Caravan, Climax Blues Band, Wishbone Ash, and Renaissance. One particularly memorable gig took place on August 17 at the Theatre Antique, a Roman amphitheater in the small town of Orange, France. The Mahavishnu Orchestra went onstage at 2 a.m. after two rain interruptions and was astonished to see an audience of approximately twelve thousand. For unknown reasons, John played "Happy Birthday" on his Les Paul at the beginning of "Open Country Joy" and seemed to be in unusually high spirits. Wishbone Ash headlined the concert, going onstage at 4 a.m.

The Mahavishnu Orchestra's last British gig of the 1970s took place at the Reading Festival on August 25, 1975. Robin Trower and Robert Fripp watched from the side of the stage. Tellingly, the setlist featured no material from *Inner Worlds*. After the last European date on August 29 in Vienna, John traveled back to England to lick his wounds for a few days, while the rest of the band went back to America. They carried on touring the States through the fall of 1975, mainly playing at colleges in the Northeast. John by now had completely severed ties to Chinmoy. His hair was long and styled, he was wearing Italian suits and shoes, and he was smoking cigarettes and enjoying a beer. His newfound freedom was apparently affecting his playing, too—Jan Hammer and Steve Kindler came to watch a show in New York and were reportedly blown away by John's performance.

The last-ever gig by the 1970s iteration of The Mahavishnu Orchestra took place on November 29 in Toledo, Ohio. "One Word" saw John quote extensively from Hendrix's famous interpretation of "The Star-Spangled Banner." John had given Walden, Armstrong, and Goldberg plenty of notice regarding the break, telling them he would be focusing on Shakti in the near future. Goldberg: "We all congratulated him, thanked him for the journey and went our separate ways."[29] He also recalls that everyone in the band got a leaving bonus. Meanwhile, Pat Metheny—who had been so taken with The Mahavishnu Orchestra in Michigan three years before and would soon become arguably the most revered "jazz" guitarist of his generation—was recording debut solo album, *Bright Size Life*, for ECM Records in Ludwigsburg, Germany, with Jaco Pastorius on bass and some very John-like arpeggios and odd-time moves on the track "Unquity Road."

*Inner Worlds* finally released in February 1976. There was no poem from Sri Chinmoy on the back cover this time, and the album received a one-star review from *Down Beat*. But John looked back with some fondness on the project. Armstrong received many offers at the end of his tenure with John—he reunited with Jean-Luc Ponty, played with Herbie Hancock's Head Hunters, and then joined Zappa for a Canadian tour and some recordings, which, at the time of this writing, are yet to see the light of day. He went on to a stellar career, mostly playing acoustic bass with a variety of jazz artists, including James Carter, Toots Thielemans, and Kenny Burrell. Goldberg worked with Alphonse Mouzon, Larry Coryell, and Gary Bartz in the immediate aftermath of *Inner Worlds*, then returned to play with John in The One Truth Band during 1978.

For Walden, though, a period of great depression followed the end of The Mahavishnu Orchestra. Fortunately, he was in demand: he flew straight from the recording of *Inner Worlds* to London to record *Wired* with Jeff Beck, reuniting with George Martin and Geoff Emerick at AIR Studios. John was mixing *Inner Worlds* down the road at Trident, where Walden wrote some material for Beck on the downstairs piano. (Walden also revealed in 2022 that John had gifted him the Fender Rhodes on which the guitarist had composed many classic Mahavishnu pieces.)

But after working on *Wired* and his debut solo album, *Garden Of Love Light* (featuring Santana and Beck), for Atlantic Records, Walden was essentially finished with jazz/rock for a while. He even turned down Weather Report: "I wanted to do more of the rock thing, with girls' panties on stage!"[30] Still, he would remain forever grateful to John: "John was my teacher, mentor and my brother. He gave me so many opportunities. I was taken out of the obscurity of being a busboy to play in The Mahavishnu Orchestra."[31]

# SHAKTI WITH JOHN MCLAUGHLIN (1976)

John McLaughlin: Acoustic guitar
L. Shankar: Violin
Zakir Hussain: Tabla
T. H. Vinayakram: Ghatam, mridangam
Ramnad V. Raghavan: Mridangam
Recorded live at South Hampton College, Long Island, New York, July 5,
1975
Produced by John McLaughlin

After mixing *Inner Worlds* and returning to New York City, John was now happily settled in a Chelsea loft, living in a veritable jazz/rock guitar community, as fellow Columbia recording artist Steve Khan recalls:

We had John on W. 23rd St.; Bill Connors was on W. 21st.; John Abercrombie had a loft on W. 18th St., John Scofield was a little further downtown in the West Village, Ralph Towner was in the area and, finally, I lived on W. 21st St. & 7th Ave! Just imagine running into any one of these great players, great artists, in your local market. There was a pretty remarkable sense of community amongst us, all totally by happenstance.[32]

In a sense, John's graduation to Shakti (a Hindi word loosely translated as "creative intelligence, beauty and power") had been on the cards for a while—he had admired Indian music as a teenager, introduced to the esteemed *vina* player Sundaram Balachander by Tom Jones's guitarist Big Jim Sullivan. John studied with Dr. Raghavan Ramanathan at Wesleyan University between 1972 and 1974, learning about South Indian (Carnatic) music and rhythm theory (*konnakol*), even though the doctor was a North Indian (Hindustani). Traditional Indian music always involves static harmony, but there are two main schools: North Indian is very virtuosic, often featuring tabla, while South Indian music is also complex but generally less ornate, more formalized.

One day Dr. Ramanathan mentioned that his nephew, Lakshminarayana Shankar, was a superb violinist. John takes up the story: "He brought Shankar around to my house and we just sat down and played. We almost composed a piece right then and there. The rapport was incredible."[33] For Shankar's part, it was the first time he found he could be "true to himself" when playing with a Western musician—John could follow and respond to everything Shankar played.[34]

Born in Madras, India, in 1950, Shankar was brought up in Ceylon—now Sri Lanka—where his father taught music at the Jaffna College of Music. Shankar learned vocals and violin at a very young age and was performing in public at six years old. He came to the United States in 1969 to study at the Wesleyan, where he also got the chance to work with Ornette Coleman and Jimmy Garrison. He got a PhD in music and took a big interest in jazz, particularly Miles and Coltrane. A friend then played *Bitches Brew* to Shankar, and he was impressed by John's playing.

As well as working with Dr. Ramanathan at Wesleyan and meeting Shankar, John began to study with sitarist Ravi Shankar, who knew both North and South Indian music. These lessons would last between 1974 and 1976. John also met master tabla player Zakir Hussain, born in Mumbai on March 9, 1951, via a Greenwich Village music shop called House Of Musical Traditions in late 1969 or early 1970. It stocked sitars, table, and tampuras; John was friends with the owner, telling him: "Jim, if ever a great Indian musician comes in, ask him would he give a friend of yours a lesson. It doesn't matter what instrument, it doesn't matter if it's North Indian, South Indian. Anything." A month or so later, Jim phoned John, telling him he had a great tabla player in the store. John instinctively asked if he would give him a vocal lesson—Zakir agreed. They immediately hit it off and later became great friends when Zakir saw John play with The Mahavishnu Orchestra in San Francisco.

John and Zakir had an immediate rapport from the very first note, as the former recounted on *The Way Of Beauty* DVD: "It was like two people, two minds, one thought, one action." They found they phrased in a similar manner, and would begin and end lines at the same point. Zakir was astonished: "It was like I was playing with my twin brother or my father. . . . It was meant to be." John, Shankar, Zakir, and Dr. Ramanathan actually recorded an album together in 1973 or 1974 that John hoped would comprise the second LP of the *Visions Of The Emerald Beyond* album, but his paymasters were not so sure: "Columbia asked me not to do it. They said people will find it confusing. So we passed that up. Maybe it was a blessing in disguise because we put a live album out later which I thought was great."[35]

For his part, Zakir remembers that his father, Ustad Alla Rakha—a renowned tabla player—was initially not overly enamored with the idea of his joining Shakti:

> In the beginning, he did have problems with it. He felt I had to make my name as an Indian musician before anything else was to happen. As a teacher, he was worried that I would drift to the other side of the world and sever my connection

with India. I convinced him that will not be and then proved that through my actions and it was fine.[36]

Shankar found he had to make some harmonic modifications when playing in Shakti: "I do not use the traditional Western violin tuning, GDAE. Instead, I use tonic-dominated tunings—EBEB or DADA—which allows the harmonics to ring, and enables me to bring my Indian soul out so I don't sound like everybody else. I have a five-string violin, too, which gives me the viola range."[37] There were other Shakti trademarks, such as the band often using the Spanish Phrygian mode, similar to a North Indian *rag Bhairavi* or South Indian *Sindhu Bhairavi* scale. Shakti summarily set out to be a true "fusion" band, melding influences of East and West, jazz and rock, South and North Indian. John himself considered it completely natural to fuse jazz and Indian music, since both rely chiefly on improvisation. It's fair to say this view wasn't always an easy sell.

But there was certainly something in the air around this time. George Harrison's *Dark Horse* tour of the United States and Canada during November and December 1974 had featured a performance by Ravi Shankar and friends. Perhaps that finally helped to solidify the Shakti concept in John's head and heart (though Peter Doggett's book *You Never Give Me Your Money* reports that a Vancouver crowd "became restless" during Shankar's set, and that, as a response, Harrison told them he was prepared to die for Indian music but not for rock'n'roll).

The South Hampton College gig that spawned Shakti's debut album—only their second concert—was co-promoted by John's roadie Greg DiGivione and featured John playing a custom-made Mark Whitebook guitar, which allowed for greater string bends than ever before. According to Zakir, they only had one rehearsal of a few hours' duration before the concert. John reported having a premonition about the gig, urging Columbia to get an eight-track machine down to the venue. They concurred, but still, *Shakti With John McLaughlin* was not released for a year. It seems that marketing the band was a problem area for the label, something that irked John from the beginning: "I got a lot of flak for that from my agent and record company. In America they were saying to me: 'What are you doing sitting on a carpet with those Indians? You've got a very successful jazz/rock band!' But I had to do it and I told them I'd accept the consequences. I ended up losing sales but at the same time I was happy. I just have to go where the music pulls me by the nose."[38]

John's instincts, in the main, seemed spot-on. The two pieces co-written by him and Shankar, "Joy" and "What Need Have I for This—What Need Have I for That—I Am Dancing at the Feet of My Lord—All Is Bliss—All Is Bliss," are remarkable onslaughts, in their own way as kinetic and striking as the original Mahavishnu Orchestra. The former featured a mode invented by the band—E, F, G#, A, B, D—and contained fast North-Indian modal melodies known as *tans*. There were breakneck unison lines and furious call-and-response sections, John firing off some remarkable bends with his new scallop-necked steel-string.

The latter is surely longest title in the history of "jazz." And, at nearly half an hour long, one can only imagine Columbia's sinking feeling, not to mention the problems with getting it to sound half decent on vinyl. But John's sheer exuberance shines through, as does his bluesy approach. "Lotus Feet," meanwhile, was a tender treasure, adding some much-needed respite and a huge improvement on the *Inner Worlds* version, if strangely curtailed just as it begins its melody and 6/8 groove.

A vital aspect of Shakti was the fact that all members were seated directly on the stage—with no chairs or stools—and in close proximity. This inspired a lack of hierarchy and an almost-perfect acoustical situation where all the musicians could easily hear each other. But from a guitar perspective, it necessitated a completely different kind of "projection"—from the gut/core, not from an amplifier or pedal. Once again, it seems John's yoga and meditation were coming in handy. And the very existence of Shakti was an important marker for racial harmony and tolerance.

## A HANDFUL OF BEAUTY (1977)

John McLaughlin: Acoustic guitar
L. Shankar: Violin
Zakir Hussain: Tabla
T. H. Vinayakram: Ghatam, mridangam
Recorded in August 1976 at Trident Studios, London
Produced by John McLaughlin

During the summer of 1976, Jeff Beck emerged with a striking version of "Goodbye Pork Pie Hat" on his million-selling *Wired* album, the Charles Mingus tune that John had covered back in 1971. Beck upped the blues quotient and played one of his finest solos on record: "John's version was so tasty, so original. I wanted to make mine more commercial, a little more rock'n'roll. It was the perfect tune for me. The melody is simple but the chords are all over the place," he told *Guitar For The Practicing Musician*. Later in 1976, Beck would tour stadia throughout the United States, Canada, and Australasia with The Jan Hammer Group.

Meanwhile, in June 1976, John recorded another striking collaboration with Stanley Clarke, "Desert Song," from the bassist/composer's Grammy-winning album *School Days*. A stunning performance on one of the key jazz/rock records of the 1970s, and possibly this writer's first-ever exposure to John's music, it was a microcosm of his burgeoning acoustic guitar style, now with superior single-note facility, unexpected string bends, unusual emphases, and original chord voicings often utilizing the thumb.

Meanwhile, as Shakti's debut album finally saw the light of day, touring opportunities were opening up for the band in the United States. T. H. Vinayakram—affectionately nicknamed Vikku—came in on *ghatam*, an ancient South Indian percussion instrument, essentially a mud, clay, and metal pot with a narrow mouth. Vikku was born on August 11, 1942. His father, Kalaimaamani T. R. Harihara Sharma, was also a noted musician, and Vikku was already playing concerts at the age of thirteen. His high-octane duets with Zakir became a vital and much-appreciated part of the Shakti live experience. Their kinship was made even more fascinating by the fact that, though both were from India, they spoke completely different languages. Vikku, as a South Indian, only spoke Tamil, whereas Hussain spoke Hindi. So, they had to compromise, communicating in broken English.

In April 1976, Shakti started opening for a Weather Report now blessed with Jaco Pastorius on bass and moving into its imperial phase, performing at American halls, colleges, and clubs to between a thousand and three thousand people. According to Weather Report's road manager, Chris Murphy, as reported in his book *Miles To Go,* Shakti always went down very well on the tour, their call-and-response sections engaging the crowd. The tour moved on to Europe in the summer, with The Billy Cobham/George Duke Band joining the bill. At the Montreux Jazz Festival on July 8, 1976, all three groups' sets were filmed. The tour ended with three nights (initially two, but an extra added due to demand) at the Hammersmith Odeon at the end of July. The last night saw all three bands gather onstage for a version of the Joe Zawinul composition "Gibraltar."

John's main Shakti guitar was now a custom-made steel-string built by Abraham Wechter, with scalloped frets (approaching the sound of the Saraswati *vina*) and an extra set of seven sympathetic strings placed across the sound hole, tuned to an open chord via a tuning box on the face of the guitar. The scalloped fingerboard allowed for more "push and pull" on the strings, more micro-tones, and a much more "Indian-sounding" guitar.

After a busy summer of touring, Shakti returned to John's beloved Trident Studios to record *A Handful Of Beauty*, assisted by engineer Dennis Mackay. Far from an attempt to "dumb down" their unique fusions and/or approach a more commercial sound, it was indeed the opposite, a full-blooded development of the debut, though the weakest of the three 1970s Shakti albums.

"La Danse Du Bonheur," composed by John and Shankar, featured a catchy melody, phrases in five over 4/4, and John comping with "Western" chords under Shankar's extraordinary feature. The two also collaborated on "India," John's opening, unaccompanied three-minute solo mixing huge string bends with the detuning of his strings on the fly. Shankar's "Lady L" touched on "Trilogy" from *Between Nothingness & Eternity*, while John's solo nodded to his contribution on Stanley Clarke's "Desert Song."

"Kriti" was a pretty, traditional South Indian composition featuring no improvisation, while John's "Two Sisters" was his composition for French pianists Mariella and Katia Labeque, the latter his new partner, too, of which much more later. It was an album standout with its elegant melody and blues feeling, later sampled by English tabla player Talvin Singh on the 1997 track "Distant God."

Rick Laird took *A Handful Of Beauty*'s back-cover photograph (at John's urging) of Shakti at the Beacon Theatre in New York City on April 17, 1976. But there were big distribution problems with the album, a sure sign that Columbia's interest was waning. Still, this meant nothing to John in real terms—he rightly felt Shakti was going from strength to strength both in concert and studio situations.

## NATURAL ELEMENTS (1977)

John McLaughlin: Acoustic guitar, vocals
L. Shankar: Violin, viola, vocals
Zakir Hussain: Tabla, timbales, bongos, dholak, nal, triangle, vocals
T. H. Vinayakram: Ghatam, nal, kanjeera, moorsing (juice harp), vocals
Recorded at Aquarius Studios, Geneva, Switzerland, July 1977
Produced by John McLaughlin
Released October 27, 1977

The summer of 1977 was a boom time for jazz/rock on Columbia Records (*Heavy Weather*, Weather Report's first and only gold record in the United States, Al Di Meola's *Elegant Gypsy*, Return To Forever's *Romantic Warrior*, and *Musicmagic*, the latter graced by keyboards and vocals by Gayle Moran, now Chick Corea's wife). But these were electric acts featuring relatively short tracks, perfectly placed for airplay. Shakti excelled in long, intense, modal improvisations, a tough sell for radio.

So, it was somewhat ironic that Shakti signed off with arguably their finest album in *Natural Elements*, certainly a more "commercial" recording than the previous two, but one that didn't scrimp on virtuosity or melodic invention. Zakir and Vikku brought some new percussion instruments into the fold— timbales, triangles, bongos—leading some reviewers to suggest an increasing Latin influence in Shakti's music. There were even elements of 1970s singer/ songwriter "pop," with more conventional chord changes and even Western-style vocals. The album also had a more direct, close-mic'd sound courtesy of a new studio for John, Aquarius near Geneva in Switzerland, also a favourite hangout for ex-Yes keyboardist Patrick Moraz.

John also reported that he and Shankar occasionally overdubbed their solos after laying down the basic tracks on *Natural Elements*: "Both Shankar and I had been deeply involved in the compositions. We had no time to even think about solos, and for a solo you really need to work, and think, and explore in your own self what it means to you, the possibilities, and how you're going to articulate them."[39]

Despite the commercial pressures being brought to bear by Columbia, there were other issues that would ultimately lead John to put Shakti on hold, as he revealed in a *Jazzwise* interview with Stuart Nicholson in February 2004:

> Vikku, the ghatam player, had a very big school in Madras and he really had to go back. And replacing Vikku was a problem . . . because he is unique. The second problem is that I was trying to bring more Western elements into Shakti. I wanted Shankar to learn more jazz harmony to come over to my side of the world. But he signed a recording contract with Frank Zappa's recording company and he got into this kind of Indian pop. Which was a disappointment for me.

But his attitude in 1977 was somewhat more combative and defiant, and he looked back a year later with some bitterness at how Shakti was treated by Columbia:

> Shakti was handled in a commercial context like everything is in America, where the basic question is "Will it sell?" If it had been taken in an artistic context, which is the only relevant context you can take music in, the approach might have been, "Listen, we have something here that is original and is happening. We have to look at it from a different point of view." It's not that Shakti has been rejected,

rather that there's been just an overwhelming indifference. That appalls me. I'd rather be abused than be treated with indifference. I've been in groups that have been booed off stage because of the music I was playing. But I don't mind that, because that makes you aware of really where you are at in yourself and what you are doing, and you either stop what you're doing or it makes you stronger.[40]

But John spoke of his pride about what Shakti had represented: "Prior to it, there was very little collaboration between North and South Indian musicians. Shakti played a role in the reunification of the North and South in the musical sense. Since Shakti, the collaborations between North and South have grown a thousand times." Zakir concurred, speaking in 1999 about the impact of the original band: "After Shakti, Indian musicians became much more open to the idea of trying things not only within the realms of Indian music, but by stepping out of Indian music and into any traditions they felt comfortable with. Shakti was one of the first combinations of musicians trying to do something that crossed all musical boundaries. We didn't approach each other thinking: 'Okay, you play South Indian, I play North Indian and he'll play jazz, then see what happens.' We just jumped into the wagon and took a ride together. It was four people as one. We were very young at that time and had no qualms about trying different things. We just sat down and played and did whatever was necessary to make it work musically and be fun. It was something unique at that time."[41]

In August 1977, as the members of Shakti were quietly going their separate ways, something was stirring at Sunset Sound Studios in Los Angeles. A young Netherlands-born electric guitarist named Edward Van Halen was busy revitalizing rock music on his so-called Frankenstrat—a homemade fusion of a Stratocaster and Gibson—putting together tracks for Van Halen's 1978 debut album. And John himself was an unlikely inspiration, as Edward recorded a pass on "I'm On Fire": "I wanted to do a melodic solo but the guys go, 'Pretend you're John McLaughlin!' So that solo came out. I don't even know what key I'm playing in! I just started playing and it fit perfect."[42] Van Halen's emergence showed the way the wind was blowing toward the end of the 1970s—and John would soon make his own dramatic return to the electric guitar.

## Mind Ecology 5:48

This fine album opener begins with the eerie sound of Vikku's *moorsing* (mouth harp) moving across the stereo spectrum. John makes extensive use of his sympathetic strings, tuned to E, F#, G, A, D, E. At 3:30, there's a motif based on the main riff of "The Noonward Race."

## Face To Face   5:58

This very complex piece moves through various time signatures, held together beautifully by Shankar and John's mostly overdubbed solos. At times, John's chords are reminiscent of America's 1972 single "A Horse With No Name."

## Come On Baby Dance with Me   (Shankar)   1:59

This is based on a traditional South Indian *kriti* (composition) called "Raghu-vamsa Sudha" in the ragam "Kadana Kutuhala." The intricate melody was a challenge for John: "The most difficult tune I've ever played in my life. This is pure classical music."[43]

## The Daffodil And The Eagle (McLaughlin/Shankar)   7:03

This joyful, brilliantly arranged standout opens with a C#m to F#m7 chord change in 6/4 time, with a melody very similar to "Morning Calls" from *Inner Worlds*. But it manages to sound very "Indian" courtesy of its minor—rather than major—pentatonic scale, and with added "blue" notes. The band change tempi effortlessly, and John's unison work with Vikku and Zakir, beginning at 2:32, showcases some of the most exciting acoustic playing of his career.

## Happiness Is Being Together   4:29

This is one of the most attractive themes in Shakti's oeuvre, outlining both Latin and Mediterranean influences and featuring some delightful harmony playing from Shankar and John. At times the arrangement is reminiscent of Crosby, Stills & Nash's 1969 single "Marrakesh Express." John's rhythmic perambula-tions, beginning at 2:48, are an absolute treat.

## Bridge Of Sighs (McLaughlin/Shankar)   3:52

This moody, effective piece in 11/4 is graced with what almost sounds like a rock backbeat from Vikku and Zakir.

## Get Down And Sruti (McLaughlin/Shankar)   7:03

This modal piece again features a double-time feel, courtesy of Vikku and Za-kir. John's solo is a mini masterpiece, with huge string bends and a remarkable series of ascending chords starting at around 1:15.

## Peace Of Mind    3:21

John and Shankar duet on this soothing album-closer. Its gentle timbres are quite a relief after the onslaught of high tempos and challenging melodies beforehand. John's sympathetic guitar strings play a key role here. "Peace Of Mind" is a fitting farewell to the original Shakti.

## *JOHNNY MCLAUGHLIN ELECTRIC GUITARIST* (1978)

John McLaughlin: Electric guitar
Jerry Goodman: Violin
Fernando Saunders: Bass
Stu Goldberg: Electric piano, organ, and mini-moog synthesizer
Billy Cobham: Drums
Carlos Santana: Electric guitar
Tom Coster: Organ
Neil Jason: Bass
Michael Walden: Drums
Alyrio Lima: Percussion
Armando Peraza: Congas
David Sanborn: Alto sax
Patrice Rushen: Piano
Alphonso Johnson: Taurus bass pedals and bass
Tony Smith: Drums
Chick Corea: Piano, mini-moog
Stanley Clarke: Acoustic bass
Jack DeJohnette: Drums
Jack Bruce: Bass
Tony Williams: Drums
Recorded at Sound Mixer Studios, New York City, and Devonshire Studios, North Hollywood, California
Recorded January 16–February 2, 1978
Produced by John McLaughlin, in association with Dennis Mackay
Released May 1978

Viewed with hindsight, *Electric Guitarist* was an unabashed attempt to win back John's old fans, those who possibly weren't enamored with Shakti. The title seems to say: *No more weird stuff!* Columbia advertised the album in the June 1978 edition of *Down Beat*—with John also the cover star—and the copy was desperate to alert potential listeners as to its intensity: "There's electricity in the air. John McLaughlin has unleashed the power and metallic beauty of his electric guitar on a new album and on a major new tour." A stern-looking John was seen playing his guitar on the roof of a tall building, overlooking what looks very much like the London—rather than New York—skyline.

*Electric Guitarist* was also, to some extent, John's ultimately unsuccessful attempt to reform the original Mahavishnu Orchestra while also rounding up some of other key collaborators of the 1970s. He asked Jan Hammer to be involved but was turned down, a source of some agitation: "He wouldn't play with me. . . . I'm too associated with jazz. It might taint his rock image," he kvetched to *Down Beat* magazine.[44] Rick Laird was otherwise engaged, touring with Chick Corea, but Billy Cobham, Carlos Santana, Jack Bruce, Tony Williams, Narada Michael Walden, and Jerry Goodman accepted. The numbers were made up with some of the greatest fusion-related musicians of the era: David Sanborn, Neil Jason, Patrice Rushen, Jack DeJohnette, Stanley Clarke, Chick Corea, and Alphonso Johnson. There were also early performances from John's future touring drums-and-bass team: Tony Smith and Fernando Saunders.

John later laid out what he had learned from making *Electric Guitarist*:

> Every piece on the album says something special to me. In a sense, I was bringing all of my influences up to date. It was great to get back together with old musical and personal friends. I'd been out of touch with these people and the electric guitar. I conceived the compositional format to be directly related to the people; having a concept of how, one, they like to play, and two, how I'd project they would enjoy playing with me in this context. Now out of all these feelings, the pieces emerged. The pieces were written before we went into the studio. That was imperative, really which is why it wasn't difficult in the actual recording; the general structure and form had been made, and so it was simple, really. The recording was completed in only two weeks. I'm happy to say that everyone played at least as well as I expected.[45]

John's main axe on *Electric Guitarist* was a modified Gibson Byrdland with a scalloped fretboard. It facilitated some extraordinary "shrieks" and string bends, as well as a new fast vibrato. Again, John found that his study of Indian music and one particular instrument helped his intonation on the scalloped fretboard immeasurably: "I know a couple of people who . . . feel a little funny because they don't have anything under the strings—it's like it's just space there, and that kind of throws them. But it didn't take me long to get accustomed to the feeling, since I had a distinct advantage of having studied *vina* somewhat, and therefore I was familiar with playing without a fingerboard."[46]

But even as Columbia delighted in John's return to the electric axe, if they were expecting a classic "fusion" album in the Al Di Meola or Return To Forever vein, they were in for a shock. The sheer variety of music on offer was dazzling, but it also reflected John's views on the "scene," as he told author (and wife of Larry) Julia Coryell in her 1978 book, *Jazz-Rock Fusion*: "How do I feel about jazz-rock? Boring! It bores me to tears; it just doesn't go anywhere. . . . I never listen to it, never. I don't want to hear it."

Indeed, 1978 seemed to be the era of "more is more"—huge drumkits, racks of guitar amps, faster and faster notes. Major labels were still signing "jazz" acts in the hope they might somehow produce the kind of runaway crossover hit that Weather Report enjoyed with "Birdland." The music business was still doubling down on "fusion" almost as a catch-all phrase encompassing anything instrumental and even tangentially jazz-related—an advertisement in the aforementioned June 1978 issue of *Down Beat* magazine said it all, trailing Lee Ritenour's album *The Captain's Journey* courtesy of the Elektra/Asylum label via Warner Bros, whose logo read: "Jazz-Fusion—A Division Of The Future." *Electric Guitarist* was a brave move away from any corporate notion of fusion, an incredibly rich, varied musical stew, only "Friendship" really focusing on "rock" textures. No other guitarist in the world could have segued from the raucous "Phenomenon: Compulsion" to the tender "My Foolish Heart."

The album was released in June 1978 to great acclaim and no little commercial success, reachng #6 on the *Billboard* Jazz chart and #105 pop, though, of course, the *Birds Of Fire* levels of success were long gone. *Electric Guitarist* was also graced with a distinctive, original cover concept. John talked about its origins in the northern England of his youth:

> Not that I was pushy, but I used to go around to all these places and say, 'Mind if I sit in?' Since I was 15 I've been doing that. And that's how I ended up on the road. But I thought I'd go classy and have a little card made. . . . I was known as Johnny in those days, that's what my mother calls me. So it had 'Johnny McLaughlin, Electric Guitarist', and the address underneath. . . . Anyway, last year I ran into two of my old friends who were part of the hard times that I mentioned when I was 14, 15, 16 years old. One of the guys had one of those cards. He had kept it all these years, and he said it would make a great album cover. Coupled with that is the fact that I am probably one of the least photographed children in the world. There's only one picture of me as a child, at 12 years old. So they (Columbia) want to put the card and picture on the cover.[47]

John formed The One Truth Band to tour the album in the summer of 1978. Goldberg and Shankar were retained on keyboards and violin respectively, joined by a young, dynamic rhythm section of T.M. Stevens on bass and Son Ship Theus on drums. They made for a very flamboyant, combustive team, coming more from a funk and avant-garde background than highly technical jazz/fusion. They were also both natural showmen: "Very different to what you'd expect in a McLaughlin show," according to Goldberg.[48] Stevens had played with Pharaoh Sanders, Norman Connors, Narada Michael Walden, and Al Di Meola before being recruited for The One Truth Band. On March 2, 1978, Stevens had also attended an aborted recording session for Miles at Columbia Studios alongside Larry Coryell and Al Foster, though the music from this gathering remains unreleased at the time of this writing.

John had got to know Theus when he drummed with McCoy Tyner and Charles Lloyd in 1977, and he was impressed with both his musical and spiritual outlook. (Bianchi reports that just before The One Truth Band tour, Theus had also just been called by Joe Zawinul to play on the title track of Weather Report's 1978 album, *Mr Gone*, but his take hit the cutting-room floor—as did takes by Alphonse Mouzon, Steve Gadd, Alex Acuna, and Zawinul himself. Tony Williams's pass eventually got the nod. . . .) Goldberg reports that Theus would often chant, with "shamanistic incantations."[49] One famous gig at the The Beacon in New York City, supported by Brand X, saw him recite poetry during his drum solo. But ultimately Stevens and Theus's personal and musical differences were insurmountable, and John had to make a change. He recruited the far-more-settled Fernando Saunders/Tony Smith bass and drums team. They were probably best known for being Jan Hammer's recent rhythm section, appearing on the albums *Oh, Yeah?* and *Melodies*, and for their work with Jeff Beck in the Jan Hammer/Jeff Beck Group. Detroit-born Saunders was influenced by the bass playing of Jack Bruce, Tim Bogert, and Paul McCartney as a teenager, and their melodic approach to the instrument remained a huge influence. Moving to New York City in 1975, he played with Larry Young and Tony Williams before being recruited by Hammer. Smith contributed to albums by Santana (*Welcome*) and Jose "Chapito" Areas before joining the Hammer Band.

John was thrilled with Saunders and Smith's immediate impact in The One Truth Band: "They had been playing together for years. They arrived with this pocket, right off! Just boom!" But whatever John had publicly said about the speed and ferocity in jazz/rock music at the expense of musical depth, The One Truth Band's live gigs featured some of his most outrageous playing and fastest tempos to date. He had clearly also been finding the time to get to the movies now and again: He would often quote John Williams's five-note theme from *Close Encounters Of The Third Kind* during the summer 1978 tour.

### New York On My Mind    5:46

It feels almost like the original Mahavishnu, helped by featuring Goodman on violin and Cobham on drums (apparently the piece was, indeed, rehearsed by the original lineup). The song is essentially in six but features strange accents. It's heavily indebted to the second section of *Apocalypse*'s "Wings Of Karma" with its four ascending chords and attendant melody. Goldberg plays his finest Moog solo to date, the result of a few years of woodshedding, inspired by Jan Hammer's playing and the fact that he hadn't liked his own sound on *Inner Worlds*: "I spent three hours a day playing scales on the Moog (pitch-bend) wheel." Goldberg apparently got a call from John's manager in Los Angeles the day before the New York recording session, telling him there was a plane ticket waiting at the airport. Goldberg sight-read his part in the studio: "It was super-fun, and based on my performance, I got the call to join The One Truth Band."[50]

### Friendship    7:02

This excellent duet with Carlos Santana has been compared to a few pieces of music: "With A Little Help From My Friends," Beethoven's "Ode To Joy." It's a clever arrangement: Santana solos over the two-chord Latin vamp, while John plays modally over one chord with some incredibly fast triads. Pat Metheny discussed the track during a *Down Beat* Blindfold Test in September 1981: "I admire both of them and I really like this performance; it was so loose, and almost free-sounding. The beginning reminded me of an Ornette Coleman thing, sort of approximate unison, a little out of tune. I'd give that five stars. That's some of the best I've heard from either one of them."

### Every Tear From Every Eye    6:53

The title is a line from William Blake's poem "Auguries Of Innocence" ("Every Tear from Every Eye/Becomes a Babe in Eternity"). The English poet, painter, and mystic certainly inspires John here, because he produces some of the greatest electric guitar playing of his entire career, using his scalloped neck to winning effect. Sadly, the track is marred by some uncertain rhythm-section playing, including an uncharacteristically out-of-tune Alphonso Johnson.

## Do You Hear The Voices That You Left Behind?  7:41

Based upon John Coltrane's "Giant Steps" chords and dedicated to the saxophonist, this is simply a killer performance from all four players—John, Chick Corea, Stanley Clarke, and Jack DeJohnette. At 2:17, we hear John repeat and then modify a fast three-note lick, developed specifically during his Shakti days. DeJohnette's breaks are remarkably complex—no matter how many times you tap your foot to keep in time, chances are you will come out at the wrong place. Clarke was clearly enthused by this track, as evidenced by his composition "Off The Planet," recorded in late summer 1978 and released on the *I Wanna Play For You* album. His piccolo bass solo is one of the greatest John imitations this writer has ever heard.

## Are You The One? Are You The One?  4:43

This was a Lifetime reunion of sorts, though sadly without Larry Young, who died on March 31, 1978. John's playful performance is augmented by a Mu-Tron envelope filter. The piece was updated regularly by John for future live performances—with the Trio Of Doom, One Truth Band, 1980s Mahavishnu, and the 1988 trio (in one of the wackiest arrangements, which often quoted Charlie Parker's "Now's The Time").

## Phenomenon: Compulsion  3:23

Just when you thought you knew where this album was going, there's an avant-garde blowout like nothing else in John's discography. It's a chance to hear what those early John/Cobham pre-Mahavishnu jams might have sounded like. Narada Michael Walden called them "duet solos" because they were so tight. The main theme is a *konnakol* rhythmic phrase, similar to one on Shakti's "La Danse Du Bonheur." In post-production, John's guitar was put through a Marshall Time Modulator envelope filter. This is as violent and unexpected as anything in the Sonny Sharrock/James Blood Ulmer canon. The virtuosity on offer somehow makes it an even more perverse piece of music.

## My Foolish Heart (Victor Young, Ned Washington)  3:25

Victor Young composed this theme for a 1949 Hollywood movie starring Dana Andrews. John detunes his low E string down to an A and puts his guitar through a Leslie speaker on this Tal Farlow–dedicated solo masterpiece.

He also uses some palm harmonics and a lot of thumb-assisted, large-interval chords. Farlow repaid the compliment in a 1980 *Guitar Player* interview with Arnie Berle: "I like John McLaughlin a lot. He's very much influenced by John Coltrane. He certainly has a lot of technique, and he can play some nice chord melodies." John played an almost-identical solo arrangement of this piece during the tour with Jeff Beck in 1975 (it's amusing to hear it in the middle of a huge arena gig), and also occasionally during concerts in 1980 and 1987.

## ELECTRIC DREAMS (1979)

John McLaughlin: Electric guitar; 6, 12, and 13 string acoustic guitar; banjo
L. Shankar: Acoustic and electric violin
Stu Goldberg: Electric piano, Moog, Prophet, Hammond organ
Fernando Saunders: Vocals, acoustic and electric basses
Tony Smith: Drums, vocals
Alyrio Lima: Percussion
David Sanborn: Alto sax
Recorded at Sound Mixers Studio, New York City, November and December 1978
Produced by John McLaughlin and John Pace
Released April 1979

John followed up his 1978 summer tour by joining some exploratory sessions for Joni Mitchell's *Mingus* album alongside Gerry Mulligan, Eddie Gomez, Tony Williams, and Jan Hammer. These were deemed unsatisfactory by Mitchell and later supplanted by a set of live-in-the-studio performances featuring Herbie Hancock on Fender Rhodes, Wayne Shorter on sax, Jaco Pastorius on bass, and Peter Erskine on drums. Meanwhile the latter three players had propelled the latest Weather Report album, *Mr Gone*, to a gold record upon its September 1978 release.

John took some of *Mr Gone*'s energy into his new studio album, *Electric Dreams*, which would arguably become his most cogent electric project outside The Mahavishnu Orchestra. (Was it a Columbia decree to feature the word "Electric" in the album title once again, just to banish any doubt?)

The Weather Report influence was increased courtesy of the recruitment of one of their alumni, Alyrio Lima, who had been a key player on the 1975 *Tale Spinnin'* album. The classically trained percussionist had enjoyed a varied career, playing with Sly Stone during his Madison Square Garden wedding to

Kathy Silva in 1974 and becoming a member of the disco-inflected Webster Lewis Band. Lima's arsenal mainly consisted of China cymbals, triangle, sleigh bells, and woodblocks, heavy on the top end, a more impressionistic, less Afro-Cuban sound than many percussionists of the 1970s. He would be granted a lot of freedom on *Electric Dreams*, and his wonderful playing became a key ingredient of the album's success.

John's main axe was now a modified Gibson ES-345, often put through a Leslie speaker, and he occasionally overdubbed a twelve-string acoustic and banjo for color, too. John Pace, the house engineer at Sound Mixer Studios, was recruited to co-produce, and together they cooked up vastly different timbres to the previous *Electric Guitarist*. A lot of time was spent getting a hefty drum sound, the snare and kick particularly supplying a lot of sonic wallop. Smith's playing, accordingly, is strong on groove and less concerned with pyrotechnics—vastly different to anything offered up by Cobham or Walden, and no worse for that. Most of the music was recorded live with all the band set up in a big room. Goldberg: "All the solos were first done live, but John and especially Shankar, being such perfectionists, would often rework their solos extensively afterwards in the studio." Goldberg reports that Pace was invaluable in that regard—"He did most of his work overdubbing, editing and mixing after the main sessions."[51]

Saunders delivers a truly great bass performance throughout, melodic, punchy, and sounding absolutely nothing like any of the other notable fretless players of the 1970s, such as Jaco, Ralphe Armstrong, Alphonso Johnson, or Brand X's Percy Jones. Goldberg's playing has come on leaps and bounds, supplying tasty Rhodes, occasional Hammond, and furious, exciting Moog solos. His performance is "revelatory," according to *The Penguin Guide To Jazz On CD*. Shankar gets a lot less solo space than he did with Shakti, but every note counts on *Electric Dreams*. As for John, he plays beautifully throughout, injecting energy and leading the band with strong call-and-response themes.

But one wonders what Columbia staffer Gene Greif was intending with the odd black-and-white album cover design, perhaps interpreting the album title a little literally. John seems to be telekinetically "summoning" a cavalcade of flying (electric) household appliances, *Carrie*-style, as a young girl (Dorothy? Alice?) holds a suitcase outside his window. One wonders how much the somewhat-forbidding cover affected sales, but for whatever reason, *Electric Dreams* didn't quite match the commercial success of the previous year's *Electric Guitarist*, hitting #14 on the Billboard Jazz charts and #147 Pop.

Despite the calming influence of Saunders and Smith, The One Truth Band also proved to be short-lived. Again, John had expressed a wish for Shankar to "bring jazz harmony into it," but the young violinist was reluctant. But there was a successful American tour during the late spring of 1979 and another famous gig at the Beacon Theatre—in tandem with master of the Telecaster, Roy Buchanan—before a short tour of Brazil and Argentina alongside Egberto Gismonti. Then the band went their separate ways. Sadly, neither Goldberg, Saunders, Smith, nor Shankar would ever perform with John on record again; the album and tour were very much a farewell to the 1970s. Goldberg moved on to his first solo album *Fancy Glance*, a mainly up-tempo set of jazz and fusion originals with bassist John Lee and drummer Gerry Brown. Shankar found himself easing into more commercial, pop-related sessions, while Saunders soon became Lou Reed's bassist of choice.

### Guardian Angels   0:51

This effective opener, featuring a fair amount of post-production echo and triple-tracked twelve-string acoustic (and a six-string doubling Shankar's violin line), was later to become an extended, popular piece (with the "s" removed) for the John/Di Meola/de Lucia guitar trio. John develops some chordal ideas he began to explore on the Shakti track "Lady L."

### Miles Davis   4:54

China and ride cymbals, snare drum, woodblocks, and timbale kick off this fascinating tribute to John's old boss (and a return gift for "John McLaughlin" on *Bitches Brew*), possibly a show of support in his hour of need. Initially built on superimposed major/minor triads over a C# tonality, Goldberg adds incisive Rhodes (with brilliant echoing of John's solo at 2:43) and ominous synth washes in the left speaker. There are shades of *Bitches Brew*'s soundworld. John quotes from "It's About That Time" at 3:43. John would sometimes quote elements of Wayne Shorter's "Nefertiti" when playing "Miles Davis" live during 1979.

### Electric Dreams, Electric Sighs   6:57

The spirit of Beethoven's "Moonlight Sonata" accompanies the opening of this album highlight. Goldberg wrote an arrangement for Shankar's beautiful triple-tracked violins during the first two minutes of the piece, sadly very low in the mix. John's guitar features a Leslie-speaker effect, but the really striking piece of musicianship is his brief banjo solo. He revealed he had been woodshedding on the instrument while working with Shakti, and he also had ideas for a modified version: "I want another banjo with some sympathetic strings and this fingerboard, because it's very percussive. There's something haunting about that sound. I only got the banjo the other day but I've been thinking about it for a couple of months. What I love about it is what I'm able to do with my left hand."[52] Goldberg and Shankar fire off superb solos, too. On tour in late 1979, McLaughlin played "Electric Dreams, Electric Sighs" as an acoustic guitar duet with Goldberg.

### Desire And The Comforter    7:34

Lima's triangle and Smith's beautifully recorded ride cymbal underpin Saunders's striking bass solo (to which Bruce added lyrics on the 1979 tour), kicking off this complex but ultimately very accessible piece of classic jazz/rock. John solos for the last three minutes, generating excitement with a hard attack and ingenious call/response patterns, answered by the band.

### Love And Understanding    6:36

Not many tracks in John's oeuvre divide opinion as much as this. Some—such as this writer—rate it among John's best work, others as an embarrassingly shallow attempt at "pop." John digs out his scalloped acoustic guitar with sympathetic strings to accompany an astonishing piece of Shankar musicianship, based around a South Indian raga called "Hamsadhwani," reminiscent of the Shakti composition "Peace Of Mind." John then digs in with emotive, hugely distorted electric guitar, obviously influenced by Santana, as Smith and Saunders enter on vocals. Their light soul voices suit the track very well, even if their pitching is not perfect.

### Singing Earth (Stu Goldberg)    0:37

Goldberg gets a writing credit for this strange synth interlude. Perhaps John had learned the hard way, or maybe it was a tip of the hat to the young keyboard wizard for five years of sterling service.

### The Dark Prince    5:15

The second Miles tribute of the album is super-fast bebop played with Smith's very heavy ride cymbal in the left channel and Lima's china cymbal in the right. John's remarkable solo ends with what sounds like him blowing a party whistle.

Kolosky lambasts Goldberg's "dated" keyboard sounds, but great Rhodes and Mini Moog playing never really dates, and this is just a world-class performance, with Miles-related quotes from "It Never Entered My Mind" at 2:07 and "Four" at 2:21 (though Goldberg claims both were "unintentional"—if so, they're a miracle of subconscious channeling).[53]

### The Unknown Dissident    6:16

In the spirit of The Unknown Soldier, John heralds The Unknown Dissident. It was written during an era of great political upheaval—The Troubles in Northern Ireland, martial law in Eastern Europe, the apartheid regime in South Africa, and various atrocities in Latin America, with journalists, poets, musicians, novelists, and artists of all stripes under threat. But the opening ambulance siren places the tune very much in the UK. The B section features similar chords to "New York On My Mind." Sanborn seems perfectly suited to this composition and plays superbly. As the music gently fades over an A/B chord, our protagonist is apparently extracted from an "ambulance" and frogmarched down a back alley before being summarily executed.

## THE TRIO OF DOOM (RECORDED 1979, RELEASED 2007)

John McLaughlin: Guitar
Jaco Pastorius: Bass
Tony Williams: Drums
Recorded at Karl Marx Theater, Havana, Cuba, March 3, 1979, and CBS Studios, New York City, March 8, 1979
Produced by John McLaughlin and Richard Seidel
Released June 26, 2007

In 2016, John reminisced about his first meeting with Jaco Pastorius: "The first person Jaco came to see in New York was me, and we jammed together at SIR (Rehearsal Studios in Manhattan). . . . He asked me for 20 bucks to fix a flat—money I never got back!"[54] John was amazed by the young tyro's playing, recommending him immediately to Tony Williams since he had already offered Ralphe Armstrong the bass gig in the new Mahavishnu Orchestra (though Williams eventually settled on bassist Tony Newton when he premiered his New Lifetime band in early 1975, also featuring guitarist Allan Holdsworth).

John and Jaco then crossed paths many times when Shakti toured with Weather Report throughout 1976 and 1977. Though Jaco's bipolar disorder went undiagnosed throughout the 1970s, his illness was doubtless exacerbated by the huge pressures of being a celebrity musician, father, and husband—to college sweetheart, Tracy—at such a young age. By the summer of 1978, though his career was going from strength to strength, things had very much changed for the worse in Jaco's personal life. Promoting the album *Mr Gone*, Weather Report embarked on a huge world tour, after which Jaco returned home to Florida to discover that Tracy had filed for divorce, in response to his infidelity with a woman named Ingrid Horn-Muller. Over dinner in January 1979, Tracy and Jaco managed to have some friendly reminiscences at their favorite local restaurant, but this was scant consolation for Jaco—he was about to lose his house, wife, and children.

So, one can only imagine the huge stress he was under as he joined John and Tony Williams for rehearsals in early March 1979 for the much-anticipated, controversial Trio Of Doom project (reportedly Jaco's choice of name). But he initially seemed to be on his best behavior and playing well. John was excited: "What a trio that was! What a pleasure it was to play with them!"[55] He has expressed dismay that those early rehearsals weren't recorded.

Williams also came into the Trio Of Doom with his own issues. He had recently released the final album of his Columbia contract—*The Joy Of Flying*, which included several duets with Jan Hammer—but he had become fairly disillusioned with his standing in the music industry, not feeling fulfilled as a composer, drummer, or bandleader.

But still, the trio was a jewel in the crown for CBS Records, and they were keen to feature their new supergroup during a series of upcoming concerts set up in Havana, Cuba, promoted as Havana Jam. The roots of the concerts lay in US president Jimmy Carter's decision to lift travel restrictions to Cuba in 1978, first imposed after the Missile Crisis in 1962. (Ronald Reagan, upon his election as president in January 1981, immediately reinstated the US/Cuba travel embargo.) A coterie of legendary jazz musicians was aboard the American cruise ship that dropped anchor in the waters of Havana for the first time in sixteen years, including Dizzy Gillespie, Stan Getz, and Bobby Hutcherson. Each performer headlined a set, and then Gillespie guested with the legendary Cuban band Irakere featuring Chucho Valdez, Arturo Sandoval, and Paquito D'Rivera, a concert that was later given a glowing review by jazz scribe Leonard Feather.

Upon his return to the United States, Gillespie waxed lyrical about the event to Bruce Lundvall, president of CBS's Pop and Jazz divisions, and the executive set about planning a three-day festival at the Karl Marx Theatre, Havana, between March 2–4, 1979. A stellar group of CBS artists made the trip to Cuba on a TWA charter flight: Billy Joel, Stephen Stills, Kris Kristofferson, Rita Coolidge, Rodney Franklin, Weather Report (who opened the series of concerts with "Black Market"), and an all-star jazz band of Stan Getz, Bobby Hutcherson, Dexter Gordon, Jimmy Heath, Tony Williams, and Woody Shaw. Irakere and other Cuban artists such as Willie Bobo, Irakere, Orquestra Aragon, and the Fania All Stars, played, too. Lundvall flew forty tons of equipment and supplies out to Havana, including a twenty-four-track recording console borrowed from the Record Plant in New York City.

There were huge expectations from fellow musicians to see John, Jaco, and Williams performing on the same stage. As Peter Erskine reported in the 2014 *Jaco* documentary: "This was the jazz/rock version of The Three Tenors." But Jaco seemed unsettled and overexcited in Havana, a situation some attributed to the fact that his new partner, Ingrid, had not made the trip with him. Erskine reports that Jaco had an aggressive exchange of views with Billy Joel. Then, after the festival-opening Weather Report set, which received a mixed reception from both audience and band, Jaco got into a *contretemps* with some members of the Fania All Stars:

> Joe had to rescue Jaco from that one because he almost got his ass kicked by those guys. Whenever Jaco lost face like that . . . boom. Weather Report had already played, so what could Jaco destroy? He destroyed The Trio Of Doom.[56]

The trio began their set with "The Dark Prince." Things seemed okay for a while, and then all hell broke loose. John takes up the story:

> It's an uptempo C-minor blues with altered changes. Jaco . . . walked back to his amp, turned it up to 11 and started playing in A major really loud against it. I was looking at Tony like, 'What's going on here?' It was nothing like rehearsals. He did the same kind of thing to Tony's tune. And then he went out and did the whole audience routine. It was a fiasco.[57]

Erskine and Zawinul were watching from the side of the stage, the former remembering: "We were embarrassed. Jaco was self-destructing up there and Tony was just furious, completely pissed off." However the crowd was going wild—though Erskine noted that it was very much an invited audience of record company employees, not the "*gente*," the common people—and Jaco was drinking a lot of *mojito* (as were many other musicians). Erskine remembers a strange mood around the whole jazz/rock contingent at the Havana Jam, though. He reported that John said to him after the Weather Report set: "I've heard all these amazing things about you, but you didn't sound that good"![58]

John recalled the scene after they'd finished playing their set: "When we got offstage, Jaco says, 'You know, you're a bad motherfucker.' And I said, 'I have never felt so ashamed to be onstage. If I never see you again it's too soon.' I was so angry because I felt he'd betrayed Tony and me."[59] John was so furious that—right up until the time of this writing—he refers to the Trio Of Doom concert as The Bay Of Gigs. Williams initially internalized his anger, staying silent. Jaco's response to the gig was to "jump into the ocean from a backstage balcony of the theatre, amidst plenty of dangerous rocks," according to Erskine.[60] Back in New York, CBS heard the live tapes and agreed with John—they were unusable. So, John recommended they wait until the dust had settled and then go into the studio:

I said, 'If Tony is ready to go, I'll go.' We went in and Tony was very angry, still. In the studio he wouldn't talk to Jaco, he wouldn't even look at Jaco, until finally Jaco said something and that was the trigger—Tony flipped. Jaco was afraid. Tony went in and destroyed his drums in the studio. And walked out.[61]

The trio had managed to record a few tunes at CBS Studios on March 8, 1979, before the blow-up. These versions of John's "Dark Prince," Williams's "Para Oriente," and Jaco's "Continuum" later appeared (with overdubbed crowd noise) on the *Havana Jam* and *Havana Jam 2* double albums, released in late 1979. They featured one of John's least-adorned guitar sounds for ten years—no effects at all, just plugging straight into an amp, reminiscent of his tone on *Extrapolation*. But there was a lot of mental turbulence from Jaco at this point, as John reported: "Jaco was acting crazy and being very obnoxious, and Tony just got fed up with it. He flipped out and smashed his drums and walked out of the studio. And that really tore Jaco to strips."[62] Sadly, it would be the last time John and Williams played together.

It seemed the sad end to a project that had promised so much. But in 2007, John was approached by Sony to oversee a remastering/remixing of the live tapes and studio sessions with a view to releasing them in their entirety. He accepted, realizing there were two other legacies involved (Jaco had died in 1987, Williams ten years later), becoming producer of the project and enlisting former Verve Records senior A&R president Richard Seidel to assist. But they had to do a lot of work on the tapes. "It was very tricky because you've got two versions of things. I wanted to get the (live) Havana part in as well, as part of the story, because it's interesting. *Trio Of Doom* is a document; it's not just a record. These two giants, they're gone. And I told Sony they had to give the money to their widows."[63]

The live tracks are, indeed, incredibly frantic and wildly inconsistent. You might even say that something sounded slightly off with this band from the beginning, and it may not be an exaggeration to say this kind of project might have contributed to Williams considering dropping out of music at the beginning of the 1980s. (In June 1991, he told *Musician* magazine: "In 1979, I was feeling in a hole, in a rut. I felt like I wasn't doing what I had the talent to do: write music, have a band, have better relationships." He subsequently moved from Manhattan to the West Coast and started private composition lessons.)

It's telling that John opens the album with Williams's inspired studio improvisation, though, a marvelous compendium of the drummer's 1970s/1980s stylings. On the notorious "Dark Prince," everyone seems to be playing at the edge of irritation; Williams is absolutely on fire but doesn't seem to like what he hears—the tune is desperate for an anchor that no one is willing to provide. Jaco's closing blast of feedback says it all. The live version of Jaco's "Continuum" is serviceable but hardly essential, while Williams's riff-based "Para Oriente" sounds a little like Cream and features several uncharacteristic fluffs from Jaco. "Are You The One, Are You The One?" kicks off with another beautiful Williams solo before breaking into a furiously fast version of John's tune, with almost a disco feel. Jaco runs through all his best licks in E, but it's hard to escape a sinking feeling about this project.

One of the first things John did to the studio tracks when remixing them in 2006 was to add a chorus-like effect on his guitar, for added resonance and a smoother attack. He was also particularly unhappy with the sound of Williams's cymbals on the original 1979 studio recordings: "I don't know why but (recording engineer) Stan Tonkel didn't open up the overheads. My engineer had a brilliant idea. He doubled up on the audio tracks—I think it was the snare or hi-hat—and EQ'd it to death to bring the cymbals out."[64] This is a strange comment, since Williams's cymbals are much higher in the mix on the original *Havana Jam* albums. But they possibly have a little more finesse on the 2007 remix. The remix also removes some "roughness" from Jaco's bass tone; it's arguably more pleasant to listen to, but it has lost a fair amount of "chicken grease," as Jaco might have put it.

The studio version of "Dark Prince"—announced by Tonkel—is certainly more successful than the live. Williams gives much-needed stability, but again it's a pale shadow of the *Electric Dreams* version—it's so hard to do the harmony justice without keyboards, despite Jaco's sterling efforts, and Williams neglects to emphasize any melodic elements of John's tune. "Continuum" has a folky cheer but doesn't add anything to Jaco's three solo versions (compare it to the version played by Hiram Bullock, Kenwood Dennard, and Jaco on the *PDB* album released by DIW Records in 1989). "Para Oriente" suffers from Jaco's extremely tangential harmony and Williams's flaccid snare drum, and the track constantly seems on the verge of breaking down.

Despite the musical and personal deficiencies and inconsistencies involved with *The Trio Of Doom*, John's hard work paid off—he received an email from Colleen, Williams's widow, saying the drummer would have been delighted with the results. "That email from Colleen brought tears to my eyes," John reported. He also reported that Jaco's widow, Tracy, had come to see The 4th Dimension in North Carolina when they played there in the immediate aftermath of *The Trio Of Doom*'s release in late 2007.

After the Havana Jam, John spent much of the spring and summer of 1979 playing acoustic guitar in his new trio—of which much more later—and then closed out an extraordinary decade of music by touring Europe with an all-star unit of Jack Bruce, Stu Goldberg, and Billy Cobham through October and November. They mainly performed material from *Electric Dreams*, plus "You Know, You Know" and "One Word," Goldberg's "The Core Of The Apple," and Bruce's "The Tightrope." Though bootleg and radio recordings demonstrate the audience reaction was generally feverish, as were some of the performances, John's old friend Pete Brown relates in Stump's *Go Ahead John* that the London Rainbow gig was exceptionally awkward: "The atmosphere was so bad, like they hated being onstage with one another."

As the decade of jazz/rock came to an end, the genre—albeit with a decidedly large dollop of R'n'B—showed no sign of losing its appeal. *Billboard* reported that 1979's top-selling "jazz" albums were by Bob James, Chuck Mangione, George Benson, and Grover Washington Jr., between them contributing 17 percent to all US record sales (compared to these artists, John's Trio Of Doom and Cobham/Bruce/Goldberg projects sounded like total mayhem, more akin to the New York loft scene, which was also coming to a close at the end of the 1970s).

However, the rest of the industry was in recession—on June 29, 1979, fifty-three CBS employees in New York, Los Angeles and Nashville were given their pink slips by president, Bruce Lundvall. (CEO Walter Yetnikoff reportedly got him to do the dirty work.) On August 10, 1979—later nicknamed "Black Friday"—another 120 people were let go. John, too, would soon negotiate his way out of the door at CBS.

# 5

# THE 1980s

From *Friday Night In San Francisco* to
*Paco & John Live at Montreux 1987*

## FRIDAY NIGHT IN SAN FRANCISCO (1981)

Al Di Meola: Acoustic guitar
John McLaughlin: Acoustic guitar
Paco de Lucía: Acoustic guitar
Recorded December 5, 1980, at The Warfield Theatre, San Francisco, and
   May 1981 at Minot Sound, White Plains, New York
Produced by John McLaughlin, Al Di Meola, and Paco de Lucía
Released July 1981

Aside from Shakti, John's chief acoustic projects of the late 1970s and early 1980s were two guitar trios, the second of which defied all record-company expectations to become an international sensation. Central to these developments was his friendship with Spanish guitarist Paco de Lucía. John had heard Paco's music on a French radio station while riding in a Paris taxi cab toward the end of 1977: "I thought: this guy's a monster. So I got back to my hotel and found out that Paco was in Paris. I mean, if that's not a sign I don't know what is. We got together a couple of days later to play and it was just unreal."[1] John would be forever marked by that experience: "After playing with Paco de Lucía, I'd have to say that flamenco technique is the most superior approach to the guitar."[2]

De Lucía had first wowed American audiences via his guest spot on Al Di Meola's 1977 album, *Elegant Gypsy*. He was born Francisco Sanchez Gomez in the city of Algeciras in 1947. A child prodigy, he won a guitar contest at twelve, and then went on tour with flamenco dancer Jose Greco and his vocalist brother Ramon. He became a household name in Spain as he led his own bands throughout the 1970s. De Lucía didn't read music but had a remarkable ear, able to pick up on melodic and harmonic lines quickly. He was also a lover of many different genres, always a dealbreaker for John.

John and De Lucía quickly hatched a plan to form a guitar trio. Paco's manager initially suggested adding folk/jazz pioneer Leo Kottke, but he wasn't available, so they went with their second choice: Larry Coryell. They rehearsed in Paris during the fall of 1978. Coryell became fascinated by de Lucía's technique, and vice versa: "He kept asking me what scales went with the chords in the songs we selected. . . . Paco learned some scales from us but we learned some scales from him too. . . . He had timing, taste and fire, and John and I ate it up."[3] But also Coryell quickly realized he would benefit from not trying to compete with these two master technicians: "I needed slower phrasing rather than just running up and down the scales as fast as I could, because John and Paco could do that to the max all night." This approach worked wonders—his "slower" licks and spontaneous melodies were strangely memorable and served as a welcome counterpoint to John and Paco's pyrotechnics.

The trio toured on three separate occasions in late 1978 and early 1979. The opening dates in Germany were a huge success, and this generally seems to have been a happy period, as John reported to *Jazztimes* in March 2015: "We were somewhere in Europe. . . . The music was just amazing this night, all three of us really burning, and it got so good at one point that Larry got up from his chair and started dancing! It was so spontaneous and funny. Paco and I started laughing out of control." Coryell also reported the three were very partial to a Nintendo game called American Football.

But Coryell was losing a battle with the bottle. During a famous filmed concert at London's Royal Albert Hall on February 14, 1979, Coryell was disturbed by the British crowd's "reserve," compared to the wild reactions the trio had been getting elsewhere. But he was also in a very bad physical and mental state: "I can't watch that performance. All these years later, I'm still disgusted with the shape I was in that night." (Coryell later credited drummer Elvin Jones for getting him into treatment during the summer of 1981: "He looked me straight in the eye and said, 'You should be in hospital.' I knew he was right. . . .")[4]

As the trio's first collection of major live dates wound down, John contributed two compositions to Fuse One's self-titled album in April 1980, recorded at Rudy Van Gelder's famous studio in Englewood Cliffs, New Jersey. This was an all-star jazz/rock studio project—alongside Stanley Clarke, Joe Farrell, Don Grusin, and Tony Williams—for Creed Taylor's reinvigorated CTI label. (Taylor and Van Gelder had worked with John back in 1970 on Joe Farrell's debut album.) John supplied "Friendship" (no relation to the composition of the same name on *Electric Guitarist*) and "To Whom All Things Concern." The former was a dry run for 1981's far superior "Stardust On Your Sleeve," but without the sweeping majesty of that later track. The latter was a middling, bop-tinged swinger and John's last electric guitar performance for a few years.

Meanwhile, McLaughlin's old *compadre* Carlos Santana was about to release his jazziest solo album to date, the entirely instrumental *The Swing Of Delight*, featuring Miles sidemen Williams on drums, Ron Carter on bass, Wayne Shorter on sax, and Herbie Hancock on keyboards. Santana was also about to finally renounce his Chinmoy name "Devadip" and cease public affirmations of his guru, urged on by his then-wife, Debbie, and appalled by Chinmoy's criticism of tennis star Billie Jean King's lesbianism. In her book *Footprints*, Michelle Mercer quotes Shorter: "Carlos was starting to question it 'cause when someone starts to tell you, 'You can't get from A to P except through me,' that's when you watch it." Shorter also reported that soon after renouncing Chinmoy, John "was also celebrating by buying drinks at a bar."

But *The Swing Of Delight*'s lack of commercial success pointed to a post-disco-and-punk record-industry slump. Columbia dropped many fusion artists—essentially only Weather Report, Stanley Clarke, George Duke, and Al Di Meola would survive the cull—and released a series of what Steve Khan wryly called the "brown paper bag" compilations, not exactly a gold watch for the recipients. Khan remembers the guitar situation at Columbia at the end of the 1970s:

> It was my feeling that you might list their guitarists in order of importance to the label in this way: John McLaughlin; Al Di Meola; and then you have to remember that artists like Jeff Beck and Carlos Santana were suddenly in this sub-genre too—bigger sellers, both of them, than all of us combined. Lee Ritenour was there too at Epic Records. Then you perhaps could include Eric Gale—and lastly me. I'm probably forgetting someone. But I never ran into any of these great guitarists at "Black Rock", as we referred to Columbia's offices on W. 52nd St. in Manhattan. I would see some of them backstage at various concerts when we might have shared a double or triple bill together. Where John was concerned, he had already reached legendary status and was on a plain all of his own making! Around the dawn of the '80s, Columbia finally realized that even they could not handle a roster a big as this. And so, sadly for me and many artists, we were dropped by the label. And then, as a nice parting gift, they released Best-Of packages on all of us.

Despite this scenario, in a move that seemed like shutting the gate after the horse had bolted, February 1980 saw the National Academy of Recording Arts

and Sciences finally adding a Best Jazz Fusion Performance Grammy Award—
won by Weather Report for their album *8:30*.

But, at least in the short term, John was a Columbia artist, and he wished to
continue a trio with Paco, despite Coryell's absence. Paco suggested Di Meola.
He had been born in Jersey City on July 22, 1954. He had attended Boston's
Berklee College of Music and was headhunted by Chick Corea to replace Bill
Connors in Return To Forever, ushering in their most popular phase resulting in the Grammy-winning albums *No Mystery* (1975) and *Romantic Warrior*
(1976). On paper, Di Meola seemed the perfect fit for the guitar trio, but there
was a little trepidation about bringing him into the fold, as John remembers:
"We'd done three tours before Al joined and that's a lot of playing. We had
become a really tight unit together."[5]

But the new trio gelled quickly, beginning a European tour in Helsinki, Fin-
land, on October 14, 1980, after only a few days of rehearsal. John's acoustic
guitar of choice was now a nylon-string Ovation. Di Meola used an Ovation
Legend with steel strings and De Lucía a custom-made, nylon-string Hermanos
Conde, named after its Madrid-based luthier. Di Meola reported sometimes
have a slightly overbearing low-end compared to the other two nylon-string
guitars, but the trio gave themselves the luxury of taking their own soundman
Vance Armstrong on tour, described by De Lucía as "the fourth musician." Di
Meola was immediately blown away by the level of musicianship on offer:

> It created a healthy competition because we were really trying to impress one an-
> other. We were really trying to grow beyond our limits and raise the bar. A lot of
> those shows, man, we were playing things we never thought we could play. You'd
> watch Paco solo and think, 'Oh my God, how am I going to play something to
> beat that?' And then you would just come up with something.[6]

John felt similarly about playing with De Lucía and Di Meola on the tour:
"It was competitive but there's no winner. There's just the excitement. When
you start playing with these guys there's a lot of love in those concerts, a lot of
affection. But it's like those guys are getting on my case! So I have to rise to the
occasion and they both feel the same way." De Lucía surveyed the audience
reaction in his home country: "In Andalucia, when I play, the audience at some
times will say 'Ole!' all at once. If they don't say 'Ole', it means that you have
played like shit!" He also pledged allegiance to his original musical inspiration:

> I play guitar not for me, but for flamenco. I don't want to be a star, or a rich man.
> I am working for my village, for my country, for my music, for the tradition of the

art form, and I want to make the music better, always better. These two (John and Di Meola) are helping me do that.[7]

John discussed his priorities onstage: "The three of us play for each other. The audience is important, but secondary. Most important to me is that I want to give something to these two men. The last thing I want is for them to get bored."[8] Writer Bill Milkowski witnessed their New York City performance on April 11, 1981:

> Paco was the portrait of studied concentration and pristine perfection: stiff backed and stern faced, with a distinguished air about him that some might misread as haughtiness. He's proud and majestic, like a regal Arabian steed prancing with grace and elegance, yet able to reveal great power. Di Meola, however, seemed merely stiff. His movements and attacks on his instrument were executed with machine-like precision and carried a hint of calculation. Like a well-trained race horse that flies to the finish line with blinders on. Di Meola seems too focused on the final effect to fully enjoy the "run" itself. Then there is McLaughlin, hunched over and boppin' in his chair, mugging and grimacing more like Stan Laurel than B.B. King, playing blues-inspired licks. He was loose limbed and fancy free, riding with his music and moving with its spontaneous flow. He's the wild and mischievous mustang, bursting with joy, romping about with no apparent plan or destination, and having a wonderful time along the way.[9]

All seemed well for the first few tours, but, according to John, Di Meola was the reason the trio split up: "For some reason, Al, at the end of the American tour, said 'Unless I get more money, I'm not going to come to Australia.' We had a world tour to finish. He had been quite annoying for a while so Paco and I said we'll just get another guitar player! So we got Steve Morse and then Al came back in saying 'I didn't mean it' and we went off as a quartet! Which was a little crazy!"[10]

But *Friday Night In San Francisco* was an unexpected smash, making #6 on the *Billboard* Jazz chart, #97 Pop, and allegedly selling around two million copies worldwide. It probably would have sold a lot more had it not become an album that everyone seemed to tape for their friends (as, apparently, was Jaco's classic 1976 self-titled debut album. He later said: "Everybody's making cassette copies of it, y'know? Everybody tells me, 'Hey man, I've got a tape of your album', which is sort of a drag—because it's illegal to do that, to begin with—and because I receive absolutely no money from people doing that. Maxell makes all the bread."[11]

John was still stunned by *Friday Night In San Francisco*'s success in 2022: "Nobody, nobody expected that album to take off as it did. It hit a nerve of some kind with the public. I think it was the joy and the love. It was the human side, the exuberance. It was three guys going bonkers!"[12] But he also revealed that he practically had to beg Columbia to record a night from the world tour: "I'd talked to CBS early on. I said, 'This trio is going to be big,' because I'd seen how the audiences reacted. And they said, 'Are you out of your mind? We want to hear electric guitar. We want to hear strong jazz-rock music.' But the sales for *Friday Night In San Francisco* were unthinkable."[13]

There was certainly something in the air on that night of December 5, 1980, at the Warfield Theatre. It was the penultimate night of a world tour during which the trio had played almost every night for two months. The presence of Di Meola and De Lucía brought out a large, very vocal Hispanic and European-flavored crowd to the venue, and sometimes it's quite miraculous to hear such a fevered reaction to wholly acoustic, all instrumental music. However, to some extent, the success of *Friday Night In San Francisco* seems hard to fathom at the time of writing, despite the giant reputation each player had garnered by 1980. John's entry into the arena for Chick Corea's "Short Tales of the Black Forest"—covered by Di Meola on his debut *Land Of The Midnight Sun* album of 1976—heralds some outrageous showboating by all three. Henry Mancini's "The Pink Panther Theme" segues into a blues boogie with John's "ringing bell" motif later used in "Little Miss Valley." John also quotes from Johann Strauss II's "The Blue Danube Waltz." Though the piece is ultimately rather rambling and dull, the trio were definitely reading the room—the audience wanted to party.

The inclusion of Egberto Gismonti's "Frevo Rasgado" was John's idea: "I like the piece very much and it's difficult. It has Spanish and Portuguese over-tones, and so it's nice for Paco, because he's at home. If he can find himself at home, he can do more or less anything."[14] John later reported that his terrific pass on the track was also directly influenced by the Spanish master: "My solo was just inspired. Paco saw me go and gave me exactly what was necessary to get higher."[15]

Di Meola's "Fantasia Suite"—originally appearing on his 1978 album, *Casino*—features some remarkable triplets from all three players, and a few fluffs, too, though de Lucía is clearly the crowd favorite. The final track, a studio version of John's "Guardian Angel" (now singular, not plural as it was on *Electric Dreams*), seems an incongruous, slightly freeze-dried addition, lacking the charm and kaleidoscopic mix of the original version, despite its new flamenco-style B section.

So, even if it's not a particularly enjoyable listen these days, *Friday Night In San Francisco* remains an extremely important album in John's career, and it's both gratifying and significant that it found such a large audience.

## BELO HORIZONTE (1981)

John McLaughlin: Acoustic and electric guitars
Francois Jeanneau: Soprano and tenor saxes
Augustin Dumay: Violin
Katia Labeque: Steinway piano, synthesizers
Francois Couturier: Fender Rhodes, synthesizers
Jean Paul Celea: Acoustic bass
Tommy Campbell: Drums
Jean Pierre Drouet: Percussion
Steve Sheman: Percussion
Paco De Lucía: Acoustic guitar
Recorded June/July 1981 at Ramses Studio, Paris, France
Produced by John McLaughlin
Released in fall 1981

In early 1981, Miles was making tentative steps toward his comeback, rehearsing and recording new material with his young nephew Vincent Wilburn Jr.'s Chicago musician friends—a process that would end with the release of *The Man With The Horn* for CBS. Meanwhile, The Young Lions—a collection of young American jazz traditionalists spearheaded by trumpeter Wynton Marsalis—were just warming up. Meanwhile British jazz was in a terrible state, desperately looking to Europe, just as it had ten years before. John's old London collaborator Alan Skidmore reported to Ian Carr in 1981: "There's no scene for me in England as a professional jazz musician. Now I just work in Europe."[16] John had once again escaped all this, enjoying his new life in Paris, cutting quite a dash with flowing locks, designer clothes, and a new partner, the gifted young pianist Katia Labèque.

During the spring of 1981, John toured France in an acoustic duo with Christian Escoudé and also wrote several new compositions showcasing a cosmopolitan, sunny sound, as influenced by Debussy and Brazilian music as they were by jazz. This new material would not be released on Columbia Records, though, who reportedly wanted him to return to "rock." John had tired of the label's lack of interest in acoustic music. "I have to leave Columbia. They have to pay me for leaving. Because they think that only electric music is worth marketing. Which I think is disgraceful to the American people. And it's patronizing." John had initially pitched them a return to the all-acoustic flavours of *My Goal's Beyond*, hoping to feature Steve Gadd or Jack DeJohnette on drums and possibly John Surman and Dave Holland, too. But Columbia's rejection of the concept caused the final schism with the label, as he remembered in July 1981:

> More than a year ago, I called CBS. I said, 'I am going into the studio. I am going to make an acoustic album. I will do it in Paris. Be prepared to accept studio bills.' And they then turned around and said, 'No, we are not going to pay for an acoustic album.' So I said, 'Okay, then, it's a breach of contract, an intolerable situation for me.' It took until last December to resolve the situation. Now, happily, I'm out.[17]

John fled to WEA—Warner Elektra Asylum—who promised artistic freedom and contractually weren't able to tell him whether he had to play an electric or acoustic guitar on his albums. Rather than pursue the "all-star" route, instead he formed a new band, The Translators, which would—as usual—be built around the drummer: in this case, a nephew of jazz organ genius Jimmy Smith named Tommy Campbell. He was yet another Berklee alumnus who had turned heads as a nineteen-year-old playing with Tiger's Baku, a fusion band led by trumpeter Toru "Tiger" Okoshi and featuring future Bill Frisell Band bassist Kermit Driscoll. They were locally famous for their Monday-night residencies at Pooh's Pub in Boston, a venue that also frequently showcased fellow Berklee alumni guitarist Kevin Eubanks, saxophonist Branford Marsalis, and drummer Marvin "Smitty" Smith. Purveyor of a florid, cymbal-heavy style (despite said cymbals being set up even higher than Alphonse Mouzon's) but with some bottom-end when needed—almost a mixture of Jon Christensen and Billy Cobham—Campbell had moved on from Berklee to land a prestige gig with Dizzy Gillespie. John liked what he heard, invited Campbell to Paris, and even rented an apartment for him while he played a residency in the city with Gillespie. They would rehearse during the day and then Campbell would perform with Dizzy in the evening. (Campbell also reports Gillespie had an endorsement deal with Zildjian cymbals and would insist on the drummer using his collection—Campbell also used Gillespie's cymbals on *Belo Horizonte*). And those cymbals were much in evidence on the album—this was the "lightest" drumming on a John record since *My Goal's Beyond*.

The Translators were fleshed out by John's new paramour, Katia, born March 11, 1950, in Bayonne, France, a classically-trained pianist (and recent synthesizer convert), who, by 1981, had already played in numerous concert halls alongside her sister Marielle, also a pianist. Their duet album *Rhapsody In Blue* had sold very well the previous year.

Then John recruited three mainstays of the French modern jazz scene: saxophonist Francois Jeanneau, born in Paris on June 15, 1935, acoustic bassist Jean-Paul Celea, and Fender Rhodes/synth player Francois Couturier. They produced a very different concept and color palette than had ever been present on a John recording—the contrast with the last "electric" band featuring Goldberg, Bruce, and Cobham could hardly be starker. *Belo Horizonte*—named for the city in southeast Brazil—foregrounded a gentler, more pastoral and lyrical sound, far less "American," less aggressive, and less in hoc to blues and jazz. However, the album had a rushed, unfinished quality, some pieces fading before their time, others featuring brief solos and less-than-memorable themes.

The opening title track set out the new band's stall—showcasing a ridiculously fast tempo and Latin feel from Campbell, then a fast post-bop section with assorted percussion instruments very high in the mix. "La Baleine"—French for "the whale"—had a bossa-nova feel, possibly influenced by Antonio Carlos Jobim's "Agua De Beber," and it was later played in duet with Chick Corea at the Montreux Jazz Festival. The tune struggles to find a clear through-line, and the synths are awkwardly superimposed. "Very Early" was John's brief take on the Bill Evans standard. (The pianist had died on September 15, 1980.) John overdubbed himself and gained a co-composer credit by virtue of a new coda. "One Melody" kicked off by referencing "In A Silent Way" and turned essentially into a one-chord jam with some flowing drums from Campbell. At 3:24, we hear some of the stacked triads later used for John's *Mediterranean Concerto*.

But it all feels a little like the prelude to *Belo Horizonte*'s one masterpiece: "Stardust On Your Sleeve." The title came from John's belief that human beings are celestial creatures, constantly in motion: "We are all flying through the cosmos. But we are not really aware of it."[18] This majestic, romantic track was adapted and expanded from *Fuse One*'s "Friendship," and it features a superb soprano sax solo from Jeanneau, every phrase memorable, a mini masterpiece of compositional structure. Elsewhere, "Waltz For Katia" benefits from the contribution of very Grappelli-like guest violinist Augustin Dumay, and the melody may refer to Gato Barbieri's "Last Tango In Paris Suite," particularly its series of modulating three-note phrases starting at 0:52. But it's essentially a vehicle for Labeque's "unjazzy" synth and piano, full of "out" notes but played with dazzling brio. At 2:25, the piece goes into 4/4 swing, Campbell's snare prelude suggesting this was pre-rehearsed, not a spontaneous moment.

The underwhelming "Zamfir," named for the Romanian pan flute player of the same name, begins with a nod to "Electric Dreams, Electric Sighs," Celea soloing over beatific, rubato Rhodes/guitar chords. The album closes with the strangely unmemorable "Manitas d'Oro," translating as "hands of gold" in Spanish, dedicated to special guest Paco De Lucía.

But *Belo Horizonte*—recorded the same month that Miles issued his studio comeback, *The Man With The Horn*—represents the beginning of one of the least-appreciated, least-documented periods of John's career. This writer— already a huge fan and owner of many John albums—was totally ignorant of the record until randomly coming across it in a secondhand London bargain bin circa 1990. This might have been done to various technical issues: there were distribution problems upon its fall 1981 release. It was also hampered by less-than-pristine production values, not helped by a rather puny vinyl pressing. And it's arguable whether WEA helped sales by placing a sticker on the LP stating that John was playing "acoustic guitar in an electric band." Still, he looked a vision of health and vitality on the cover.

Soon after recording *Belo Horizonte*, John dueted with Chick Corea at the Montreux Jazz Festival in Switzerland on July 15, 1981, a superb performance available to watch on YouTube.

## MUSIC SPOKEN HERE (1982)

John McLaughlin: Acoustic and electric guitars
Katia Labeque: Acoustic piano and synthesizer
Francois Couturier: Acoustic and electric pianos, synthesizer
Jean-Paul Celea: Acoustic bass
Tommy Campbell: Drums
Recorded June and July 1982 at Ramses Studio, Paris, France
Produced by John McLaughlin
Released in fall 1982

The spring of 1982 found John living a happy and settled life with Katia in Paris, thrilled to be in the city of his childhood dreams:

> I've always loved France since the first time I came here. I love the food. I love the language, the culture, the architecture. So I feel happy to be here. To be here gives me the possibility to participate more than I can do in New York because the media in America, in relation to music, is much more precisely defined than

here. In Europe, it's much more possible for me to appear on television—simply because I don't play a very popular kind of music. Here there's less emphasis on what is sellable.[19]

John was also drawn to Paris due to its much greater emphasis on the arts and culture than in Britain or America, an environment where one could actually see jazz on primetime television; during this period, he performed duets with Brazilian superstar Gilberto Gil and Stéphane Grappelli, and in a guitar quartet with Larry Coryell, Philip Catherine, and Christian Escoudé, all of which are available to watch on YouTube.

For his next recording project, John stuck with the core quartet from The Translators: Labeque, Couturier, Celea, and Campbell. But he had never re-peated himself over a two-album cycle, no matter how settled the personnel, and this era was no exception. The year 1982's *Music Spoken Here*—though generally ignored on its original release—has a very different mood to the previ-ous *Belo Horizonte* (and hangs together much more successfully), in some ways looking forward to his mid-1980s sound, with more power coming from the rhythm section and an increasingly experimental approach to production and mixing. Still, John was keen to avoid the "fusion" tag, in the sense that most people would understand the word: "I think a lot of fusion music is not true fusion. The fusion has to happen inside you. . . . You can't say: Let's put it with a disco beat. Or let's do it with a rock beat. It won't have any weight. I want something to really grab my insides."[20]

John was true to his word—no notes were wasted on *Music Spoken Here*, and composition was much more important than instrumental virtuosity, despite moments of individual brilliance. It was also notable for featuring John's return to the electric guitar, albeit in a far subtler form than during his 1970s pomp. Labeque stunned with some extraordinary, drastically improved synth solos, always original but certainly not "jazz." The whole album was wildly eclectic—never a reassuring aspect for critics, but always John's *raison d'etre*.

"Blues for L.W." emerged as *Music Spoken Here*'s centerpiece and enduring classic. It was named for Lech Welesa, the Polish union leader who led a revolt against the Communist party in 1981 and was imprisoned for his troubles. Three ominous bells introduce this quintessential John blues, frequently played in various forms throughout the years. At 0:58, there's a quote from "Blues For Pablo" from Gil Evans/Miles Davis's *Miles Ahead*. The descending chords at 1:18 are borrowed from "New York On My Mind" and "The Unknown Dissident," and John plays a remarkable, uncharacteristic run at 2:06. Labeque then performs her best synth solo with John, truly conjuring the sound of surprise, an outrageous piece of musicianship helped by the exciting "big band" arrangements underneath. Couturier's acoustic piano solo, beginning at 4:14, sounds uncannily like the playing of Zawinul, helped by the liberal deployment of echo.

"Honky-Tonk Haven," co-written with Shankar, is an electric rehash of Shakti's "Get Down And Sruti," an enjoyably outre slice of modal, avant-jazz/funk. Campbell lays down a slamming proto go-go beat, later sampled by The Real Roxanne for their hit single "Bang Zoom (Baby Let's Go-Go)" in 1986 and by Janet Jackson for "If" in 1993. Celea's acoustic bass makes for a lovely counterpoint to the weirdness. The track ends with what sounds like Synclavier-generated sirens—a warning to the jazz police, indeed.

"David" is John's heartfelt, complex tribute to the elder brother who gave him his first acoustic guitar at eleven years old. John's enigmatic introduction is accompanied by lush chords from Couturier's Prophet-5 synth. At 2:17, there's a familiar descending chord pattern, reminiscent of similar sections from "New York On My Mind," "The Unknown Dissident," and "Blues For L.W." Celea chips in with a fine, expressive bass solo, somewhat in the Eddie Gomez mode. Many elements of this excellent composition were later recycled for the second movement of John's *Meditteranean Concerto*.

"Brise De Coeur"—roughly translated as "heartbreaker"—is one of John's most romantic compositions, with a possible influence from the work of Pat Metheny and Lyle Mays, particularly their 1981 album, *As Falls Wichita, So Falls Wichita Falls*. The track is also shrouded in a distinctly ECM-like reverb, and Labeque stuns with some breathtakingly clean piano runs on a beautifully recorded Steinway. The cover of Gismonti's "Loro" is taken at a ferocious clip, Campbell finding an ingenious samba groove featuring a particularly fleet-of-foot hi-hat part. John later performed the tune with its composer in Rio de Janeiro in 1994.

Then there are the album's tone poems: "The Translators" again brings to mind Gil Evans's soundworld with its lush chords and syncopated basslines (and John's return to the electric guitar), superimposed over a drum machine groove and Campbell's bombastic fills. "Negative Ions" is reminiscent of Allan Holdsworth's work, via John Coltrane—a meandering, through-composed voyage through various modes and chords, with searching solos superimposed over the top.

*Music Spoken Here*'s bizarre album cover showed a shirtless John apparently attempting to "put a square peg in a round hole," as the saying goes—perhaps an ironic statement on the supposed folly of trying to "fit" so many genres together, or maybe his comment on the idiocy of putting music into strict delineations/genres (on the back cover, he's pictured trying to measure the length of a piece of string . . .). The title seems to say: "There are no boundaries here—it's all just music." This was relevant as jazz took another turn toward conservatism in 1982, typified by The Young Lions' debut album for Elektra/Musician, recorded live at New York City's Carnegie Hall on June 20, 1982, and—ironically—produced and devised by Mike Gibbs, orchestrator of *Apocalypse.*

Such traditionalism held no appeal for John. And despite the lack of blazing electric guitar, John's more aggressive new music wasn't a million miles away from Miles's sound during the summer of 1982 (Stump claims that "Nem Um Talvez"—the Hermeto Pascoal composition recorded by Miles for his 1971 album *Live-Evil*—was laid down during the *Music Spoken Here* sessions but left off the album at the eleventh hour) with its nods to Flamenco, blues and swing. Miles was touring with guitarist Mike Stern to less-than-ecstatic critical notices (documented on the live album *We Want Miles,* issued in May 1982), but John was generally supportive of the new direction and the playing of Strat-adorned, jeans-wearing, long-haired Stern: "I like Miles' new guitar player. I like what he's doing. It reminds me a little of the *Jack Johnson* era. It's not, I guess, a new conception, a new way, but I enjoy the guitar player."[21]

The record business, meanwhile, was in its latest slump, now attacked by the twin threats of video games and rerecordable cassettes, emphasized by the "Home Taping Is Killing Music" sticker that appeared on many LPs of the era. Columbia Records—still Miles's home—let three hundred employees go and closed nine regional sales offices around the United States in August 1982.

But the live arena was John's chief focus, and The Translators set off on tour throughout the spring and summer of 1982, kicking off in Detroit on April 14, then moving to Europe, including a prestige, televised gig at the Antibes Jazz Festival on July 21. John gave an insight into the music he was listening to on his travels: Coltrane, Miles, gypsy music, Indian music, Chopin, and Schumann. This was a strikingly different band setup for John—he sat at the front of the stage with a very close-mic'd nylon-stringed acoustic guitar (necessitating some very hard picking to be heard above the electric elements in the band), Labeque facing him alongside and Campbell usually set up side-on to the crowd. But the tour was fraught with sound problems, hastening the band's dissolution. It's also fair to say that some of the synthesizer sounds being utilized in the band were not particularly subtle—apparently "factory presets"—and compared to Zawinul or Hancock, fairly primitive. Nor did they gel too well with the acoustic elements of the band—predictably, the best moments were when the Fender Rhodes provided a foundation. Also, it has to be said that the material on the two albums was very hit-and-miss—apart from "Stardust On Your Sleeve," "David," "Blues For L.W.," and arguably "Aspan" and "Brise De Coeur," the era didn't provide many classic John compositions.

But despite the fairly muted response to *Belo Horizonte* and *Music Spoken Here* (neither, at the time of writing, have seen the light of day on streaming platforms), the early 1980s had been a rewarding era for John, and he found a lot to admire about his short-lived Translators band. After *Music Spoken Here* slipped out without much fanfare in the fall of 1982, the French contingent of the band returned to their jazz (or, in Labeque's case, classical) day jobs, while Campbell moved on to being much in demand, quickly picking up work with Sonny Rollins, Kevin Eubanks (a big Mahavishnu Orchestra fan), and Manhattan Transfer.

Meanwhile, Elektra/Musician—Bruce Lundvall's new Warners-bankrolled jazz label—rereleased John's 1971 album, *My Goal's Beyond*, in the fall of 1982 with a striking new cover, a black-and-white shot of John in intense, "thinking man" pose. It made a brief appearance on the *Billboard* Jazz charts at #34. The nostalgia business was always in fashion, and John would shortly be presenting his own version of it.

## *PASSION, GRACE & FIRE* (1983)

John McLaughlin: Yamaha classical Flamenco-type (gut-strung) guitar
Al Di Meola: Ovation 6-string steel-string acoustic guitar
Paco De Lucía: Spanish gut-strung Flamenco guitar
Recorded at Marcus Studios, London; Eras Studios, New York City; and
    Wizard Recording Studio, Briarcliff Manor, September–December 1982
Produced by John McLaughlin, Al Di Meola, and Paco De Lucía

On August 14, 1982, John performed a solo acoustic guitar concert at the University of British Columbia in Vancouver, Canada, on a bill opposite Katia and Marielle Labèque. Returning to Paris in September, he produced *Gladrags* for the piano-playing sisters, released on Warners in 1983, an album mainly consisting of classic Scott Joplin compositions. This was immediately followed by a reformation of the guitar trio alongside Di Meola and de Lucía. They had a stockpile of material to record and a world tour booked between April and October 1983.

Sessions for *Passion Grace & Fire* began in September 1982 at Marcus in Fulham, West London, hitherto best-known as the studio of choice for British pop acts like Thomas Dolby, Gary Numan, Imagination, and Level 42.

Expectations were very high after the success of *Friday Night In San Francisco*, and the album certainly doesn't disappoint, even if sales figures fell short. One might imagine the relative sterility of a studio might blunt the trio's creative and virtuosic impulses, but quite the opposite occurs: three beautifully recorded guitars (courtesy of Femi Jiya, later in the 1980s to become Prince's engineer of choice), a sympathetic mix with clever stereo separation, and minimal but telling digital reverb bring out the best in all three players, and, frankly, removes all the unnecessary showboating of *Friday Night*. The album is also made for CD, sounding excellent in the current Philips version. (A curious anomale, though, for those brave enough to try to play along, is that some of the album seems to have been sped up at the mixing stage by almost a semi-tone, possibly to equalize out a little of that excessive low-end that concerned Di Meola.)

"Aspan," previously recorded on *Music Spoken Here*, is rearranged mostly as a fast waltz with a "straight" feel, adding some syncopated flamenco sections in 4/4. On Di Meola's gorgeous "Orient Blue Suite," John tunes down his low E string to an A, repeating the trick from "My Foolish Heart," and the piece showcases phenomenal solos by all players, including a strikingly "out" lick by De Lucía at 5:44. The pair of de Lucía compositions—"Chiquito" and "Sichia"—hang together beautifully; the former is dedicated to Chick Corea, while the latter is a fast samba built around a catchy vamp with some ridiculously fluid triplets from John. "David" is another adaptation from *Music Spoken Here*, a terrific band performance with nevertheless a big and uncharacteristic fluff from De Lucía at 5:30. Di Meola's winning title track closes the album with a fond homage to Stevie Wonder's "Masterblaster (Jammin')."

Despite its artistic success, *Passion, Grace & Fire* is yet to be considered one of the strongest acoustic albums of John's career—it's another early 1980s project ripe for reappraisal. The trio set out on tour again in early 1983, supported by Steve Morse on solo acoustic guitar. John traveled with De Lucía alone for the final Australasian leg.

## MAHAVISHNU (1984)

John McLaughlin: Synclavier II digital guitar, Les Paul special
Bill Evans: Soprano and tenor saxes, flute
Mitchel Forman: Fender Rhodes, Yamaha DX-7 "Blow torch," acoustic piano
Jonas Hellborg: Fretless bass guitar, fretted bass guitar
Billy Cobham: Drums, percussion

Danny Gottlieb: Percussion
Katia Labeque: Synclavier II, Yamaha DX-7, piano
Hariprasad Chaurasia: Indian flute
Zakir Hussain: Tablas
Recorded April and May 1984, Ramses Studio, Paris, France
Produced by John McLaughlin
Released in the fall of 1984

Right up to the time of this writing, John claims the title of his 1984 studio album and subsequent reignition of The Mahavishnu Orchestra moniker was not his idea but prompted by an unnamed tour manager: "I wanted to make him happy so I used the name. I didn't feel I was betraying anything."[22] Despite John's insouciance, this must have delighted WEA after a few years of so-so record sales.

John once again attempted to get all four members of the original Mahavishnu Orchestra onboard, but he was once again snubbed. However, one original member who heeded John's call was Billy Cobham. He had relocated to Switzerland in 1980 at the end of his solo contract with Columbia Records (1977–1979), formed a new band featuring guitarist Mike Stern, played several prestige gigs in Europe with Herbie Hancock and Ron Carter, in duet/big-band configurations with Louie Bellson, and also recorded two solo albums (*Observations & Reflections* and *Smokin'*) for Elektra/Musician.

After getting the invitation from John, Cobham probably had good reason to believe he was in with the new Mahavishnu for the long haul. He told *Down Beat* in April 1984 what he was expecting from the forthcoming album and subsequent world tour:

> As much as I know is that the material . . . will be, I suspect, a lot of stuff that we'll put together as a group as opposed to the old Orchestra concept, where 98 percent of all the material was John's. I think there will be more input this time, so it'll be interesting to see what comes out of it. John talked about the idea of hopefully working with a singer . . . maybe somebody like Bobby McFerrin. But we'll see. I know that the bass player is real good—Jonas Hellborg from Stockholm. He's a very eager young fellow, and he's got a lot to say. He made a couple of albums in Europe where it's only him on the records, and you wouldn't believe it's only him—that four strings would do all that. It's like he's the next Jaco. In fact, it's a step beyond, a little bit more complicated than Jaco. It's exciting to see him play.[23]

In the same interview, Cobham also reported that Katia was expected to appear on keyboards for both the album and tour (only the former occurred), and that he hoped to play some keyboards on tour, too (which didn't happen, for reasons soon to be divulged). He also confirmed that John had attempted to involve Hammer, Laird, and Goodman again, too, and let slip that he was listening to Kajagoogoo and Van Halen for inspiration.

Once John knew that only Cobham would return from the original Mahavishnu Orchestra, he looked for new recruits. First on his wish list was bassist Jonas Hellborg. He was born in Gothenburg, Sweden, in 1958. A Monkees, Beatles, Hendrix, and Cream fan at eight years old, he "wanted to be a pop star."[24] At sixteen, he moved to Lund, got into heavy metal, and started playing in cover bands and doing studio sessions. He found that his neighbor was a major Albert Ayler fan and subsequently began to teach himself jazz harmony over the next few years, transcribing solos by McCoy Tyner, John Coltrane, and McLaughlin. He also started doing solo concerts: "Since I didn't have a piano or guitar playing with me, I was forced to learn all the chords on bass just to get by. I learned a lot of jazz standards that way."[25] This aspect of his playing would come in particularly handy when playing with John.

Hellborg's major debut on the scene was a solo bass gig at the 1981 Montreux Jazz Festival, supporting Steps, an all-star band featuring Michael Brecker on saxophone. Brecker was blown away by Hellborg's playing and urged him to move to New York, which he did, quickly picking up regular gigs at the Brecker brothers' Seventh Avenue South venue. After one such concert, Hellborg met a suitably impressed John and passed him his demo tape. He then moved back to Sweden, but almost two years later, he got a call from John, who invited him to join up with Cobham for a trio performance on French TV, playing "Blues For L.W." and "Are You The One? Are You The One?" (during which Hellborg broke a G string but somehow continued playing, to much amusement from John).

For the keyboard chair, John chose New York–based Mitchel Forman. Born January 24, 1956, he studied classical piano and then attended the Manhattan School Of Music (alongside fellow piano master Kenny Kirkland), studying jazz for three years, joining Gerry Mulligan's band straight from college, working extensively with Stan Getz, and also recording jingles with NYC studio players such as Steve Gadd, Don Grolnick, and Will Lee. Forman's solo performance at the 1980 Newport Jazz Festival caused a stir, and this led to two unaccompanied albums for Soul Note Records, *Childhood Dreams* and *Only A Memory*.

Once again, it was the rhythm section that John felt was so vital to glue his new project together, connected closely to his musical sensibilities and his emotions—not so much the top-line players, who were generally left to look after themselves. But this time around, he neglected to include a lead violinist for the first time ever in one of his working electric bands. Instead he turned to gifted young multi-reedist Bill Evans, who had accompanied Miles on the trumpeter's comeback trail since early 1981.

Born February 8, 1958, in Clarendon Hills, Illinois, Evans had grown up on the outskirts of Chicago and was somewhat of a piano prodigy, classically trained and playing recitals by the age of just six. He moved on to saxophone in his teens and relocated to New York in 1979 to study and join the jazz scene. A recommendation from fellow saxman Dave Liebman led him to Miles's door, and he became a trusted collaborator, confidante, and friend of the trumpeter. But by the summer of 1983, Evans's role in the Miles band was drastically diminished. Evans signed a solo record deal with Elektra/Musician—Bruce Lundvall's new label—and also received a call from John inviting him to join the revamped Mahavishnu Orchestra. (It's not known if John canvassed Miles's opinion before contacting Evans.) On October 31, 1983, Evans informed Miles that he would be leaving. (Ironically, his replacement was Bob Berg, an influence on Evans when he was growing up.) Evans's last gig with Miles before joining John was at the Radio City Music Hall on November 6. Miles, true to his word, didn't harbor any resentment to either Evans nor John, proving it by drawing the back cover illustrations for Evans's debut album, *Living In The Crest Of A Wave*, released in November 1983.

The sessions for *Mahavishnu* kicked off at Ramses—John's studio of choice for the third album running—in April 1984, but he wasn't making things easy for himself; he was playing a new axe, a Synclavier guitar made by New England Digital. It enabled John to create horn-like timbres and lent itself more to *legato* phrasing, closer to the great saxophone players he admired. John waxed lyrical about the guitar to writer Howard Mandel in his book *Future Jazz*: "For me, the Synclavier is a revolutionary instrument. It's infinite, as far as sounds are concerned. There are sounds I've created via computer that are very personal, that belong to me and have become my voice." John estimated he used thirty different timbres on the album—all well and good, but to the uninitiated ear, the guitar and synth tones might have been hard to distinguish. John complimented Forman's attention to detail on this topic: "The minute a synthesizer guitarist starts playing with a synthesizer keyboardist, you become aware. Mitch Forman has done so much work on his timbres that they're his and nobody else's, so there's actually quite a bit of contrast."[26] Still, this was a hard sell for those who had grown up on the original Mahavishnu Orchestra, longing to hear John tearing it up on a Les Paul or double-necked Rex Bogue. (*Jazz Times* lamented John's "horribly flaccid timbre of flute and other assorted woodwinds.")[27]

But it's important to put John's choice of guitar in context: this was an era when his near-contemporaries Al Di Meola, Pat Metheny, Jimmy Page, Vernon Reid, Andy Summers, Lee Ritenour, Allan Holdsworth, Bill Frisell, Robert Fripp, and Adrian Belew were also experimenting with guitar synthesis, looking for—and largely succeeding in—finding individual voices on their instruments. (John's "smooth" lead sounds were completely different than, say, Fripp and Metheny's relatively harsh timbres.) Elsewhere, sequencers and click tracks were extensively used for the first time in John's music, albeit generally more for "time-keeping" purposes rather than as genuine musical accompaniment.

Forman, however, prioritized a Fender Rhodes and acoustic piano over his Yamaha DX7 while Hellborg, Evans, and Cobham were similarly old-school: Hellborg played fretted and fretless basses; Evans soprano, tenor and Oriental wind instruments for color; while Cobham achieved a superb all-acoustic drum sound in the studio. John didn't scrimp on some raucous, red-blooded lead electric guitar at times either, blazing his Les Paul through a Scholz Rockman unit. He recruited noted Weather Report soundman Brian Risner to mix *Mahavishnu* alongside Ramses house engineer Jean-Louis Rizet. They did a sterling job—it's a sumptuous-sounding record without too many concessions to the 1980s clichés of big drums and scary synths.

Soon after recording *Mahavishnu*, John was back in the same studio producing the *Gershwin* album for the Labèque sisters in June 1984, the same month Miles's *Decoy* was released. *Mahavishnu* was then issued in the fall, a period when neo-conservatism in jazz was reaching a peak. Blue Note Records was about to be relaunched, and the Young Lions were at full strength. Wynton Marsalis would soon release *Hot House Flowers*, which—outside of the title track—featured compositions all dating from pre-1955. Meanwhile Marsalis's "feud" with Miles was being given a lot of media space. Needless to say, John had no truck with neo-conservatism in jazz, and his album seemed relentlessly futuristic in comparison (though some critics lazily claimed he was simply after Miles's mid-1980s electric sound), and he was adamant about featuring only original compositions.

*The Wire* in the UK gave *Mahavishnu* a glowing review: "Absolutely superb . . . Billy Cobham shows himself capable of a hitherto unimagined degree of sensitivity while Bill Evans' performances are a joy to perceive."[28] A world tour was then booked, scheduled to last for the rest of 1984. Once Cobham had been approached to record the album, he assumed he would do the tour, too. It wasn't to be. John replaced him with ex–Pat Metheny Group drummer Danny Gottlieb, a decision John has never fully explained, but one that drastically disturbed Cobham, as he explained in 1987:

The Hahavishnu became a real bad joke. I extended myself to a point with John McLaughlin and his ideas, and I chose to really push it. It became more an obsession for me, in a way, than for anybody else, and I ended up being the one hurt most. It cost me almost a year's setback in work. I had nothing; it was the closest I've ever come to being destitute, because I lost all of the work that I could've had that summer. About three weeks after the tour started I found out from a guy who works at Paiste cymbals that Danny Gottlieb was doing the job. And I said, "Well, it's the first I've ever heard of it." I was still getting ready to go. The last time I spoke to John McLaughlin, he was supposed to get back to me with information on how I was supposed to transport my equipment. And I never heard from him again. But I know one thing—I'll never play with John McLaughlin again.[29]

Thankfully this was not the case—they buried the hatchet eventually, but it took a long time. But it was a dream come true for Gottlieb, being a huge John (and Cobham) fan:

In 1971, I started at the University of Miami. I remember being told about an upcoming concert that would feature this unbelievable band, The Mahavishnu Orchestra. We all went and stood there with our mouths open for the entire set. Billy on drums—we had never heard ANYTHING like that! And it changed our lives. I became a lifelong fan of John's music and playing from that day forward— Shakti, everything. He was one of the gurus, along with Miles, Herbie, Chick, Jack DeJohnette, Keith Jarrett, Elvin, that we all followed and studied. I never thought that I would get to meet him, let alone play with him, in a million years.[30]

In early 1984, Gottlieb was on a mid-tour break while playing with singer/ songwriter Michael Franks alongside his colleagues from the band Elements (Bill Evans, Mark Egan, keyboardist Clifford Carter, guitarist Joe Caro, and percussionist Manolo Badrena) when he got wind of some interesting developments:

We all knew Bill would be leaving Michael and going to play with John's new Mahavishnu band, and we were all so thrilled for him. And being such a fan of Billy Cobham, I was hoping just to get to hear them, never dreaming I would ever be asked to play in the band! Bill called out of the blue and said, "You may be getting a call from John. Billy is not doing the tour and he may ask you." I was half asleep and really didn't believe it wouldn't happen but shortly after, John called and said, "Bill recommend you and we need someone to do the summer tour, and I would love to have you play!" I told John I would love to do it, but I just had to make sure Michael was covered.

Franks gave his blessing, and Gottlieb had to get over to Paris immediately for rehearsals: "I can't remember if I had to leave the next day, but it was very quickly. And when I asked about drums, he said: 'You can bring your own drums, and I know you like cymbals—bring a lot of cymbals!" Initially Gottlieb was given a lot of freedom in interpreting the new material: "I remember just playing the way I played. The songs were complicated, but nowhere near as crazy as the original Mahavishnu Orchestra, not too much odd-time playing. John didn't give me exact instructions, but just the way he played had so much power! I was just trying to keep up with him! I thought the band sounded great, and I was so proud to be in it."

And playing with Hellborg opened a lot of doors: "I loved playing with Jonas, and we really had a good time together from the start! He was wild—I had never heard anyone play like that. We really didn't have to talk about the rhythm section that much although I do remember talking about some of the busy songs—we discussed who would keep a groove and who would play more busily around the soloists."[31]

The reignited Mahavishnu Orchestra went out on tour throughout the summer and fall of 1984, starting on July 12 at the legendary Hammersmith Odeon in London. Gottlieb remembers the gig well: "I remember someone yelling: 'Where's Billy?' at the beginning of the concert!"[32] Major festival gigs followed at North Sea Jazz (July 14), Montreux (July 18), and Antibes (July 27). Gottlieb enjoyed these big events: "They were all so much fun and special. I am so glad a video from Montreux was finally released and is available, as there is so little documented from that band."[33]

John had a very different onstage persona in 1984 compared to the mostly seated acoustic performer of 1980–1983—he was now striking "rock star" poses at the front of the stage, apparently relishing his return to loud electric guitar and enjoying the more outgoing personalities of his bandmates, particularly Forman and Hellborg.

A US tour followed in the fall of 1984. By now, Hellborg was often living up to his "new Jaco" tag—a famous Beacon Theatre gig on October 13 saw the bassist quote from Hendrix's "Little Wing," twirl his bass around his head, and then throw it across the stage, earning a standing ovation. The tour ended in some style, but for one member of the revamped Mahavishnu Orchestra, it would be a rather tense period, as Gottlieb remembers:

I could tell John wasn't 100% happy. My memory is that we finished the tour in the Basque Coast of France and John was able to give us a full week's vacation just to relax, which we all did. But I was hearing rumors that John might want to get another drummer, and I was very uneasy about it. Finally he came to me and said, "I really enjoy your playing, but there were some things that are missing for me. I would like you to go home to New York, and in two weeks, I'd like you to come back to Monte Carlo, and I'd like to work with you, just the two of us, for two weeks before the next tour. I worked with Billy in the beginning, and I'd like to work with you. What I am after is more power and passion and I'd like to work with you on the basics of Indian rhythm. Also there is a great drummer in New York, Jamey Haddad, who studied Indian drumming, and he could really be helpful for you." I was ecstatic! I was going to stay in the band, and I would get to spend two weeks with John in Monte Carlo! It was amazing![34]

Gottlieb took a few informal lessons with Haddad in New York, then headed back to Monte Carlo for extensive rehearsals and training sessions with John:

John had two apartments. I stayed in one next to his. We got into a routine where we would go to the sea, swim, get coffee and croissants or a fresh baguette, and then work. We would ride to the rehearsal place and he would play Indian music in the car, explaining what the rhythms were. We played just drums and guitar, playing through the tunes. At night he showed me Indian rhythmic subdivisions and breakdowns, and he explained how I could integrate these rhythms into the songs of the band. He showed me, for example, that you could take a measure in 4/4 time, with sixteen 16th notes, and then divide those notes into any combination that would work, like 6-4-6 (which equals 16). He then showed me the basic Indian syllabus, which allowed me to orchestrate the 6-4-6 on the drums, ending in a resolution point on 1. He then showed me if I wanted a group of 15 notes (three fives, for example), I could leave the first 16th note silent, and then play three fives and it would equal 16 (1-5-5-5), I would then play this on the drums between phrases of the band songs, and we both laughed and had a great time with it. I was still able to keep the subtlety of the Metheny approach, but also add some extra power and rhythmic variety.[35]

Gottlieb also reports that John wished him to play with more of a groove feel, with less emphasis on cymbals, a marked contrast to how he was asked to play with Pat Metheny:

Mark Egan and I always talked about how I had approached the drums in the Metheny Group from the top down—with cymbals as the priority and the rest of the kit around it. (With John) there needed to be a priority of (playing) more from the bottom up—bass drum and snare. I practiced some of Gary Chester's exercises (later contained in his book *The New Breed*), and it really helped me develop a stronger groove feel. I also started incorporating more arm strokes that I was studying with Joe Morello, which allowed for louder playing.[36]

## Radio-Activity   6:52

Was John on the hunt for some radio airplay? It seems unlikely, but this is a generally successful introduction to his new soundworld. Triggered by Forman's sequencer—reminiscent of *Inner Worlds*' title track—this is essentially a one-chord modal blowout in the manner of "Honky Tonk Haven" and "One Melody." It could easily have gone much more "disco"—imagine Hellborg playing the bassline from Material's punk/funk classic "Bustin' Out"—but Cobham saves the day with an exciting performance. His stop/start fills are models of ingenuity, and he brilliantly displaces the beat at 1:40, aping his playing on "Opelousas Lady" from his 1978 solo album *Simplicity Of Expression—Depth Of Thought*. There's also a great moment at 4:48 when he echoes three Forman keyboard stabs. John digs in with a stunning solo, his guitar synth "screaming like Thomas Pynchon's missile arcing across the empty sky," according to Howard Mandel in his book *Future Jazz*, presumably a reference to Pynchon's novel *Gravity's Rainbow*.

## Nostalgia   5:56

This was the second notable track with the title "Nostalgia" released in 1984; British singer/songwriter David Sylvian had also recorded one in June featuring Kenny Wheeler—John's old London collaborator—on flugelhorn for the *Brilliant Trees* album. John's composition can't avoid comparisons with Miles's "In A Silent Way," though, courtesy of its scene-setting drone, key of E, and opening four-note melody. Forman's lilting Rhodes/piano vamp, first heard at 1:49, may reflect a Lyle Mays influence. A classic 1980s composition from John's pen, "Nostalgia" was often played live right into the 2000s. During the 1986 tour, he played the piece on steel-stringed acoustic guitar.

## Nightriders   3:47

John begins this slight but likeable track with a Wurlizer-style electric-piano patch on his Synclavier guitar. Cobham's intro fill seems designed to wrongfoot the listener, not helped by his hitting of the crash cymbal on the "four" of the bar. A "clap track" is heard throughout, suggesting the song was recorded to a click or percussion sequence. Evans overdubs himself to create a horn section and plays his first meaningful, gutsy solo of the album—but it's overshadowed by two of John's, the first on the Synclavier, the second on a hugely overdriven Les Paul, reminiscent of similar passes on *Visions Of The Emerald Beyond*. The track retains a bluesy mood courtesy of its recurring seven-note motif.

### East Side West Side    4:55

John describes the title as something that "can only be understood by people who live in Manhattan—there are two different cultures."[37] As such, the track becomes another ode to the Big Apple, a fast, bebop-tinged blowout in the spirit of Weather Report's "Fast City." John's miraculous solo is augmented by Cobham's uncanny high-speed grooving and oddly emphasized fills. Evans plays his best tenor solo of the album, with a lick at 2:52 very reminiscent of Michael Brecker. It's possible this tune is also John's tip of the hat to Miles's then-wife and native New Yorker, Cicely Tyson, whom many observers credit with saving the trumpeter's life in the early 1980s. *East Side West Side* was a CBS TV series that ran for one season in 1963, starring Tyson (reportedly the first time an African American had starred in a US TV drama) and George C. Scott. It was a gritty, but short-lived show that dealt with controversial subject matters.

### Clarendon Hills    (Bill Evans)    6:03

Side two of the original LP kicked off with an Evans composition named for his birthplace. But sadly it's a portentous, unattractive piece, with very obvious harmony and "whitebread" chords, not helped by Forman's blaring synth sound. It leans more to instrumental rock/pop than jazz. The head, played by Evans on soprano and John on synth guitar starting at 0:17, is guaranteed to raise the hackles. Cobham tries his best to inject some energy and plays brilliantly again, with some outrageous accompaniment. "Clarendon Hills" tries but fails to reach a Metheny-esque "Midwestern" lyricism—it probably should have been left off *Mahavishnu*.

### Jazz    1:43

There's a touch of John's "Miles Davis" and Gil Evans's voicings about this impressionistic, through-composed piece. And is that a quote, in the ascending bassline at 0:25, from Leonard Bernstein's "New York"? If so, we can read this as John's tribute to jazz of all shades and stripes, and the city that enabled it to truly come of age. The title seems to say: "It may not sound like 'jazz', but this is 'jazz' to me. Why not?" Cobham provides another superb commentary alongside a shaker and cowbell, and it's possible the melody is shared by Evans on soprano and John on Synclavier guitar.

### The Unbeliever   2:47

This short, effective tone poem is apparently heavily influenced by Hermeto Pascoal's composition "Nem Um Talvez," recorded by Miles on the *Live-Evil* album. Cobham's kit is treated with all sorts of gated reverbs, while the final, menacing chord and general unease throughout suggest that the protagonist of the title is in for a bumpy ride.

### Pacific Express   6:30

Over a synth/percussion sequence very much in the Joe Zawinul vein, the Japanese-accented voice says: "Too dark! Use flash!" recorded from a Minolta "Talker" camera (the photo is finally taken at the end of the track!). Hellborg plays his first solo on the album using his double-knecked Wal bass. *The Wire*'s Calvin Smith called it "the best Jaco Pastorius copy I've ever heard." Some tasty Fender Rhodes from Forman and excellent Evans, Cobham and John solos round off a superb composition and band performance. "Pacific Express" was covered by Miles during concerts in the summer of 1985. He filleted the piece in his trademark fashion, zooming in on just two key phrases from the head. When John played the tune live during 1986, it was often preceded by a section from "The Dance Of Maya," and sometimes also quoted "A Love Supreme." John reports that the tune and title "came basically from all the images I had from around-the-world trips."[38] The title might also refer to an airline that operated in the western United States from 1982 to early 1984.

### When Blue Turns Gold   3:19

John ends the album with a doorway into a new musical style. Zakir's tablas double Katia's piano while John's strummed steel-string acoustic is buried deep in the mix. John and Zakir add *konnakol* vocals and clapping at the fade. "When Blue Turns Gold" was performed live on French TV during the summer of 1984 with the same personnel, John digging out his scallop-necked acoustic and Marielle Labeque joining on tambura. The opening piano/tabla duet was performed exactly like the album version, suggesting it was originally scored by John and not improvised in the studio.

## *ADVENTURES IN RADIOLAND* (1986)

John McLaughlin: Gibson Les Paul special, Mike Pedulla Guitar (for controlling Synclavier Digital Guitar), acoustic guitar
Bill Evans: Saxophones, keyboards
Mitchel Forman: Keyboards
Jonas Hellborg: Wal Double Neck bass guitar
Danny Gottlieb: Premier Drums and Paiste Cymbals, Ludwig Drums, Simmons SDS7, Sycologic PSP Drum Interface
Max Costa: Computer programs and drum sequences
Recorded in January and February 1986, at Psycho Studios, Milan, Italy
Produced by John McLaughlin
Released January 1987

John received an invitation to appear on Miles's *You're Under Arrest* album during the first two weeks of 1985. He arrived at the Record Plant in New York City to record "Ms. Morrisine" (named for keyboard player Robert Irving III's then-wife), "Katia Prelude," and "Katia." The latter features some phenomenal playing by John, "one of his most thrilling solos on record," according to Tingen (*Miles Beyond*)—it's hard to disagree. The full twelve-minute studio take (now available to hear on Miles's *Bootleg Series Vol. 7*, released in 2022) was a blast, but Miles somehow edited it down to seven minutes: "When I went into the studio to edit it, everybody acted like somebody died. It was so good they wanted to leave everything on. Every time John starts some runs on guitar, I just took it out."[39] It is, indeed, a superb editing job from Miles—to the untrained ear, John's solo sounds like a complete performance.

*Aura* (recorded January 31 to February 4, 1985, at Easy Sound Studio, Copenhagen) was another very special Miles project to which John contributed hugely. Composed by Danish trumpeter and arranger Palle Mikkelborg, the album was one of the most critically lauded in the last decade of Miles's life. Miles reportedly directed John to "play downtown New York, you know what I mean?"[40] The directive worked: it's some of McLaughlin's most unhinged, exciting playing on record. On "Orange," he generates incredible rhythmic tension, and also catches the ear with the use of his low E, even though the vamp is in F. Miles then plays one of his greatest recorded solos. On the slow-burning

"Violet," John trades fours with Miles to winning effect. Tellingly, he was also tasked with playing Miles's ten-note "code" in the "Intro." Katia, who accompanied John to the Copenhagen sessions, later commented on the remarkable rapport between Miles and McLaughlin.

The revamped Mahavishnu Orchestra, now featuring Jim Beard on keyboards in place of Mitchel Forman and John exclusively playing a Les Paul, then played a short European tour in late February 1985. Meanwhile, Blue Note Records—now spearheaded by Bruce Lundvall, previously the head honcho of Elektra/Musician—celebrated its resurgence with an event at New York's Town Hall called *One Night With Blue Note*, featuring Tony Williams, Bobby Hutcherson, Freddie Hubbard, Grover Washington Jr., and Herbie Hancock, among many others.

Two months later, Hancock invited John to work on a feature film, and what a film—Bertrand Tavernier's *Round Midnight*, starring Dexter Gordon as Dale Turner, a role that earned the saxophonist a Best Actor Academy Award nomination. This was a labor of love for all involved, not least Hancock, who had been recruited to devise the score and take a major acting role in the film. In his liner notes for the soundtrack album, Tavernier remembered receiving a call from Hancock just before filming started, the pianist exclaiming: "I just finished reading the script and I cried. I felt so proud to be Black and a jazz musician." It was a feeling shared by many of the musicians involved with the project.

Many of John's scenes were shot between July 1 and 12, 1985, at Studio Éclair, just outside Paris in Epinay Sur Seine, in which the old Blue Note club—active between 1958 and 1968—had been reproduced by legendary Hollywood set designer Alexandre Trauner. This was the first fictional movie in history to use a completely live music score, recorded in real time. (Hancock marveled at the sound captured on the set: "If only every jazz club could have such good acoustics!")[41] However, John's brief piece of "acting" didn't impress everybody; Norwegian jazz writer Randi Hultin was a guest on the set, reporting of his performance: "I had just seen him (playing guitar) at the Kongsberg Festival in Norway and now he had a role in the film—but he was more proficient as a guitarist"[42] John, looking serious and dapper in black suit and tie, played alongside Gordon, drummer Billy Higgins, bassist Pierre Michelot, and Hancock on a memorable version of "Body And Soul," among other highlights. The whole project was a dream come true for the Englishman.

Immediately after *Round Midnight* wrapped, John hooked up with Hellborg to play a series of duets, including a date at London's Royal Festival Hall on July 19, 1985, supporting Lee Ritenour. The Mahavishnu Orchestra then toured the United States in August 1985. The following month, John spoke to *Guitar*

*Player* about the state of jazz, a fascinating interview that also gave hints as to the schizophrenic nature of his forthcoming album:

> There seems to be a kind of hiatus going on. Today, rock and jazz are rhythmically, harmonically, and experimentally inferior to what was happening even as far back as the '60s. But this kind of backlash against intellectuality of any kind is more of a sociological problem than it is a musical one. It's cyclical, and a more receptive mood will return. However, you can't deny that a lot of pop music—including the type of easy-listening funk by so-called jazz musicians—is terribly banal. It's superficial, and it is not even covertly commercial; it's unashamedly blatant. Jazz is vital, living music that should be about life. Don't misunderstand me, because at the same time I don't knock any kind of music. I like Billy Idol, you know what I mean?[43]

In his crosshairs might have been some of the "smooth jazz" albums being churned out by the likes of Freddie Hubbard, Stanley Turrentine, and Stanley Jordan on Blue Note Records (and Elektra/Musician . . . ). Meanwhile Jan Hammer's music for the *Miami Vice* television show became nothing less than a sensation. The soundtrack album went to number one on the pop charts, and Hammer won two Grammies (but no Emmy—*Murder, She Wrote* pipped *Miami Vice* for Outstanding Achievement in Music Composition for a Series, the winning composer John Addison also publicly criticizing Hammer's use of synthesizers).

But all wasn't lost for fans of old-school, quality jazz/rock in 1985—alongside the updated Mahavishnu Orchestra, bands such as Scott Henderson's Tribal Tech and The Chick Corea Elektric band were forming, while Steps Ahead and Weather Report were also releasing strong albums. Meanwhile ex-Police pop star Sting was incorporating elements of jazz into his music, employing noted jazz/rock players such as former Weather Report drummer Omar Hakim and ex-Miles bassist Darryl Jones for his debut solo album, *The Dream Of The Blue Turtles*, and subsequent world tour.

On November 19, 1985, a very merry John guested on *The Tonight Show Starring Johnny Carson* playing the Ray Noble jazz standard "Cherokee" with the house big-band at an extremely swift tempo—it was a reminder to American audiences just how astonishing McLaughlin's acoustic guitar work could be (and, conversely, a shameful reminder of how British television had ignored John's work throughout the 1980s). John joined Carson for a quick chat too (alongside a smiling Grace Jones), revealing he was due to be divorced from his third wife, Eve, the very next day and acknowledging that touring a lot "hasn't really helped the marriages too much . . ."

John then performed his *Mediterranean Concerto* (of which much more later) on November 27 and 29 at the Dorothy Chandler Pavilion in Los Angeles, and then it was back to Europe at the start of 1986 and a visit to the aptly named—considering the sheer outrageousness of the resulting music—Psycho Studios in Milan to record *Adventures In Radioland* (officially credited to "John McLaughlin & Mahavishnu"). Gottlieb remembered the happy atmosphere around the sessions (despite the whole band watching the tragic Space Shuttle *Challenger* explosion in his hotel room on January 28), and reports that John was utilizing the Charles Mingus method of teaching the band his new material:

> We were in Milan for a month. It was a fun, loose recording. I remember John would come in with a song fragment and play it for us. There was nothing written down. We would have to transcribe this hard piece of music and then figure it out. It took more time but we were also able to get inside the music as it developed. We pretty much had to just play everything over and over again until we memorized the material. I loved the music! And John was great, and fun! I remember taking the train every day to a workout facility and doing aerobics classes in Italian, which I totally did not understand. We had a great time during that month. And the food—unbelievable![44]

Gottlieb was also incorporating electric drums into his setup for the first time:

> Electronic drums were coming into fashion and they were fun to use. I remember John liking the sounds of the Simmons 7 (kit), and he asked me to get it. It was really expensive, like $4000. I also bought a Lexicon (unit), as it had a gated reverb sound that was popular from that famous Phil Collins "In The Air Tonight" fill. John liked the electronic drum sounds, and I did as well, because I could imitate Billy Cobham with easy rolls around the toms![45]

What emerged from Psycho Studios was one of the strangest and least-heralded albums in John's career, albeit one that arguably showed off his reformed Mahavishnu band (sans Cobham) to greater effect than the previous self-titled album. *Adventures In Radioland*'s watchword was variety—John absolutely refused to get bogged down with the latest Jazz Revival (despite his *Round Midnight* experience), ploughing on with his unique vision, which took in everything from funk, blues, Occidental music, Brazilian rhythms, Zawinul-inspired fusion, and, this time, an increasing reliance on technology, the Synclavier digital sampler and Gottlieb's Simmons drums particularly prevalent. In many ways, *Adventures In Radioland* was analogous to 1976's *Inner Worlds*, a mixture of intense band burnouts and briefer "experiments" mainly designed to push the sonic envelope.

The main problem is the lack of major John compositions: "Jozy," "Florianapolis," "Reincarnation," and "The Wall Will Fall" (all of which would make regular live appearances over the next five years or so) are obvious standouts, but two or three more of a similar quality could have pushed *Adventures In Radioland* into the category of a minor classic. The album might even be called—invoking David Bowie's first studio project of the 1990s—John's *Tin Machine II.* "The problem lies not with the playing but the writing, which is uniformly drab and unconvincingly macho," according to Cook and Morton in *The Penguin Guide To Jazz On CD.* But John was taking inspiration from mid-'80s pop production techniques and trying to find some material to match those parameters. The album features some terrific music—and some of John's finest electric guitar work—if one can somehow accommodate the huge drum sounds and curious lack of bass in the mix.

While recording at Psycho Studios, Gottlieb persuaded John and Mitchel Forman to guest on a few tracks for his debut album *Aquamarine,* released in 1987. John featured on an entirely improvised, acoustic piece ("Duet"), while Forman appeared on the more conventional "Being." Other guitarists on *Aquamarine* included John Abercrombie, Steve Khan, Jeff Mironov, and Joe Satriani.

John and the band set off on a US tour alongside Weather Update—Zawinul's post-Weather Report unit featuring Peter Erskine, Khan, and Victor Bailey—during the summer of 1986. Mitchel Forman had left to play with both John Scofield (appearing on the guitarist's classic album *Blue Matter*) and Wayne Shorter (John's old collaborator Stu Goldberg also joined Forman on Shorter's 1987 album, *Phantom Navigator*). Jim Beard came in on keyboards, and his compositions "The Wait," "Diana" (with a bass vamp borrowed from Herbie Hancock's "Hornets"), and "It's Up To You" were regularly played on tour. Evans's "Flight Of The Falcon," "Let The Juice Loose," and "Living In The Crest Of A Wave" were also often performed, the latter sometimes featuring elements of "Phenomenon: Compulsion" and "The Dance Of Maya."

The contrast between this tour and the previous two was marked—the band seemed to be enjoying themselves more, and there was more stage "presentation" and audience participation in the tradition of other mid-1980s fusion bands like Steps Ahead and Chick Corea's Elektric Band. John had also amended his guitar style for the 1986 concerts—he generally stuck to single lines or vamps on his Les Paul, leaving the comping to Beard. The net result was a drastically improved live unit that regularly upstaged Weather Update. Khan: "Just about everywhere we played, they kicked our asses six ways from Sunday, mostly because their presentation was in so much better shape than ours. We had no new music and unless everything went perfectly for us (which it never did), we would always be a mess."[46]

As the tour moved to Europe (now without Weather Update), the band played a prestigious British gig at London's Royal Festival Hall on June 24, 1986. John made a guest appearance with the Gil Evans Orchestra at the Ravenna Festival on July 2, then reconvened with the band for a show at the Antibes Jazz Festival, later broadcast on French television. Saxophonist David Sanborn guested in Milan, Italy, on July 20, and then Miles unexpectedly made an appearance in Copenhagen. According to John, he "sat at the side of the stage for the whole show. At the end . . . he came on stage and saluted the audience with us!" Then it was back to the States in the fall of 1986, again with Weather Update in tow. Bill Milkowski posted a rave review of their September 5 show at The Ritz in New York City: "Mahavishnu . . . is smokin' so hard now it's frightening. The core of Danny Gottlieb on drums, Bill Evans on saxes, and Jonas Hellborg on bass has been together long enough (nearly three years) to reach that level where they're playing instinctively, almost telepathically, just like the Mahavishnu Orchestra of old."[47]

Despite these kinds of positive notices and generally enthusiastic audiences, John clearly had an eye on the bottom line as the tour reached its conclusion. Gottlieb: "I do believe the tour was not a big money-earning venture. I remember hearing that it was a struggle to keep the band going financially, as it cost so much to be on the road."[48]

Another issue seems to have been that *Adventures In Radioland*'s release was delayed when Warners declined to take up the option for another album. Who knows what would have happened had it been issued during the summer of 1986 and become a decent seller. Instead, it crept out in early 1987, long after the band had gone their separate ways, and its release was hampered by faulty distribution and a lack of promotion. But the album did feature a strikingly effective cover design—inexplicably changed by Verve for the 1993 CD rerelease—though there was a confusing credit on the back sleeve of the original LP: "Acoustic Guitar by Abraham Wechter," listed among the musician credits, led some (including this writer) to wonder if Wechter had played acoustic guitar on the album. He was actually John's luthier of choice.

It's hard to disagree with Milkowski, though—despite the 1980s Mahavishnu's dependence on burgeoning technologies, the band had forged its own identity against all the odds while barely playing any of John's 1970s music (possibly why he decided to jettison Cobham after the recording of *Mahav-ishnu*). In the age of Prince, Van Halen, and Billy Idol, John wanted to crank it up and explore some of these modern production techniques, and a lot of it worked—he played some of his greatest-ever electric guitar solos in concert with this band, in particular at the televised North Sea Jazz and Antibes 1986 gigs. But Hellborg looked back at the group—and the whole "fusion" scene—with very mixed feelings in 1993, as he embarked on a solo career:

> Getting away from the fusion connection, the McLaughlin thing, has allowed me to grow. I escaped from that whole mentality of competitiveness in music. Playing with John I was automatically thrown into that, whether I wanted to or not. And because I had some technical ability, I was immediately faced with the 'obligation' to fulfill certain expectations of virtuoso playing. I got a lot of stuff from McLaughlin, and that was a great period of my life, a great experience. But that whole mentality kind of sidetracks you. All those guys, that whole generation of musicians—they missed the boat somehow. When I talk to John, he says all the right things—but when I listen to what he's doing, it's still all this really fast stuff. You can hardly hear what he's playing because he's playing too fast.[49]

Gottlieb felt differently, though, and learned not to look too far ahead during his time with John:

> Things ended very positively with John as far a musical and personal friendship goes. There was never a thought on my part as to how far it would go, or how many recordings, or really anything other than to follow John's lead and see how long he wanted to keep this particular band. And the reality was, just to even GET a chance to play with John was something I never thought would happen! It was a life-changing musical experience and I am forever grateful.[50]

### The Wait (Jim Beard) 5:35

To a generation—like this writer's—brought up on Phil Collins's "In The Air Tonight," Peter Gabriel's "Intruder," and David Bowie's "Let's Dance," this track was an exciting development in John's career. After all, it was an era (Billy Cobham's 1985 album *Warning!* came with a disclaimer printed on the back reading: "Severe damage could result to your sound system if played at extremely high levels"!) when studio technicians were trying to get as hot a signal as possible, looking for that ever-elusive Big Drum Sound. Gottlieb recalls giving the mastering engineer some real problems when utilizing electric drums on "The Wait": "I remember being proud of the fact that there was something like a 50-decibel difference from the beginning to when the drums entered, to shock the listener. I heard that the mastering engineer was not told about the upcoming louder part, and that it blew out the speakers!"[51] John outlines the melody with great elan before embarking on a memorable solo featuring some of the fastest picking in his entire career, taking on 1980s "shredders" such as Satriani, Steve Vai, and Steve Stevens, but using completely different intervals to all of them. One such miraculous run ends with John trying to hit a high C# and just bending it sharp. Evans's subsequent soprano solo is distinctly "white-bread" and somewhat shrill in comparison—at this point, though, John was a particularly hard act to follow.

### Just Ideas (Mitchel Forman)   2:00

A rather odd bit of sequencing places Forman's mercifully brief "Just Ideas" as the album's second track, its saccharine major chords completely incongruous after the onslaught of the previous tune. Originally featuring on the composer's 1982 album *Childhood Dreams*, here it is hampered by a rather undignified soprano sax/guitar-synth melody.

### Jozy   5:25

This is one of the most sheerly enjoyable recorded performances from the 1980s Mahavishnu Orchestra and a key John composition of the era, a tribute to Weather Report keyboardist/co-founder Josef Zawinul, and influenced by his tunes such as "Mr Gone," "Madagascar," and "Night Passage." The modal "one-chord" melody can be traced from Shakti's "Get Down And Sruti" via "Honky Tonk Haven," "One Melody," and "Radio-Activity." But there's a lot more drive and compositional elan here—"Jozy" is deceptively complex. John's solo sound seems to be based on an accordion patch, with a fair amount of digital delay added. Gottlieb marshals the band superbly, starting out with the legendary "Purdie Shuffle" and then easing eamlessly into double-time. It's not surprising that he is heard whooping for joy at the tune's denouement. Tribal Tech guitarist Scott Henderson waved lyrical about John and "Jozy" during a September 1990 Blindfold test for *Down Beat* magazine:

> I can't say enough about him; he's the greatest. The tune was great, obviously in-
> fluenced by Weather Report—particularly the tune "Madagascar." Great compo-
> sition. John McLaughlin is playing his ass off, as always. I think that's Bill Evans

playing sax, and Mitchel Forman. I like the way the tune built, really melodic and with great harmony. That's a 5-star tune, for sure. John McLaughlin was one of the first guys I was influenced by. *Birds Of Fire* is still one of my all-time favorite records. I look up to him because he's such an overall great musician, not just as a soloist but also as a composer and a legend.

When "Jozy" was played live during 1986, John and (sometimes) the band would don Ray-Bans. Was this a parody of "jazz"? Or a homage to Graham Bond and band, who would often wear shades during their performances in true Mod style (as in the cult film *Gonks Go Wild*)?

### Half Man—Half Cookie (Bill Evans)   2:56

If jazz purists weren't already running for cover, here was a clear invitation. Evans's composition is a pure studio confection, virtually impossible to play live (though the band did try). But John and Evans's unison heads are quite fun, and there's a witty big-band interlude featuring some robust tenor blowing from the composer. With its tight sixteenth notes and intricate arrangement, it sounded like Evans had spent some time listening to Scritti Politti's *Cupid & Psyche 85*. He pursued similar timbres on his second solo album, 1985's *The Alternative Man*.

### Florianapolis   (McLaughlin, Forman)   5:21

This resplendent tribute to the Brazilian city was possibly influenced by the music of Egberto Gismonti, particularly up-tempo tunes such as "Loro." The chord movement in the middle-eight sounds very similar to Pat Metheny's "James," but then again *that* tune's bridge also sounds a bit like "Electric Dreams, Electric Sights" . . . John plays one of his greatest-ever acoustic guitar solos here. The sampled "trombone" toward the end of the tune sounds like Forman rather than John—the keyboard player used a similar sound soloing on John Scofield's "Heaven Hill" recorded for the *Blue Matter* album six months later. "Florianapolis" became a favorite of John's over the next few years, in duet with de Lucía and also with the Trilok Gurtu trio of 1989/1990. It was also covered by The Labèque Sisters on their 1991 album, *Love Of Colours*.

## Gotta Dance    4:18

This is one of the oddest pieces in John's entire recorded repertoire, but it encapsulates the eclectic mood of *Adventures In Radioland* very well. The title comes from a 1952 Gene Kelly/Cyd Charisse movie, but John clearly uses it for humorous purposes. A beatific acoustic guitar/soprano sax melody, accompanied by softly undulating synths, is rudely interrupted by a swinging horn section, a deafening sequence of Gottlieb's gated acoustic/Simmons drums, and a slapped Hellborg bass solo that sounds uncannily like Level 42's Mark King. Then the serene acoustic guitar melody returns at the end, as if it had never been away.

## The Wall Will Fall    6:00

The title of this turbo-charged blues/bebop composition (only John could find the rhythmic connection between a slow 6/8 blues and super-fast bebop in 4/4) may refer to the Berlin Wall, which finally fell on November 6, 1989. Gottlieb's count-in ushers in a brief trading of fours between John and Evans, before a four-note head that derives from a live version of "Electric Dreams, Electric Sighs" played during the late 1979 tour with Jack Bruce and Billy Cobham. John shed some more light on the tune's structure to *Guitar Player* magazine in 1987:

> It starts on the blues but the center part belongs to the tradition of "The Dark Prince" or "Do You Hear The Voices You Left Behind" which are definitely Coltrane inspired, using Gmaj7, Bb13 to Emaj7, Gb13 to B, progressions of major thirds, which is all Coltrane. There's also a tonal modulation which is interesting to play, and it's very uptempo, so you really have to know the chords to find something, because you can run the changes, but to find something is very difficult. What I like to do is stack modes sometimes; you can just stack a minor third up on top of it. Sometimes I'll hear a tonal chord, say Cm7, and I'll play the notes Ab, B, C# against the C minor modal chord. You're really pushing the issue there.[52]

John achieves that "tonal modulation" brilliantly with a stirring solo, blasting through a very elaborate set of chord changes, and Evans digs in on tenor, too. Hellborg apparently detunes the low string on his five-string bass from a B down to an A—but playing along to this track reveals it was sped up a little during post-production. "The Wall Will Fall" was reformated very effectively for the 1994 organ trio with Dennis Chambers and Joey DeFrancesco, and also treated to an interesting all-acoustic cover version by The Groningen Guitar Duo on their album *The John McLaughlin Suites.*

### Reincarnation    2:57

John's fourth excellent composition on *Adventures In Radioland* benefits from Hellborg's sweet-toned bass melody—with a hint of "Nostalgia"—and also its beguiling harmonic architecture. It's hard to ascertain whether John plays on this—he possibly doubles Evans's soprano sax melody on guitar synth during the middle eight. John obviously had a soft spot for "Reincarnation," though, returning to it on *Que Alegria* six years later.

### Mitch Match (Forman)    3:54

A quirky Forman composition with a stop/start structure and strangely jolly major-key feel, "Mitch Match" was often played live during 1984, including on the *Live At Montreux* DVD. But it's not much of a composition and points to a dearth of quality material on *Adventures In Radioland.*

### 20th Century Ltd.    2:31

The title may refer to an express passenger train that ran through New York City between 1902 and 1967. John's steel-string acoustic makes its third and final appearance on the album, and he plays his familiar triplet chordal hammer-ons. Kolosky claims that the tune's melody, such that it is, is similar to "Arjen's Bag" and "You Know You Know." In any case, it's another interesting—if minor—ending to a McLaughlin album, suggesting he will be sticking to the acoustic guitar for the foreseeable future.

## *PACO & JOHN LIVE AT MONTREUX* (RECORDED 1987, RELEASED 2016)

John McLaughlin: Nylon-string acoustic guitar
Paco De Lucía: Nylon-string acoustic guitar
Recorded at the Montreux Casino, Montreux Jazz Festival, Switzerland, on
    July 15, 1987

In December 1986, John traveled to Oslo's Rainbow Studios to play on Zakir Hussain's *Making Music* for ECM Records in the illustrious company of Jan Garbarek on saxophones, the first time John had performed with the European jazz legend. John, playing steel-string acoustic guitar, enjoyed the music but was slightly peturbed by one of jazz's most singular impresarios: "Manfred Eicher was a bit, shall we say, overpowering to work with, but it was a wonderful project to be involved in."[53]

John cut a much more conservative figure during this period, having very much shed the "guitar hero" image that had prevailed toward the end of the 1986 tour. Seated, serious, and sober, he also reported that he was once again falling in love with the acoustic guitar, finding ever new ways to communicate on it. Meanwhile he had forged a duo with Hellborg, concocting a beguiling contrast of styles and sounds. They had first played live together in 1985 and continued to tour in early 1987 with a setlist that mixed covers (Pascoal's "Nem Um Talvez," Luiz Eça's "The Dolphin," Charles Mingus's "Goodbye Pork Pie Hat") and John originals ("Guardian Angel," "Zakir," "Follow Your Heart," "Electric Dreams," "Blues For L.W.," "Are You The One?" and "Pacific Express"). Themes—some from the original Mahavishnu Orchestra era—were mixed and matched, arrangements changed on the fly, and there was a joyous, flexible feeling to these concerts. They traveled to Japan in January, then toured in Europe, including notable gigs in Bourge, France (later shown on British TV as part of the excellent jazz series *Sounds Of Surprise*), and the Fairfield Halls in Croydon on March 6, 1987. Hellborg reminisced about this period:

> With just the two of us . . . of course, it was totally dominated by John's musical persona but we could go in lots of spaces within that, in terms of his history and also other things that he enjoyed playing. For example, we did a lot of Brazilian stuff, which I know John loves. And that has never really come out in a big way. We did a piece by Hermeto Pascoal and some other beautiful stuff, just beautiful melodies. And sometimes we would just play a beautiful song like that without soloing on it, which is a great idea.[54]

John then reunited with Paco de Lucía for a summer tour. The repertoire was a mixture of originals, standards, and familiar pieces by Chick Corea and Egberto Gismonti. They were joined by French wunderkind Biréli Lagrène—who had just released *Inferno*, his debut album for Blue Note Records—on June 17, 1987, in Freiburg, Germany, then dueted at London's Royal Festival Hall on June 26 and at the Montreux Jazz Festival on July 15. The latter concert was filmed for posterity, released on DVD and CD in 2016. It was an extremely "hot" concert recording, full of room ambience and presence, though slightly hampered by what sounded like a little chorusing added to John's guitar.

Two solo performances kick off the concert: John begins with "My Foolish Heart," complete with low E tuned down to an A, bookended by blues themes with elements of "One Melody." De Lucía then performs "El Panuelo," co-composed with his father, Antonio, a fast 6/8 with deliciously ambiguous chords and a florid middle section. John and de Lucía's duet begins with a furious take on Chick Corea's "Spain," and then John beautifully reharmonizes the *rubato* opening to De Lucía's "Chiquito"—the piece is a highlight of the album and concert.

A fiendishly fast "Florianapolis" is delightfully rearranged with John soloing over a major-flavored three-chord vamp, before de Lucía and John in turn solo over the entire song architecture. It's an absolute classic of John's 1980s output. "Frevo" is greeted like a hit single by the Montreux crowd—courtesy of its inclusion on *Friday Night In San Francisco*—and features some of John's fastest playing on record, while de Lucía seems slightly uncomfortable with the relatively simple melody of "David."

His "Sichia" is slowed down from the version on *Passion, Grace & Fire* to winning effect, and given a pleasing samba feel, including a bizarre end section when both players duet frantically on their string trees. A relatively laidback version of "Guardian Angel" concludes a rousing concert full of controlled virtuosity, a vital document of this very special musical and personal friendship and a thrilling fusion of flamenco, jazz, Latin, and blues.

The summer of 1987 ended with some tragic news for John and every music lover: Jaco Pastorius died on September 21 after a difficult five years of intermittently brilliant music blighted by bipolar disorder, poverty, and trauma. Attempting to gain entry to the Midnight Bottle Club near Fort Lauderdale, he sustained life-ending injuries at the hands of the venue's manager, who also happened to be a martial artist. Jaco was just thirty-five years old. John later paid tribute:

> In the bass guitar firmament, he's unique. And nothing can take that away. Nothing. Whatever happened afterward is just tragic. Because we all loved Jaco. He was a loveable guy. He had his faults too but who doesn't? He was a lovely person. And everybody just wanted him to . . . to be alive and just play. That's what we're here for.[55]

On a brighter note, in 1987 John met an extraordinary drummer and percussionist named Trilok Gurtu, who would soon play a very important part in the guitarist's career. Born in Mumbai on October 30, 1951, Gurtu grew up among a family of musicians: his grandfather was a music scholar and sitar player; his mother, Shobha, a revered singer; and his older brother a tabla player. Picking up the basics of the tabla himself, he became interested in pop music before jazz, devouring The Beatles, James Brown, Motown, and Jimi Hendrix. "Anything I heard, I would try to figure out how they did it. But I would imitate it in my own way, with tabla, the way the South Indians would do it." [56] Inspired by his brother, he moved on to a drum set but continued to augment it with tablas and various other shakers and cymbals, and also developed his trademark stance, kneeling behind the kit and using a floor-tom instead of a bass drum. He started working with a jazzier group in a Mumbai hotel, one member of which played him Elvin Jones's playing with John Coltrane, and a door opened up: "I thought, 'Wow, what is this?' It was so nice, but how was he doing it? I thought I could never learn to play like that because there was no one to teach me."[57]

Gurtu quickly became an accomplished jazz player, and, at the age of twenty, he toured Europe with a fusion band called Waterfront, then returned to Mumbai to play with established players like John Tchicai and Charlie Mariano. A period in New York led to a vital meeting with Don Cherry, with whom he played for two years. He then settled in Hamburg, Germany, where he met Collin Walcott in 1984 and started playing with Walcott's world/jazz supergroup Oregon. Gurtu also formed his own group and, in 1986, found himself playing opposite John's revived Mahavishnu Orchestra at a European jazz festival. "Afterwards, John came up to me and said, 'Maybe we should play together.' So he came to my house and we played. And we've been playing ever since."[58]

It's hardly surprising that John and Gurtu should find so much in common, both "jazz" players who happen to be classically trained Indian musicians, too. John elaborated on their kinship to Bill Milkoswki in *Jazz Times*, April 1992:

> Trilok is an Indian musician by training and a jazz musician by affection, so we have a lot in common. He can shift at a moment's notice from an Indian groove to an Elvin Jones kind of groove. So we're able to move together in a very easy way . . . very instant communication. At any point, we can dramatically change the musical derivative, and this means we have a big field to play in. We're not restricted to just one or two particular ways of communicating. And he has a great sense of humor too in the way he plays.

The first port of call was a trio featuring John, Hellborg, and Gurtu that rehearsed a lot but only seems to have played once in concert, in Detroit, Michigan, in 1988. (Hellborg also reports the concert may have been recorded.) But this trio was short-lived—John and Hellborg's musical association finally ended after a very fruitful decade together. John would soon put together another trio, though, and the guitar/bass/percussion format would be his principle musical vehicle of choice over the next five years.

Meanwhile, in November 1988, John produced the Labeque sisters' album *Symphonic Dances And Songs From West Side Story* at Davout Studios in Paris—it was a harbinger of John's first major solo project of the next decade.

John, Miles, and Dave Holland at Hill Auditorium, Ann Arbor, Michigan, on February 21, 1970. *Photo credit*: Mike Dibb

John soundchecking at the Towne Cinema, Bloomington, Indiana, on April 24, 1972. *Photo credit*: Peter Erskine

L. Shankar and John fronting The One Truth Band in 1978. *Photo credit*: Chris Hakkens

John and a sleeping Tony Williams travel to Havana on March 1, 1979.
*Photo credit*: Peter Erskine

Jaco Pastorius in Havana on March 3, 1979, just before the infamous Trio Of Doom concert. *Photo credit*: Peter Erskine

John in Havana on March 3, 1979. *Photo credit*: Peter Erskine

John duets with Al Di Meola in 1979. *Photo credit*: Craig Howell

Danny Gottlieb and John soundchecking in Ravenna, Italy, on July 15, 1986. *Photo credit*: Danny Gottlieb

John at The Old Fruitmarket in Glasgow on July 7, 1995. *Photo credit*: William Ellis

Dennis Chambers, Joey DeFrancesco, and John at House of Blues in Los Angeles on February 11, 1996. *Photo credit*: Dennis Chambers

John speaks to Ian Carr for *The Miles Davis Story*. *Photo credit*: Mike Dibb

John and Chick Corea perform with Five Peace Band at Cork Opera House on October 24, 2008. *Photo credit*: William Ellis

# 6

# THE 1990s

## From *The Mediterranean Concerto* to *Remember Shakti*

### *THE MEDITERRANEAN CONCERTO* (1990)

John McLaughlin: Acoustic guitar
The London Symphony Orchestra
Michael Tilson Thomas: Conductor
Michael Gibbs: Orchestrator
Katia Labeque: Yamaha piano and MIDI grand piano
Recorded at CTS Studios in Middlesex, England, 1988, and Studio Davout in Paris, France, 1988
Produced by Steven Epstein (concerto) and John McLaughlin (duets)

John's fabled work of the 1970s was finally creeping out on CD in the late 1980s as the format hit boom-time. He took a philosophical view during a July 1988 interview with Richard Cook of *Wire* magazine: "Oh, I think it's always flatter-ing that people find your previous work interesting for a number of years. Any artist has delusions of immortality. My personal view is that when it's finished, it's done. There's nothing you can do with it any more. What's important is today."[1] It was an admirable stance for a world-renowned musician, but also perhaps recognition of the fact that his peak 1970s Mahavishnu work had not yet reached that point of critical "untouchability" that it has at the time of this writing. There was also the tacit acknowledgment that he hadn't released a major-label album for four years and showed no sign of setting down his acous-tic guitar any time soon.

But as 1990 approached, John was on the cusp of a purple patch, full of ideas for future projects and with a seemingly endless pool of genres and styles from which to choose. He also had some serious competition in the guitar department, with Bill Frisell, Pat Metheny, John Scofield, Mike Stern, Bireli Lagrene, John Abercrombie, Vernon Reid, Allan Holdsworth, Hiram Bullock, Scott Henderson, Steve Khan, and Frank Gambale, among others, receiving critical plaudits and gaining cult followings among jazz/rock fans. John opined on the state of the art at the dawn of a new decade: "Sco (John Scofield) I love. He's maybe my favourite jazz guitarist playing today. (Bill) Frisell, it's funny but I've never heard him. I heard a guy called Scott Henderson who I was very impressed with. If there's a good guitar player then I want to hear him. I should know if I want to send someone out to break his hands." In the same interview, while pledging allegiance to the acoustic guitar, he also made a particularly prescient comment when asked whom he would play with if he ever returned to the electric: "If the great Larry Young were alive, I'd have him with Elvin Jones. I'd just go in with a few heads, a few tunes. Maybe I'll get to do it one day."[2]

In the meantime, John started the new decade back with CBS Records, and with the long-overdue release of his *Mediterranean Concerto*. John explained the genesis of the piece in the album's liner notes, written at his Monaco home on September 10, 1989, and containing one crucial error:

> It was in 1981, after a concert at the Hollywood Bowl (during which the pianists Katia and Marielle Labeque also performed), that we were having dinner with Ernest Fleischman, the Executive Director of the Los Angeles Philharmonic. During the dinner Ernest asked if I would come to play Rodrigo's famous "Aranjuez" Concerto for guitar and orchestra. Very flattered, I replied jokingly that I would come to play if I were to write a new piece. Much to my surprise, he agreed immediately, and because of his constant enthusiasm—without which the piece would not exist, and for which I shall always be thankful—*Mediterranean* was written and premiered in Los Angeles on Thanksgiving 1984.

The premiere performance actually took place on November 27, 1985, rather than 1984, at the Dorothy Chandler Pavilion. A second performance was added on November 29. On the eve of the first concert, John revealed to *The LA Times* what was at stake for him:

> This is such an experiment for me. We have no idea if it will work. I finished my work only six weeks ago. All along, my friend Michael Gibbs was working on the orchestration, but the conductor (Jan Latham-Koenig) got his score for the last two movements only today (Thursday, November 21), so I have thus far never

actually heard the finished concerto. But I feel good (about writing for orchestra), now that I've gotten my feet wet. Not to be in a vulnerable situation is a mistake. Being there enriches me. Even if the concert is a disaster, had I not done this, I would have lived with regrets.[3]

It was a typically brave statement from John. Pianist Keith Jarrett is also known for his classical work—performing Pärt, Bach, and Mozart among others—alongside his jazz and related music, and religiously avoids playing jazz when preparing for a classical performance, and vice versa—for him, the two styles involve completely separate techniques and mind-sets. (He said in the documentary *The Art Of Improvisation*: "I always thought I had to be way over-prepared for classical performances because I was coming from this weird world that wasn't accepted, I was like an invader in the ranks. If I want to do justice to Mozart, I have to stop playing jazz for that period of time.") But we don't get this sense from John; he integrated a lot of previous work into his concerto and synthesized many of his chief interests: flamenco, Indian, jazz, blues. It's possibly why the piece is so rich and difficult to categorize, and possibly why it lay on CBS's shelf for over a year.

But if the orchestrations and general logistics weren't giving John enough to think about as he prepared for the premiere, there were also challenges in using a nylon-string acoustic guitar with an orchestra. He again turned to his favorite luthier for the solution:

Abraham Wechter, who has made four guitars for me over the years, is building a nylon-string instrument with a large body to naturally bring out a rich bass midrange. I've asked him to concentrate on the upper register, in order to have a special brilliance. It'll have a cutaway, which I believe will be adopted by classical players eventually because it facilitates things that are impossible otherwise. Another unclassical aspect is that I'll be using a mic.[4]

John's Los Angeles premiere turned into quite the cultural event. Miles was there, as John told Kolosky in *Power, Passion & Beauty*: "He came with Burt Bacharach. I played every note for Miles that night. Eventually I gave him a cassette of the piece . . . which he listened to attentively on a ghetto blaster while eating a late night supper in his hotel room. 'John, now you can die!' he said. Really cool." It was certainly a rare treat for a "modern composer" to have a premiere during his lifetime—John was vividly aware of this, as he told writer Howard Mandel in *Future Jazz* a few years later:

Think of Charles Ives. I went to London to hear the New World Orchestra—conducted by Michael Tilson Thomas—play Ives' *Fourth Symphony*, a staggering piece, and you know Ives never heard his piece played? So let's keep perspective with regard to artistic music success and commercial success.

The concerto had been gestating since 1983, inspired by John's new home in Monte Carlo, right by the Mediterranean. In the liner notes, John expounded on his classical influences:

> One can detect immediately my continuing affection for Hispanic and French cultures of the 20th century, particularly in the first and second movements. The third movement will perhaps reveal more of the New-World influence. In any event, should any of those who listen to this piece then accuse me of creating a vast "potpourri" I shall be delighted, for it is nothing if not that, and if it gives pleasure to only one person, then all the work would have not been in vain.

John was very keen for the orchestra to get fully involved and be flexible in their approach. Improvisation was also still a nonnegotiable aspect: "What's interesting for me is that all the cadenzas are improvised. That's something they like very much in the classical world, because they've lost that way of working."[5]

The huge CTS Studios in Wembley, northwest London—the first purpose-built studio in the UK—was chosen to record the concerto. Grammy-winning New Yorker Steven Epstein, then senior executive producer at CBS Masterworks, was charged with the technical challenge of documenting the work. John opted to bring back the London Symphony Orchestra conductor Michael Tilson Thomas and orchestrator Mike Gibbs from the *Apocalypse* sessions over a decade before.

Taken as a whole, the concerto is indeed a landmark piece for John, an extraordinary statement from a "jazz" musician and one of the most timeless artefacts in his catalog. It's a great shame that—at the time of this writing—it isn't available on streaming platforms. The opening movement, "Rhythmic," may bring to mind the soundworlds of Stravinsky, Khachaturian, Ravel, and Bizet. The fast 6/8 section also seems influenced by Rodrigo's "Concierto De Aranjuez." "Slow & Sad," the second movement, is based around John's "David," here given a very tender reading with a French horn taking the melody and a touch of Debussy's soundworld. John told *The LA Times* about "Animato": "The third movement comes closest to jazz, though it's more contemporary. There's tremendous harmonic movement, but the rhythms? That's another story: they are directly inspired by Indian beats."

John decided to augment the concerto with a series of duets with Katia to boost the running time for the CD and cassette. These five pieces—three old and two new—were recorded live at the Davout Studios in Paris. He relayed in the liner notes:

> The realization of the duos with Katia Labeque is one of the high points of my musical life. She is an exquisite musician endowed with the most fabulous means. These five pieces offer a view into an intimate world, one that holds great promise for future harvests. The pieces are themselves simply "songs" that are more or less abstract but nevertheless very personal.

If the John/Katia duets are less inspired than the concerto, with a peculiarly soulless quality, they are nonetheless a fascinating document of an unusual musical pairing. The arrangement of "Brise De Coeur"—first heard on *Music Spoken Here*—is the pick, totally acoustic with a beautifully played melody and a majestic Katia run. "Two Sisters"—a rehash of the Shakti composition from *A Handful Of Beauty*—is a success, too, taken almost completely *rubato* with pleasingly ambiguous chords and a great blues section.

"Until Such Time" is initially minimalist, almost to the point of invisibility, but then John's fast 3/4 vamp almost takes it into "My Favorite Things" territory, alluded to by Katia. "Montana" is a cheery (or cheesy) throwaway, despite the treacherous B section, the title possibly evoking the same kinds of terrain mapped out by Pat Metheny, but it's hampered by Katia's dated Midi piano.

Finally, there was John's tribute to his friend and Shakti collaborator Zakir Hussain, first recorded on the tabla player's *Making Music* album. Here it's rather saccharine, not helped by Katia's Midi string swells and a strangely weightless guitar tone.

John performed the *Concerto* and duet pieces with Katia during the summer and fall of 1989 at selected cities in the United States and Europe, including a televised performance on July 11 with the Orquesta Filarmónica de Munich, where he brilliantly incorporated themes from his whole career into his improvisations. It's also fascinating to watch him in full evening dress and showing real signs of pressure and intense concentration. Incredibly, he appears not to read a note—his parts were all memorized.

Meanwhile, Miles's autobiography was issued in September 1989 to healthy sales but also criticism for its blunt language and *laissez-faire* approach to detail. John was only mentioned four times, with very little material about his contributions to the fabled *In A Silent Way*, *Bitches Brew*, and *Jack Johnson* sessions.

# *LIVE AT THE ROYAL FESTIVAL HALL* (1990)

John McLaughlin: Acoustic guitar, Photon guitar synthesizer, voice
Kai Eckhardt-Karpeh: Electric bass
Trilok Gurtu: Percussion, voice
Recorded at the Royal Festival Hall, London, on November 27, 1989
Produced by Stefan F. Winter
Released in April of 1990

The roots of this excellent album were laid down in 1988, when John and Trilok Gurtu's short-lived trio alongside Jonas Hellborg came to an end. John then asked bassist Jeff Berlin to come onboard. Born January 17, 1953, in Queens, New York, Berlin was yet another attendee at the Berklee School in Boston, where he had studied modern composition with Gary Burton and also became part of *Apocalypse* orchestrator Mike Gibbs's ensemble. Upon leaving Berklee, Berlin joined a trio with Tony Williams and Allan Holdsworth, gigged with Al Di Meola and Gil Evans, and then rejoined Holdsworth in Bill Bruford's groundbreaking fusion band.

Berlin talked about how he first met John and how the trio came to be:

> Back in 1977, I was hired to be the house bassist for Atlantic Records at the Montreux Jazz Festival by Herbie Mann. There were a lot of musicians coming and going. We'd play all night 'til four in the morning. One evening, I'm walking down a hallway and I hear my bass sound—someone was playing my bass. I walk in the room and it's John McLaughlin. Ten years later, he called me. He said he never forgot what I did as a bass player at the festival in 1977.[6]

Audio evidence of the short-lived John/Berlin/Gurtu trio—which toured Europe twice between April and September 1988—is available to hear on the bootleg CD *The One In Bremen*. Indeed, it was a striking evening of musicianship—who but John would form a trio consisting of electric bass, acoustic guitar, and percussion? But the latter term hardly does Gurtu justice; by now he had settled on a novel setup incorporating water pail, gong, tablas, temple blocks, bells, ride and splash cymbals, two pairs of hi-hats, and some Roto-tom-styled drums. He knelt on a Persian rug to address the kit, never using a stool, and removed his shoes out of respect for the playing area. Gurtu also sometimes reversed usual jazz logic by neglecting to use his ride cymbal when accompanying a soloist, picking up a tabla or triangle instead. He could swing on anything.

So, John's new trio was certainly groundbreaking, but it also asked a lot of the bassist. Berlin, like Anthony Jackson, was and is a purist who refuses to slap his bass in the traditionally "funky" style. Maybe that didn't help his cause in the long term, but it was also suggested that John believed he was always too loud onstage. Still, Berlin was nothing but complimentary about John and the trio in the years to come:

> Musically, it was an astonishing experience. I learned a lot. Trilok [Gurtu] is brilliant too. I became a better musician. I hope I contributed a lot to it too. We'd rehearse eight hours a day at his girlfriend's chateau. I had never been in a chateau. There were acres of vineyards and it was fantastic. After rehearsing, we'd just play jazz tunes for our own entertainment.[7]

So, a new bassist was needed for the US tour of the summer of 1989. The man chosen was Kai Eckhardt. He was a German-born Berklee graduate, another bassist who attended Gary Burton's improvisation classes. After Berlin's departure, John had asked Burton for some bass recommendations. Burton suggested Baron Browne—lately of Billy Cobham's quintet—Jimmy Earl and Eckhardt. It was pure luck that John phoned Eckhardt first. After a brief conversation, John went round to the bassist's Boston apartment to hear him play and join him in a blues jam. Then John attended a gig Eckhardt did with drummer Bob Moses (after which John helped Eckhardt carry his equipment to the car), and the young bassist was hired. "This is going to work out very well," Eckhardt remembers John saying.

The trio format was a tough initiation for Eckhardt, and he recalls a lot of support but also some impatience on the part of Gurtu and John with regard to his understanding of compound time signatures. But the situation quickly improved, and the first gig for the new trio was at an Italian club in December 1988. Eckhardt was amazed at the striking intensity of his two bandmates when playing in concert, compared to during rehearsals:

> They literally left me in the dust! I didn't know where 'one' was. I'm sweating and uncomfortable . . . but at the end of the night, there was a standing ovation, and John said, 'Kai, you have a way to go, but that's a good start'. So I was kind of on the bandwagon, but for a good year I was trailing behind.[8]

The summer 1989 North American tour saw the trio develop into something very special. They could play aggressively, funkily, or very quietly, performing some new John material, a few standards, and one or two compositions from the 1980s Mahavishnu era. Eckhardt mostly played a double-necked bass—one fretted five-string and the other a fretless four-string—but with a lot more bottom than Hellborg and Berlin, while obviously influenced by them and other usual suspects of 1970s and 1980s jazz/rock bass. Most importantly, he played John's music with heart and soul.

But it was sometimes a troubled tour. Possibly this wasn't a great time in John's career or personal life. He was a very buttoned-down, fairly serious character in concert, dressing very smartly and generally keeping a fairly low profile, not embarking on dramatic or humorous announcements from the stage. Eckhardt told Anil Prasad of the kinds of circumstances that John sometimes needed to create magic during this era:

> In the dressing room of the Montreal Jazz Festival (July 2, 1989), we were about to go on. There was a little window and John is leaning out of it to catch some fresh air. The window comes down on his finger—it's one of those old Victorian ones that comes down like a guillotine. He yells in agony and somebody comes rushing in with a bucket of cold water. Within seconds, his fingernails are turning black. He's in terrible pain and we're thinking 'Oh God, the gig's screwed.' Then they announce the start of the show and he goes onstage and plays and sounds killer the whole night. The crowd is ecstatic and it was a great show. And he's hurting so bad after the gig. He did not have a good time. But he gave everybody else a good time. That was something I learned from him. You have performance standards. He would never go onstage stoned or drunk—never. In two years that we were on the road, not once did I see him wasted. The stage was his sacred space.[9]

There were also many moments of humor onstage. Eckhardt's beatboxing and natural stage presence were a plus, and one March 1989 concert in Stuttgart saw John reduced to tears of mirth courtesy of Gurtu's wordless vocalisms and water-aided sound effects (available to watch on YouTube).

The volume levels of the trio had gradually been going up since the Jeff Berlin days, as Gurtu remembered: "We started off acoustic but we couldn't get enough volume on stage, so after a while, John put a synth in the guitar. I remember it was in Ft. Worth (June 8, 1989); and wow, the whole music changed after that . . . I could really bite into the drums."[10] John's Abraham Wechter gut-string acoustic guitar was now equipped with a Fishman Hexaphonic transducer capable of providing a separate output signal for each of its six strings. Those signals were sent to a Photon Guitar Synthesizer, and then MIDI connections were forwarded to two Yamaha TX-7 synthesizers. The result was that John could both "loop" sounds—for example, if he wanted to solo over a pedal point or sustain a chord indefinitely—or he could augment his regular acoustic guitar tone with elements of guitar synth, giving it more color and body.

After various late summer concerts in Europe, the trio played just two UK dates in November 1989—in Edinburgh and London—with the latter night digitally recorded at John's expense, with the intention to release it on CBS Masterworks. However, this arrangement fell through, so John decided to tout for a one-album deal. First in line was JMT (Jazz Music Today), a Munich-based label run by Stefan Winter, and a vital imprint for releasing M-Base music earlier in the 1980s. This mixture of jazz, funk, hip-hop, and Harmolodics—a vital antidote to the so-called Young Lions movement—was established by youthful US-based players and singers such as Steve Coleman, Greg Osby, Cassandra Wilson, Lonnie Plaxico, Robin Eubanks, and Gary Thomas (the latter soon to collaborate with John).

*Live At The Royal Festival Hall* kicks off in somnambulistic style with "Blue In Green," famously a key ballad on Miles's *Kind Of Blue* (and, at the time of this writing, by far that album's most streamed song on Spotify), though there is debate as to who exactly composed it. Miles has sole credit on that 1959 album, but Bill Evans recorded his own version on *Portrait In Jazz* from the following year. Evans recorded it again in 1974 for a live album bearing the same name. Either way, the *Live At The Royal Festival Hall* version makes very little impression, save for showcasing John's chordal mastery and featuring the opening section from the *Round Midnight* soundtrack version of "Body And Soul."

"Just Ideas/Jozy" demonstrates the sense of space in John's new music, making the entry of Gurtu's half-time shuffle even more powerful, his floor toms echoing around the hall. "Florianopolis" is another intricately rearranged piece from *Adventures In Radioland* and *another* chord masterclass from John, while Gurtu's "Pasha's Love" is an onslaught of complex time signatures, mostly in 9/8 (counted 2-2-2-3) with some delightful Spanish elements and ferocious riffing from John and Eckhardt. It was previously recorded as "Pasha Love" on Nana Vasconcelos's 1989 album, *Rain Dance*.

"Mother Tongues" originated back in 1988 with the Jeff Berlin trio and would become a key John composition over the next few decades. Gurtu makes full use of his water pail and gong, then repeats the trick with sleigh bells, creating a hissing sound like a skillet. "You can make a lot of sounds with water. I think it's becoming my trademark," he told *Modern Drummer* magazine in November 1992. He also paid tribute to John's subtle harmonic accompaniment in 9/4: "John takes care. You can depend on him. It's never a competition. That's what is special with this group. I would leave a situation if I felt there was competition."[11]

The album rather outstayed its welcome (at least on CD format) with a new version of "Blues For L.W." featuring a long *konnakol* vocal section by John and Gurtu over the "Miles Beyond" riff, with Eckhardt even throwing in a little beatboxing, some references to "Are You The One? Are You The One?" and John's homage to Hammond organ trios.

Despite a less-than-extensive release in the spring of 1990, hampered by minimal promotion, uncertain sequencing (it takes a long time to get going), and a strange cover—just a very humdrum photograph of London's South Bank Centre—*Live At The Royal Festival Hall* quickly became one of JMT's bestsellers, reaching #3 on the *Billboard* Contemporary Jazz Albums chart. It's another classic John album awaiting proper reassessment, at the time of this writing not available on streaming platforms.

The second leg of the US tour was set to resume in early 1990, but then disaster struck. While he was moving some belongings around in his home, a TV set fell onto John's right hand. He couldn't touch a guitar for two months. Once he had finally recovered, there were a few European dates in April, then the trio took some time off, and then the US tour continued in October 1990. John promoted it via an amusing double interview with Swedish rock guitarist Yngwie Malmsteen published in the September 1990 edition of *Musician* magazine. There was some good-natured joshing between the two players, of vastly different generations and musical/personal outlooks, and John spoke candidly about his accident: "I was having nightmares. I was waking up in the middle of the night sweating. But there's a good side. Already this accident has affected the way I think."[12] He was also asked about his relationships with the original Mahavishnu Orchestra: "Billy was always cool, but I had problems with Jan Hammer and Jerry Goodman. They were fucking jerks! And you can print it, it's all right. Jerry's cool now but Jan still has some weird problem with me after 20 years."

## *QUÉ ALEGRÍA* (1992)

John McLaughlin: Acoustic guitar, Photon MIDI Interface
Trilok Gurtu: Percussion
Dominique Di Piazza: Bass
Kai Eckhardt-Karpeh: Bass
Recorded in Ludwigsburg, Germany, November 29–December 3, 1991
Released March 1992

Sadly, Eckhardt's time with the trio came to an end in November 1990, at the end of the American tour. His foster father had been diagnosed with both Parkinson's and Alzheimer's disease, though at first Eckhardt didn't reveal this to his bandmates. "I started to withdraw from John and Trilok, I became a different person. I did my job but I wasn't happy."[13] John offered his help but acknowledged it was perhaps best for Eckhardt to move on from the trio (though he was invited to record a few tracks on *Què Alegría* and paid handsomely for his time).

An enlightened character, Eckhardt's reflections on what he had learned about playing with John and Gurtu give an interesting perspective—he described playing in odd-time signatures as something akin to an actor's "invention" of a character's backstory when performing onstage:

> When you're playing with Trilok and you're playing in a cycle of nine, you have to hold your independent cycle. You're in four and someone else is in three, but you're agreeing on the same rate of subdivision. If one groups four together and the other groups three together, but they keep going as three against four, you cannot get pulled to the other side. Playing with the trio, I learned that we always have to keep playing inside our own internal centre.[14]

Eckhardt was also amazed at the standard of playing in the trio: "I learned how deep human creativity is. I didn't even know the level of musicianship existed on this planet until I met these two guys. Wow! This is what a human being can do!"[15] Eckhardt went on to work with Steve Smith's Vital Information, Billy Cobham, Patrice Rushen, and Wayne Shorter, and later began a solo career.

The trio's new bassist was the Frenchman Dominic Di Piazza. Born into a musical family in 1959, he grew up listening to bebop, Flamenco, *manouche* jazz, and Indian music, first picking up the guitar. Di Piazza was a late starter on bass at twenty years old, inspired by hearing Jaco for the first time. He quickly developed an unusual technique of "picking" the instrument with thumbnail, index, and middle fingers, leading to an extremely fluid, "guitaristic" style. Di Piazza played with Gil Evans in 1987, but John first heard him when he was given a cassette of his solo bass playing while on tour in Paris. John summoned Di Piazza to Monaco to audition, as the latter remembers:

> I knew that he played tunes like "Giant Steps", and at that time, I was very proud of what I could do . . . so I was very at ease as we played through that tune and a number of other Coltrane songs. When we were done, he said, 'OK . . . now we're going to try something in 5/8 . . .' 5/8? I didn't even know how to count it!

As I began to sweat, I thought to myself that this was it—he was going to kick me out. After we played through that piece, he proceeded to call a tune in 9/8. As we played through, I was watching his foot tapping and was completely lost! After that, I was telling myself, "OK, I know that this is not going to happen." But he told me that we'd meet in about six months to play through the songs again.[16]

Despite Di Piazza's nerves, he passed the audition. He also developed a strange five-string bass for playing with the trio, as a result of being asked by John to "comp" (play chords) under his solos, so he added a top C rather than the usual bottom B.

John took a little time out from rehearsing with his new band when, on July 10, 1991, he joined a host of musicians gathered backstage at Paris's Grande Halle de la Villette for a very special concert honoring Miles. It was titled "Around Miles Davis," and his paintings (some in collaboration with his partner/artist, Jo Gelbard) were draped and spread all around the stage. Miles played with his usual touring band for the first half of the concert, and then was joined by a star-studded line-up of key collaborators through the years: John, Herbie Hancock, Wayne Shorter, Jackie McLean, Steve Grossman, Chick Corea, Joe Zawinul, Al Foster, Dave Holland, and John Scofield. (Tony Williams claims he was not asked to appear.) John borrowed a Les Paul for the gig, joining Foster, bassist Richard Patterson, Zawinul, and Scofield on "It's About That Time" and "Katia." The latter in particular made for a fascinating study of John and Scofield's contrasting soloing styles. John later spoke about the concert:

> The way Miles set it up, each tune . . . as was Miles' wont . . . had a kind of op-position element happening. He would pair up players, Scofield and myself, Wayne (Shorter) and Bill Evans, Jackie McLean and Steve Grossman, Herbie and Chick . . . so that there were always two soloists on the same instrument, which was nice for us. I don't get much chance to play with Scofield, whom I love. So every tune was from a different era . . . different feeling, different sound, different attitude. Each piece had its own life to it. And it's just amazing to think that it all came from one person.[17]

John reports he spoke to Miles one last time after the concert before the trumpeter's death on September 28, 1991:

> The last time he called me—this was after the last Paris concert—he was down in Rome . . . and I knew he was already not well in Paris, and he called me at home, and he was just talking about his Ferrari car, he just wanted to chat. He just wanted to hear a friendly voice. We just shot the breeze basically. We didn't

talk about anything specifically—definitely not music. Miles would never speak about music on the telephone. I don't remember him ever speaking about music. He was old-school. Beautiful-school.[18]

The Seville Guitar Festival, taking place during October 1991, also became a tribute to Miles. It was a weeklong Spanish sojourn, including a thrilling "jazz fusion" night featuring John, Larry Coryell, Paco De Lucia, Stanley Clarke, George Benson, and MD George Duke. Coryell dueted memorably with Clarke on "School Days," and De Lucia performed a section from "Concierto De Aranjuez," then dueted on a spirited "Zyryab" with John. John played "Que Alegria" with Gurtu and Di Piazza and also jammed on Miles/Ron Carter's "Eighty One" and Miles's "It's About That Time" during the finale. The drummer in the house band was Dennis Chambers, that great player who had turned heads with Mike Stern, Scofield, the Brecker Brothers, and Parliament/Funkadelic. John was very much aware of his work, but they had never played together before that night. Apparently, he sidled up to the drummer before the concert and whispered: "I heard about you." John would soon be seeking Chambers's number (and would also look up bass player James Genus, who had played with Chambers in Seville). The excellent concert was later shown in full on British television.

John's new trio then performed a few European gigs in November 1991, including a date at the Royal Festival Hall in London, in preparation for another studio album. Meanwhile Polygram had reignited Verve Records, that famous Norman Granz–founded jazz imprint that had lain dormant between the late 1960s and early 1990s. New executive Jean-Philippe Allard signed John to the French arm of the label, while other luminaries such as Joe Henderson, Herbie Hancock, Wayne Shorter, Betty Carter, Charlie Haden, Abbey Lincoln, John Scofield, and Shirley Horn, as well as younger stars Roy Hargrove, Christian McBride, Chris Botti, and Nicholas Payton, also signed to Verve. This was a serious cadre of players, and John was given carte blanche by the label. He responded by recording the trio (almost) totally live in the studio:

We set up and just played a concert. What you hear is what you get. In the trio, the playing together is so important, we have to get that on record, and not just put a rhythm track down and put a solo on top. We could have done it in a concert hall. The difference is basically psychological and physical, in the sense that in the studio you don't start indulging in things and letting pieces go long. You have to be more restrained and economical, which is not so bad. It obliges you to be more essential, and I'm able to put more pieces on the record.[19]

There were definite advantages to being on a major label again with *Què Alegría*: the marketing and distribution clout, along with an attractive album cover featuring a smiling John looking every inch the debonair man about the arts. It hadn't been a particularly easy few years, and in Howard Mandel's book *Future Jazz*, John admitted that "there are times when business pressures were brought to me. You're taking risks and that's part of the deal. If you're going to follow your instincts, you've got to assume the risks, which I'm very happy to do."

Upon *Que Alegria*'s release in March 1992, it was a critical and commercial success for John. The trio set off on an extensive US tour, including a memorable week at New York's Blue Note club in April. The trio was his "jazziest" band for a long time, a situation that excited John:

> We do a lot of unison playing together, which is something that goes back to bebop, exemplified by Charlie Parker and Dizzy Gillespie. I love that. It's been a part of my music all along, even with Shakti. Curiously enough, unison playing is a tradition you find in India too. This is one of the aspects of this complicity that is growing between Dominique and myself. We have this kind of guitaristic relationship developing that's very interesting. And I still have a great complicity between the two of them. And so the group itself becomes more whole now than it's ever been. The record is great, but some things have started to happen in live situations that are truly amazing. It's like we planted a flower that's blossoming now.[20]

During the summer of 1992, the studio house band of American TV show *The Tonight Show With Jay Leno*—featuring Branford Marsalis and Kevin Eubanks—began playing The Mahavishnu Orchestra's "Lila's Dance" and "Meeting Of The Spirits" before commercial breaks. (Eubanks once revealed his high-school nickname had been "Mahavishnu.") It's unknown whether their endorsement of John's 1970s music did much for his record sales, but concert attendances were much healthier in the States than they'd been for a long time. But John wasn't looking too far back. He even revealed to one stunned interviewer of his admiration for pop/R'n'B star M. C. Hammer.

Meanwhile, Gurtu appeared on the cover of *Modern Drummer* magazine in November 1992 and spoke extensively about working on *Que Alegria*, but the album also marked the end of Gurtu's involvement with John's music—apart from a brief reunion in 1996—and there are clues it might not have been an entirely happy parting. Speaking to Joe Zawinul biographer Brian Glasser, a few years after a reported power struggle with the Weather Report keyboardist, Gurtu said, "It was the same thing with John McLaughlin, all this mental manipulation. With John, I was a sideman, the only time I was, because he'd called me." John had a different take on the end of the trio: "Trilok became so busy that he needed to have my gigs nine months ahead of time, which made life pretty impossible for me."[21] Straight after leaving John's trio, Gurtu continued his solo career for CMP Records, recording his best album by far, 1993's *Crazy Saints*, with key guests Zawinul and Pat Metheny.

Di Piazza meanwhile left with far happier memories of his time with the trio: "I am grateful that John hired me and gave me a tremendous musical experience while performing in some of the most beautiful venues with great conditions. I am also grateful that John would allow me to feature solos on stage. It is because of this experience that I can play on stage alone now! When you work with an icon of his stature, your name is forever associated with his."[22]

Despite that, Di Piazza gave up music briefly to work in a factory and devote himself to religious studies during the mid-1990s, but he returned to performing in 2000, recording a well-received trio album with Bireli Lagrene on guitar and Chambers on drums.

### Belo Horizonte  6:35

This was a thrilling reinvention of the title track of John's 1981 album, a great arrangement and fine introduction to Di Piazza's playing. John's low-key opening uses arpeggios that bring to mind "This Is For Us To Share" from *Extrapolation*.

### Baba (for Ramana Maharshi) (Trilok Gurtu)  6:51

John's wonderfully dark chords open Gurtu's tribute to Maharshi, the Hindu sage. His Hammond organ patch looks forward to The Free Spirits band a year later. Gurtu recorded this piece for his 1991 solo album *Living Magic*.

### Reincarnation  11:52

This was a fascinating revamp of John's composition first heard on *Adventures In Radioland*. Eckhardt's fretless bass theme is beautifully played, while John's extended chordal improvisation is adapted from "Rockabilly Bootleg," a track played on tour with Hellborg during 1987. The eerie two notes concluding "Reincarnation" pay homage to the final two notes of "Blues For Pablo" from Miles and Gil Evans's epochal *Miles Ahead*.

## 1 Nite Stand    5:25

John yelps with delight through this exciting piece, full of trapdoors, stop-start figures, and false endings. The main melody may reflect an influence from Ornette Coleman's "Broad Way Blues." Eckhardt gets a superb bass tone, adding some much-needed bottom end via his low B string. The reason for the American spelling is unknown.

## Marie (Di Piazza)    1:59

John was delighted with Di Piazza, and he celebrated by giving him a solo piece on *Que Alegria*: "It's beautiful what he's doing there. I think the only other person who did that is Jaco. And I encourage Dominique to keep going as much as he can in his own direction, to grow and evolve."[23] Di Piazza ends the piece with descending three-note chords over an A pedal point, possibly a nod to Jaco's version of "Blackbird."

## Hijacked    8:35

John's arpeggiator kicks off one of his best compositions (and performances) of the 1990s. "I can start to play a phrase and it keeps going on. Or I hit some notes or chords and hold them while I play. You can have layers going. There are many possibilities, and this can provoke Trilok and Dominique into different directions."[24] The piece is indeed "hijacked" to become a swinging blues in the middle. John uses some very Gil Evans–like chord voicings, especially in the stop/start sections.

## Mila Repa    7:31

This tone poem, composed by John on piano (his demo is available to hear on the 2021 album *Liberation Time*) and named for the Buddhist disciple of Tibetan descent, has echoes of "The Translators" and "The Unbeliever," as well as Mark Isham's 1980s ambient music, with its deliciously suspended chords and minimalist drums. It's a powerful piece with a unique atmosphere.

## Qué Alegría    10:32

This is a cheerful piece with a Brazilian flavor and more jazz chords than on the rest of the album put together. It also seems to have been mastered more loudly than the other tracks. The middle vocal section features *konnakol* rhythms. Gurtu was amazed at John's facility with the system: "Time is very strong with him. He studied it and he's very precise—more than I am, sometimes. He needs to know every value of every beat. Me, I just hear it and play."[25]

### 3 Willows   5:14

John ends *Que Alegria* in melancholic mood, demonstrating his mastery of voice leading and overdubbing a solo for the first time on the album. "3 Willows" was written on piano and originally titled "Shade Of Blue," the demo of which is available to hear on 2021's *Liberation Time*. It's an understated farewell to jazz/rock for a while, and it stylistically looked forward to his next album project.

## TIME REMEMBERED: JOHN MCLAUGHLIN PLAYS BILL EVANS (1993)

John McLaughlin: Acoustic guitar
Yan Maresz: Acoustic bass guitar
The Aighetta Quartet
Francois Szony: Acoustic guitar
Pascal Rabatti: Acoustic guitar
Alexandre Del Fa: Acoustic guitar
Philippe Loli: Acoustic guitar
Recorded at Regson Studios, Milan, Italy, March 25–28, 1993
Produced by John McLaughlin
Released in August 1993

*Time Remembered* is a tribute to pianist Bill Evans, one of John's all-time musical heroes. John had first heard Evans on Miles's *Kind Of Blue* at seventeen years old, beguiled by his poignant harmonies. During the 1960s, he got the chance to see Evans several times at Ronnie Scott's in London, and then regularly at the Village Vanguard in New York City in the following decade. During one such concert, Evans played an introduction to "Nardis" that amazed John, as he reported in *Time Remembered*'s liner notes: "Some of the most beautiful music I have ever had the privilege to witness. I was there with saxophonist Dave Liebman, and we were both in a state of total astonishment."

John had been thinking about an acoustic tribute to Evans's music since the early 1980s. There had been many individual tributes to the pianist, not least

Pat Metheny and Lyle Mays's "September 15" (the date of his death in 1980), but very few whole albums. In 1986, The Kronos Quartet had recorded their *Music Of Bill Evans* collection, also featuring frequent Evans collaborators Jim Hall on guitar and Eddie Gomez on bass, but John wasn't blown away by this blending of different elements (though he remains a fan of the Quartet).

In early 1992, John began to work through Evans's material, enlisting his young French guitar student Yan Maresz, a Berklee graduate, to help arrange it. There would be no piano, nor contributions from any Evans alumni—just John with his trusty Abraham Wechter nylon-string acoustic, Maresz on acoustic bass guitar, and the Aighetta Quartet. They were a group of acoustic guitarists based near John's home in the south of France, who, according to John's liner notes, weren't familiar with Evans's work at all before recording *Time Remembered*, "but subsequently became enamoured with the compositions and devoted hundreds of hours to mastering the parts."

Clearly a labor of love, the resulting tribute album was something approaching "chamber jazz" and like nothing else in John's catalog, but still a heartfelt, major undertaking: "It was just five months of just writing and rehearsing, rewriting parts, rehearsing again, rewriting, back and forth until they started to sound right. I was tearing my hair out. But when I heard it, boy, I was so happy, so much so that I'd like to do it again with some of my favorite tunes, whether it's Victor Young or Lerner and Lowe, the great Broadway songs of the '40s and '50s."[26] Indeed, John would honor that wish later in his career.

In the manner of Evans's own *Conversations With Myself*, John had even initially considered making *Time Remembered* an overdub record, playing everything himself: "In the beginning, I thought I'd do all the parts. But when I really started to analyze it, I felt it would be too much me. I like the fact that you hear different sounds and different tones on the guitar. And we played together. That's the really important thing, that we played together; I think it's much more beautiful this way."[27]

A solution was to mainly tackle ballads rather than Evans's more up-tempo work. This was a decision informed by the presence of six acoustic guitars playing together, and the large, resonant live room at Renson. But the relatively somber material chosen opened John up to criticism that *Time Remembered* didn't feature some of the more upbeat Evans material: "It's a more classical, maybe more European view of Bill's music. I think we should remember that in this period of the late 1950s with Miles, Bill and Gil Evans both brought this very strong color of the French impressionists, Ravel, Debussy, and Satie. This was a predominant color and influence he brought into jazz music. So it's true, it doesn't have this nightclubby atmosphere. But it has this atmosphere of a studio in Milan, and we're playing his music, and it's beautiful music."[28]

The opening "Prologue" makes for an excellent microcosm of John's methods, a subtly building arrangement with attractive stereo placement for the four guitars. "Very Early," a new version of the *Belo Horizonte* composition, again showcases the different acoustic timbres well, John concentrating on triplets and a few "outside" notes for his short but memorable solo. "Waltz for Debby," Evans's tribute to his niece, written with Gene Lees, is a winner, too, with John uncharacteristically sticking closely to his guitar's upper register.

"Song for Helen," written for Evans's producer and friend Helen Keane, was given a glowing review by guitarist Henry Kaiser during his *Down Beat* Blindfold Test of February 1996: "It gets five stars. John has gone so many places with the guitar before anybody else, and he's been to so many places guitarists have yet to go. He's a master, and here he is playing the music of one of his masters. And he plays it with such love, depth and feeling. A person would have to have something wrong with their soul to not be moved by this track. But why does he use all that digital reverb?"

John gives "Only Child" and "My Bells" a strange up-and-down rhythmic quality, in very constrained 4/4. He takes a composition credit for the underwhelming "Homage," which nods to Evans's "Turn Out The Stars" and "Time Remembered." The full-length version of the title track is somewhat stodgy, as is "We Will Meet Again," Evans's elegy for his brother Harry.

Despite its longueurs, *Time Remembered* maintains a special mood. It works as background music, but close listening reveals layers in the arrangement and moments of glowing improvisation from John. The question is, does he go too far with the "chamber jazz" sound, and is it too close to easy listening or Muzak? Rhythmically, it's certainly somewhat limp. "The music has no tension," according to Richard Cook and Brian Morton in *The Penguin Guide To Jazz On CD*, rather missing the point.

But *Time Remembered* was ahead of its time—the 1990s jazz landscape would soon be littered with tribute albums and reversions of classic works. (Verve itself released Joe Henderson's tributes to Miles, Antonio Carlos Jobim, and Billy Strayhorn, and Herbie Hancock *Gershwin's World*, within five years of *Time Remembered*.) John never considered touring to promote the album. By its May 1993 release, he had very quickly moved on to the next—completely different—project.

# THE *FREE SPIRITS—TOKYO LIVE* (1994)

John McLaughlin: Guitar
Joey DeFrancesco: Hammond XB-3 organ and trumpet
Dennis Chambers: Drums
Digitally recorded live on December 16 and 18, 1993, at The Blue Note,
   Tokyo, Japan
Produced by John McLaughlin

John had predicted he might return to the organ trio, one of his musical passions, and by the spring of 1993 he had found his ideal combination of musicians to form what became known as The Free Spirits (borrowed from a Larry
Coryell band in the late 1960s). The result was his first electric guitar album for
eight years, featuring all original material except a cover of Miles's "No Blues."
   Some have said that John's trio was influenced by guitarist John Abercrombie's return to the organ trio (*While We're Young*, recorded for ECM and
released in early 1993), others looked at John Scofield's recent career, the so-
called Blue Matter Band featuring Chambers and also his New Orleans–flavored
album *Flat Out*. John's take on the format was completely different to both.
He would supercharge the organ trio, bringing odd-time signatures, slamming
funk, blues, Indian rhythms, and high-speed jazz/rock. In other words, it was
business as usual. But he was under no illusions that The Free Spirits was a return to his roots nurtured on the London R'n'B circuit: "I remember playing at
Ronnie Scott's with the Mike Carr Trio with Jackie Denton on drums—that was
some trio, I tell you!" he told Stuart Nicholson of *Jazzwise* in 2004. John had
also worked in organ trios and quartets with Georgie Fame and Graham Bond.
   At last, Dennis Chambers had freed up his schedule to join John, and, on
paper, he was his ideal drummer. A chops phenomenon, he was also a good
listener and conversant in all jazz styles from bebop to fusion. He had the uncanny knack of memorizing the most complex compositions after only one or
two hearings—he couldn't read music. According to guitarist Steve Khan, who
would borrow Chambers in December 1993 to record his classic album *Cross-
ings*: "Every band has a book of music and Dennis has all those books in his
brain. He just has to access it and he's ready to play again."[29]
   Chambers was born in Baltimore, Maryland, on May 9, 1959. His mother
was a backing vocalist for Motown Records. She spotted Chambers's obvious
talents from a young age—he started on the drum set at just three years old and
grew up inspired by the sounds of Roy Haynes, Elvin Jones, Lenny White, Billy
Cobham, Tony Williams, Buddy Rich, Louie Bellson, Steve Gadd, Zigaboo

Modeliste, Melvin Parker, and David Garibaldi. But instilled in him from an early age was the need for originality: "It was blasphemous to play like anyone else," he said later.[30]

At thirteen years old, Chambers was performing in a covers band at a Baltimore nightclub owned by James Brown. Brown dropped in and, mightily impressed by the young drummer, offered him the drumming chair in his band, but his mother insisted that he stay in school instead. (At the time, Brown had a saying: "Don't be a fool, stay in school.") Around this time, Chambers also saw The Mahavishnu Orchestra live for the first time: "It was an experience I will never forget. It felt like I had stuck my finger in a light socket. I couldn't sleep for 48 hours."[31] Cobham became a huge inspiration for Dennis: "Billy was the innovator with Mahavishnu, playing fusion music with the double bass drums . . . and the way he'd play the fastest single-stroke rolls you ever heard, or playing odd-time signatures."[32]

Chambers's career went from strength to strength with Parliament/Funkadelic and the P-Funk All Stars in the late 1970s and early 1980s, and then with guitarist John Scofield on his classic albums *Blue Matter* and *Loud Jazz*. There was also high-profile session and live work with Hue & Cry, Bireli Lagrene, Gary Thomas, Khan, Stanley Clarke, George Duke, the Brecker Brothers, and many others. Chambers finally met John at the Guitar Legends Festival in Seville, Spain, in 1991:

> (John) said he was a big fan and had a lot of records I'd played on. I was blown away. He said, 'Hey man, we've gotta play,' and smiled, so I knew something was up. Sure enough, two years after that I get a phone call and he says, 'Man, are you ready to play?' I said, 'Sure. What about Trilok?' He said he was going to put that band on hold because he wanted to play electric guitar again.[33]

John's Free Spirits band provided Chambers with the chance to show different sides of his drum personality, including playing with brushes, something he wasn't usually known for, and executing authentic bebop with a traditional grip.

The drummer came over to the UK in early 1993 for five days of rehearsals with John at Nomis Studios in Hammersmith, West London. One day, during a kitchen break, Chambers came across Jimmy Page, who, when hearing that John was in the adjacent studio, blurted out: "That's my teacher next door!" Page hugged John, and they reminisced about the old days—it was their first meeting for almost twenty years.

Joining Chambers and John at Nomis was Joey DeFrancesco, the new superstar of the Hammond organ. He was another recommendation from Miles.

DeFrancesco was born in Philadelphia on April 10, 1971. A natural musician from a very young age, he started playing the organ at four years old and was soon learning Jimmy Smith's famous solo from "The Sermon" by ear. He was influenced by his organ-playing father, "Papa" John, as well as John Coltrane and Frank Sinatra, and he went to high school with future luminaries Christian McBride and Ahmir "Questlove" Thompson. DeFrancesco joined Miles's band at seventeen years old, after Davis saw Joey play when the trumpet legend was the special music guest on a local Philadelphia TV show called *Time Out*. De-Francesco can be heard playing synthesizers on the Miles albums *Amandla* and *Live Around The World*. He also signed for Columbia in the late 1980s, making his debut with *All Of Me* and eventually recording five albums for the label.

The chemistry between John, DeFrancesco, and Chambers was electrifying from the beginning, as the latter reported: "The band is phenomenal. It's sort of like Tony Williams' Lifetime, but it's not as wild. . . . It's more musical. John wrote all the music and he wrote his backside off. And he's playing his back-side off. He's one hell of a guy, very intelligent and a very giving person too."[34] John wanted quick reactions from the other two band members. Chambers was ready: "We were cracking up on stage a lot of nights because, all of a sudden, John would start playing 'The Dance Of Maya' in the middle of some other tune, over the drum solo or something. . . . At any given moment, he could bring a classical or Indian vibe into a piece and make it work."[35] Chambers also dug the fact that John was such a fan of his instrument: "He just loves drums. You can't play enough for him. The more you play, the more he'll just stand there and smile."[36] Chambers also reports that John discussed *konnakol* with him from time to time, sharing some of his study: "He even gave me some tapes to watch. It's very fascinating and very complex."[37] But the trio also encountered volume problems onstage from time to time, with Chambers occasionally strug-gling to lock in with DeFrancesco's bass-pedal work.

The Free Spirits played live for the first time in Paris during May 1993, and the band would be a going concern for all three members over the next year. John's guitar of choice for the project was a long-scale Gibson Johnny Smith. (Smith was an influential guitarist and teacher, recording three late-1960s al-bums for Verve and counting Bill Frisell as one of his students.) He was now favoring a fairly clean sound with a little chorus/flanging and the very occasional use of ring modulator. It was a tone that divided opinion, but John seemed a far more jovial character during this period, looking healthy and happy, usually decked out in a Hawaiian shirt and loafers. The music reflected that—the trio demonstrated more of a dedication to good-time swing, jazz, and R'n'B than there had been in John's music for a while, with a nod to his bebop heroes, particularly Thelonious Monk. ("Round Midnight" and "Rhythm-a-Ning" were occasionally played in concert.)

John decided that his next Verve album would be recorded live, so three concerts were documented at the Blue Note club in Tokyo, Japan, between December 16–18, 1993. But disaster nearly struck when John pulled his shoulder muscles and was barely mobile during the second night of the residency. For a while, it was touch and go whether he would be able to make the third and final gig. But he recovered quickly, and the trio got enough material for the album, though Chambers reports: "I was more worried about him than playing the gig."[38]

Though overlong, *Tokyo Live* is generally upbeat, energetic, and exciting. "McLaughlin really sounds like he's having fun for the first time in a long while," according to Morton and Cook in *The Penguin Guide To Jazz On CD*, and it's hard to disagree. DeFrancesco kicks off with a delicious solo blues intro on "1 Nite Stand" while the excellent "Hijacked" comes with a frantic new opening soli section. (DeFrancesco later quotes from Harry Warren's "Gold Diggers' Song [We're In The Money].") The organist then demonstrates his formidable trumpet chops, delivering a superb Miles impression on "When Love Is Far Away," originally written by John for the Labèque sisters' 1991 album *Love Of Colours*.

Thanks to Chambers, "Little Miss Valley" is the funkiest of John's pieces to date, and the drummer also excels on "Juju At The Crossroads" (the title perhaps hinting at a Wayne Shorter–meets–Robert Johnson vibe?), delivering a masterclass in beat displacement. Fellow drummer Marvin "Smitty" Smith commented on the track during an August 1995 *Down Beat* Blindfold Test:

> Dennis, that's my man. And I really do like John. So their playing I appreciate greatly. But as far as this group concept here, it misses the mark for me. I got the feeling that John was selling himself short, as if he were making an effort to sound like John Scofield's group. And it probably doesn't help that feeling that Dennis is playing drums, because he played with Scofield. It's just not a strong enough group concept. It doesn't have enough projection and impact for me. This music needs movement, harmonically, rhythmically, so it really helps when you have a moving bass line, a linear aspect that is really missing here. The musicianship is high here, but in terms of performance, I have to give it two-and-a-half stars.

"Vukovar" commemorated the site of a bloody battle during the Croatian War Of Independence in 1991, and the head seemed a variation on the theme from "Radio-Activity" and also hinted at "Electric Dreams, Electric Sighs." The final two tracks were tributes to Miles. There was a no-frills version of "No

Blues," while "Mattinale," named for the monastery attended by John during the 1970s, became a kind of "greatest hits" of his late composition style. There were elements of "Mother Tongues" in the pedal-point solo sections, a Spanish-sounding chord progression taken from 1981's "Aspan" and a hint of Miles's "Solea" from *Sketches Of Spain*.

The critical and commercial success of *Tokyo Live* would keep The Free Spirits on tour for much of 1994 and 1995. Meanwhile, in August 1994, John did his first Blindfold Test for *Down Beat* magazine. He was asked to opine on Tal Farlow, Al Di Meola, Derek Bailey, Kenny Burrell, Frank Sinatra, and Ronny Jordan. Jordan, Bailey, and Burrell didn't escape his rancour, and he was ambivalent on Di Meola, Sinatra, and Farlow.

John was also less than impressed with a recent superstar guitar collaboration, Pat Metheny and John Scofield's *I Can See Your House From Here*, released in 1994 on Blue Note Records: "I thought that was dreadful. I couldn't believe it actually. There's a minimum you can expect from them, but the minimum wasn't even there. I threw it out of the window, I couldn't stand it. But it doesn't lessen my admiration of either of them."[39] But in the same interview, he professed a great interest in Frank Gambale and Allan Holdsworth's playing. John's next project, however, could hardly be less related to the classic jazz/rock style.

## AFTER THE RAIN (1995)

John McLaughlin: Guitar
Joey DeFrancesco: Hammond B-3 organ
Elvin Jones: Drums
Recorded at Clinton Studios, New York City, October 4 and 5, 1994
Produced by John McLaughlin

John was not finished with the organ trio yet, and the fall of 1994 brought the opportunity to explore the format with one of his musical idols: drummer Elvin Jones, most famous for his work with the fabled John Coltrane Quartet of the 1960s. But John's main touchpoint was Jones's collaboration with organist Larry Young on the latter's 1962 Blue Note album, *Unity*:

> Every time I play I'm paying a tribute to Trane, to Miles, to Bill Evans, people I love and who inspire me, even non-musicians. I feel very sensitive to drummers in general and Elvin in particular, because of what he and Trane did to my head,

opening my eyes to seeing music and rhythm. I knew Elvin loves Hammond organ trios because the first time I heard Larry Young was with Elvin on records with Grant, and with Woody Shaw and Joe Henderson. To hear Larry and Elvin swinging away—oh! I've played with organ trio a lot, even when I lived in the UK I thought of the formation as a nice tribute to Larry too. He's been dead for a long time, but I still miss him.[40]

So, *After The Rain* was ostensibly a tribute to Coltrane, but it also became a tribute to Jones and Young, and the organ trio format in general. Recorded over two days at Clinton Studios (where Miles had laid down parts of *Tutu*), it was another "covers" album (with one semi-original composition), and arguably John's first all-jazz solo recording since 1969's *Extrapolation*.

While the improvisation is at an extremely high level and the album gains from a consistency of sound and tone, it seldom works up any real steam and feels like a retrograde step after *Tokyo Live*. *After The Rain* is also too waltz-heavy and lacks memorable moments. Still, judging by Jones's regular vocal interjections, he seems to be very much enjoying the music.

The album kicks off with a serviceable take on Duke Ellington's up-tempo blues "Take The Coltrane," originally appearing on the 1962 album *Duke Ellington & John Coltrane*. John reimagines Gato Barbieri's "Encuentros," first appearing on the Argentinian saxist's 1973 album *Chapter One*, changing it from a 6/8 tango into waltz time and adding various sections, but his soloing is ungainly and lacks an effective through-line.

The Coltrane classics "Naima" and "Crescent" are more successful, Jones providing some winning dynamics, while John's "Tones For Elvin Jones" is a modified blues in 5/4 with nods to "The Wall Will Fall" and Grant Green's "Lazy Afternoon." Perhaps the slightly lackluster nature of *After The Rain* is best emphasized by a less-than-essential version of "My Favorite Things" (and its incorrect songwriting credit—the CD mistakenly lists Lorenz Hart instead of Oscar Hammerstein II).

John was thrilled to secure Jones on drums for four live dates in France during 1995 and 1996, even if the guitarist essentially had to be a "sideman" for these concerts: "It had to be set up where I'm his employee. He's a legend. Even unknowingly, I couldn't be in a situation that was disrespectful."[41] The gigs generally featured epic, fifteen-minute readings of "My Favorite Things" plus "Naima," Carla Bley's "Sing Me Softly Of The Blues" and "Encuentros." But again, the music at these concerts was somewhat one-dimensional, with very little light and shade, and would have worked better in a club rather than on a festival or concert stage.

During this period, John made the occasional guest appearance playing "In A Silent Way" with Joe Zawinul, who was concurrently moving through Europe with his Syndicate. The Free Spirits—with Chambers back onboard—shared the bill with the Syndicate at London's Royal Festival Hall on October 29, 1995. It was a strangely inert affair, and John's band seemed strikingly insular compared to the cosmopolitan, hot-rodded Syndicate. Even the encore jam session combining the two bands failed to catch fire.

John needed a change. He would soon ditch the organ trio and embark on his most "star-studded," fusion-styled album since 1978's *Johnny McLaughlin Electric Guitarist*.

## *THE PROMISE* (1995)

Don Alias: Percussion
Jim Beard: Keyboards
Dennis Chambers: Drums
Vinnie Colaiuta: Drums
James Genus: Bass guitar
Zakir Hussain: Tabla
Nishat Khan: Sitar, vocals
Yan Maresz: Arranger, acoustic bass guitar, bass guitar
John McLaughlin: Acoustic guitar, electric guitar, keyboards, MIDI guitar
Mark Mondesir: Drums
Pino Palladino: Bass
Mariko Takahashi: Vocals
Jeff Beck: Electric guitar
Michael Brecker: Tenor sax
Joey DeFrancesco: Hammond organ, trumpet
Al Di Meola: Acoustic guitar
Trilok Gurtu: Percussion
Tony Hymas: Keyboards
Paco de Lucía: Acoustic guitar
David Sanborn: Alto sax
Sting: Bass
Recorded at The Blue Note Jazz Club, Tokyo, Japan
Studio Ygmas, Monaco
Tribe Studio, Milan, Italy
Sumit Bernet Studio, Dallas, Texas, United States

Studio Ferber, Paris, France
Clinton Recording, New York City, New York, United States
Mill House Studio, Wiltshire, England
Wessex Studios, London, England
Produced by John McLaughlin and Eddie Kramer ("English Jam")
Released on December 21, 1995

John ended 1995 in one of the busiest periods of his entire career. He had found a new trademark electric guitar sound (with some chorusing via a Sony M7 effects processor, and a stereo output going into two amps) and was financially on an even keel, courtesy of regular touring and healthy album sales with major-label backing. Meanwhile he had separated from Katia Labeque, though he continued to feel very much like a European at his Monte Carlo base, finding much to dislike about the new celebrity culture developing in the United States and England:

> I moved from New York in '82. Frankly, I missed the linguistic diversity of Europe. I suppose I just got fed up of hearing English all the time. I don't come back to England much now. What really pisses me off is this Anglophonic arrogance, this English-speaking domination of the world. I bullshit my way in German, I bullshit my way in Italian . . . and I enjoy that and others enjoy it because it shows you're making an effort to speak their language and accept it and them. England I don't care too much for anymore. London's OK. But elsewhere . . .[42]

Meanwhile the mid-1990s recording studio was becoming a treasure trove of new technologies, with hard-disc recording, looping, and sampling very prevalent, and John was determined to explore these avenues. Indeed, *The Promise* would even flirt with jungle/drum'n'bass, a London-born, hyperactive fusion of techno, acid house, and funk based around drum loops, samples, and vintage synthesizers. It's tempting to draw comparisons with David Bowie, John's near-contemporary and onetime boss, who tapped in to similar soundworlds while making mid-1990s albums *1. Outside* and *Earthling*. John outlined his predilection for drum'n'bass:

> There's a lot of it that's garbage, but there's some very nice things in there such as D*Note, Lemon D and Grooverider. I really enjoy them. I've also got a record by Colonial Cousins with Hariharan and Lezz. What's really amazing to me is that some of these young, English underground people don't really know too much about music. Their musical knowledge is very limited, but it's what they do with

that knowledge that is very interesting and really attracts me. They've got great imagination.[43]

Like Bowie, John risked the scorn of the critics for being a man in his fifties attempting anything outside the accepted norm. But—also like Bowie—there were only partial elements of drum'n'bass incorporated into his new music. Another British "jazz" musician looking into similar areas from somewhat of an outsider's perspective was saxophonist/composer Courtney Pine (and it's a shame John and Pine have never worked together) on albums like *Modern Day Jazz Stories* (1995) and *Underground* (1997).

*The Promise* was also another attempt to reunite some of John's favorite past collaborators:

> For me, this whole record was joy from start to finish. I actually would have liked to reunite Shakti, but I haven't been able to get hold of Shankar for a long time. And the original Mahavishnu Orchestra—that would have been nice, but I gave up on that ten years ago. I was stubborn; I always felt music was stronger than petty feelings, but I was wrong. Originally the holdouts were Jerry Goodman and Jan Hammer, and then Jerry was cool and Billy Cobham wanted to do it, and Rick Laird would have done it. But to hold a grudge for so long, you've got to be really weird.[44]

John would, indeed, assemble a remarkable cast of players from almost every era of his musical life for *The Promise*. David Sanborn made his third guest appearance; Al Di Meola and Paco de Lucia joined John for the first time for nearly thirteen years; Trilok Gurtu returned from the 1988–1992 trio; percussionist Don Alias returned from Miles's *Bitches Brew* sessions in 1969; and there were superstar guest appearances by Sting, Michael Brecker, and Jeff Beck. John revealed he also had wanted to include a live improvisation with Cuban pianist Gonzalo Rubalcaba, but it didn't fit onto the album. (Rubalcaba would go on to dedicate a composition to John, 2007's "Infantil.")

Put simply, John seemed to have his mojo back again, eager to experiment. Nothing was off-limits—Flamenco, jungle, organ jazz, "rock," Indian music, and yet another tribute to Miles ("No Return"). He put a serious dent into his air miles with *The Promise*—it was recorded in no less than nine locations. It was also arguably his first album explicitly designed for CD, a very long collection with interludes and sound effects, playing out like an aural movie:

> From the start, I intended to string these pieces together with certain transitions, specific verses of poetry—a whisper of Dante, a burst of rain, a haiku, chirping

cicadas, a Lorca couplet, temple bells, a 72-second 'English Jam'. It all fell into shape in the mix, done by Max Costa, with whom I always work. Recording is easy if you prepare well. Logistically, this album was tricky—going here, recording there, in the middle of tours, everyone else on tour, too. For the dates with Brecker and Sanborn, I flew from Japan to New York for three days, had sessions on two afternoons, the third day flew back to South Korea. Nutty, but it was that or not have them.[45]

But to what did the title allude (apart from also being the name of a John Coltrane composition from *Live At Birdland*)? John explained its meaning to *The Wire* magazine in March 1996:

> It's life. I've been at rock bottom and now I'm up. Who knows what'll come next? It's the way it goes. You can't expect music to stand still because your life doesn't stand still. It doesn't always reflect your life, doesn't always change like your life changes, but it does change. It's got to. There's always the promise of something new, good or bad. That's what the title means. You don't know what it is, but you know there's the promise of something different around every corner.[46]

Despite its disparate recording dates/locations and huge stylistic range, *The Promise* hangs together superbly, a testament to both Max Costa's engineering and John's production skills. It was rightly seen as a huge return to form, no doubt helped by John's most serious media offensive for years. The cover artwork didn't hurt either, a striking 3-D image put together by Alberto Mayer. *The Promise* was "a valid experiment by a major artist," according to *The Penguin Guide To Jazz On CD*. The audience agreed: thanks to its big-name guests and excellent music, it sold approximately twice as many as John's other 1990s albums right off the bat—around ninety thousand—and reached #4 on the *Billboard* Jazz Chart.

Somehow John also seemed to be tapping in to the cultural zeitgeist. A generation of young British-Asian musicians such as Talvin Singh and Nitin Sawhney, loosely described by the media as being part of the so-called Asian Underground, had emerged as big fans of John's work with Shakti and The Mahavishnu Orchestra. John's groundbreaking fusions of two decades ago were gaining traction with the younger generation.

### Django (John Lewis)    7:24

Recorded at Wessex Studios in London, here was the summit meeting everyone had been waiting to hear: John's first recorded duet with Jeff Beck. John paid

tribute to his friend: "He's number one in that style. A killer. He plays that guitar, man, like nobody I know. I wanted to record 'Django' forever. It's apropos,
written after Django Reinhardt's death, really lyrical, and who better to play it?
It's very slightly modified. It just used to be a little more dainty. We walked in,
plugged in, and we had it so easy. In the end, that what's beautiful about music,
because with people you love and admire, you can go into the unknown. Some
wonderful things happen on that take."[47] And on this John Lewis composition first performed by The Modern Jazz Quartet, the contrasting styles work
a treat—Beck's unreconstructed sound with no effects processing, and John's
highly refined, DI'd, stereo-chorus attack. It's also a very clever arrangement
with Beck investing the famous melody with his usual lyricism and then both
players soloing over the changes (including a brilliant moment at 2:23, when
Beck changes his pick-up mid-lick). Phil Collins was earmarked to play drums
but was busy, so "Django" marked the debut of Mark Mondesir (his surname
roughly translates from West Indian patois as "my desire") on John's music.
Their collaboration would seem a natural fit—Mondesir shared that treasured
Cobham ability to groove hugely while also featuring some serious instrumental
chops. He was born in 1965, the son of St. Lucian parents, who had moved to
London five years earlier. Mondesir was enraptured by music from a very young
age, taking up drums totally by accident at the age of twelve when a school-
teacher thrust some sticks into his hands, tiring of his incessant tapping on his
desk. To his amazement, Mondesir found he was a complete natural. At sixteen,
he was flicking through the radio dials and found a German jazz/rock station:
it was The Mahavishnu Orchestra with Billy Cobham. Mondesir was amazed,
immediately pledging to take the drums seriously as an art form. He also took
great inspiration from Narada Michael Walden, Tony Williams, and particularly Tommy Campbell. Mondesir's career began in earnest in 1984, when, attending one of Ian Carr's London-based Weekend Arts Center workshops, he
met saxophonist Courtney Pine. He then spent a long period in the bands of
Pine, Julian Joseph, Kevin Eubanks, and Steve Williamson, earning plaudits
from Trilok Gurtu, Tony Williams, and Dennis Chambers. Mondesir spoke of
finding himself in the studio recording "Django" with two of his all-time heroes:
"So, I find myself at the studio with John to my left and Jeff to my right. It was
unbelievable to have two of my favorite guitarists on the same session."[48] The
band is completed by Beck's regular touring keyboard player Tony Hymas and
bassist Pino Palladino, famous for his expressive playing for everyone from Gary
Numan to D'Angelo.

## Thelonius Melodius  5:22

This tribute to pianist Thelonious Monk (despite the disappointing misspelling of his Christian name), recorded during a soundcheck at the Blue Note Japan during the *Tokyo Live* sessions, was first played in duet with Chick Corea at the Montreux Jazz Festival in 1981. It begins with elements of 1978's "Phenomenon—Compulsion." At 2:00, John quotes John Coltrane's famous solo from the "Acknowledgement" section of *A Love Supreme*. Both John and DeFrancesco's solos conclude with the main melody from Monk's "Little Rootie Tootie."

## Amy and Joseph  2:28

This short, beguiling piece, written for John's friend and former road manager Joseph D'Anna and his wife, Amy, begins with a verse of Dante's "Divine Comedy," read by Stephanie Bimbi, loosely translating as: "When halfway through the journey of our life/I found that I was in a gloomy wood/Because the path which led aright was lost." John's rich chordal accompaniment suggests both "Reincarnation" and "Mila Repa."

## No Return  7:20

A drum'n'bass loop and snippet of Miles saying, "You ready?" (presumably John's impression of the trumpeter) usher in another classic composition. But its arrangement divides opinion courtesy of a go-go-influenced, drum-machine groove and John's guitar synth (or keyboards?) taking care of the chords. One can only dream of, say, Vinnie Colaiuta and Jason Rebello guesting on this (not to mention Miles), but it's still one of John's most enduring post-1970s compositions, with gorgeous harmonic movement and a winning guest spot from trumpeter Joey DeFrancesco. John's sixteenth-note lick at 4:57 sounds uncannily like one from Jaco's bass solo on Weather Report's 1980 track "Port Of Entry."

## El Ciego  9:10

Written by John in 1990—the title translates as "the blind"—this tremendous piece was originally meant for de Lucia to record solo, but ended up as a reunion of the classic Guitar Trio: "Paco, who I see every year at the holidays, said, 'Juanito, I need a piece for recording.' So I gave him the cassette. Two months later I asked him how he liked it. and he said, 'It's great, but I don't know what you're doing, so I didn't do it.' Paco does read very slowly, but then he plays the stuff marvelously. If he had the score it could have worked, but he likes to figure it out with his ear, which he wasn't able to do. But we both liked the piece, so later we recorded it with Al in Paris."[49] John also experimented with different stereo panning for the three players: "This is the first time we recorded with Paco panned to the middle. Usually, I'm in the middle, and Al's to the left, but the way the melody was, I thought Paco should be in the middle."[50]

## Jazz Jungle   14:45

Percussionist Don Alias shouts his encouragements ("Let's go! Do it!") at the top of yet another tribute to New York City's rich jazz heritage. This hard-driving jazz/rock epic seems very much inspired by John's appearance with the James Genus/Dennis Chambers rhythm section at the Seville Guitar Festival, and the B section also refers to "Pacific Express." According to Stump in *Go Ahead John*, "It seems to be a conscious attempt to recreate the Miles Davis era of *Jack Johnson*." This aspect is very difficult to hear, though John's melody apparently does take some impetus from Joe Zawinul's compositions such as "Directions" and "Gibraltar." It's certainly an epic of collective improvisation, though—"We get this structure but only as an anchor, as a launching pad for . . . delirium, where we can play alone but also play with and over each other, to get up each other's noses."[51] "Jazz Jungle" is the long-overdue collaboration between John and saxophonist Michael Brecker. John explained how they first met in Bill Milkowski's book *Ode To A Tenor Titan*:

> I arrived in New York early January 1969 and found a really good underground scene for young jazz musicians. It consisted primarily of organized jam sessions in various lofts around the city. I recall very clearly the jam where I first met and heard Michael Brecker play. Drummer Barry Altschul had a loft on Bond Street, and I arrived with bassist Dave Holland for the jam. We were in a circle of around eight or nine musicians and basically improvised "round robin" style, one after the other. Michael, who looked no older than nineteen or twenty, was opposite to me, and when he began playing, I was blown away. Even then, Michael had the gift of liberating the listener simply because his playing was already masterful. Of course, from that time on, I became one of his greatest admirers. I continued to follow his career and buy his recordings. On "Jazz Jungle", there was a vibe in the studio that affected every one of us. After this recording, Michael and I became much closer and began spending time together whenever possible. And now, after more than twenty-five years, every time I listen to this track, Michael still blows me away.

John and Brecker remained friends until the saxophonist's death in 2007. Sadly the piece, for all its wholehearted soloing and Chambers's remarkable solidity, is difficult to get through, not helped by a very "roomy" production. It ends very abruptly with a rare Chambers fluff and John's half-serious outburst—"Why did you stop there? When I just got my second breath?"—amid general amusement.

## The Wish    8:39

A charming piece in 9/8 based around a C# tonality, "The Wish" marked the end of John's musical relationship with Gurtu. He rued the direction the percussionist's career would take as the 1990s wore on, saying in 2008: "I think he was listening to his manager, who wanted him to maybe try to reach a bigger audience."[52] The solos are in Lydian mode. At 6:26, John nods to Miles's "Jean Pierre."

## English Jam (Vinnie Colaiuta, John McLaughlin, Sting)    1:12

This brief but potent piece was recorded with Sting and Vinnie Colaiuta during the sessions at Sting's home studio for the excellent version of "The Wind Cries Mary," which appears on the Jimi Hendrix tribute album *In From The Storm*. It was John's first exposure to both players: "Sting's into it. He likes to play. After all these years, we'd never met, so it was a good opportunity. He's not just a pop star, he's very aware."[53] As for Colaiuta, John rated him a "beautiful, crazy drummer. We plugged in and that was it. I mean, Vinnie's unchained. I heard the first ten seconds and called Sting and said I'd just like to use that little bit, and he said 'Yeah!' There's about 15 minutes of it."[54] This is one of the great missed opportunities of *The Promise*—it would have been fascinating to hear more of this jam.

## Tokyo Decadence    0:39

John waxed lyrical about the new beat: "Jungle is brilliant! I took some drum'n'bass tapes and played them to Dennis Chambers. He couldn't believe it. He said: 'Who the fuck is that?' Of course it wasn't anybody playing, nobody could play like that, not even Dennis. But that's the technology now, that's what you can do, and you have to use the technology to its full extent if that's the music you want to play, if you want to do new things. I intend to do plenty of things with this technology."[55] The drum'n'bass beat may also have reminded

John of some of the displaced, double-time grooves laid down by Miles's drummers of the early 1970s: Al Foster put together a proto-jungle beat for "Rated X," while Jack DeJohnette played similar grooves with Miles on pieces such as "What I Say," "Black Satin," and "Funky Tonk." Brief as "Tokyo Decadence" was, John was pleased that the end result was "completely twisted. But without madness or fantasy, music's boring."[56]

### Shin Jin Rui    10:47

The Japanese title loosely translates as "Generation X." This is the third and final David Sanborn guest appearance with John, and he makes another excellent contribution. "Shin Jin Rui" recycles some older John material to impressive effect—the bass vamp is very reminiscent of "Jazz," the descending chords in the B section nod to "New York On My Mind" (revamped for "Blues For L.W."), and at 3:51 we hear the speeded-up chords from "Reincarnation." It's a terrific band performance, with Alias's congas a particular highlight.

### The Peacocks (Jimmy Rowles)    5:53

This gorgeous all-acoustic-guitar version was possibly inspired by the inclusion of pianist Jimmy Rowles's standard on the *Round Midnight* movie soundtrack, with Wayne Shorter memorably playing the melody on soprano sax. But the piece fits perfectly into John's *Time Remembered* soundworld. Maresz plays a five-string acoustic bass guitar (with his low B string apparently tuned down to Bb), while Philippe Loli accompanies John on nylon-string acoustic. John ends this impressive album with two lines from Federico Garcia Lorca's poem "Si Mis Manos Pudieran Deshojar," loosely translating as: "Will it be tranquil and pure/If my fingers could only strip the moon."

## *THE GUITAR TRIO* (1996)

John McLaughlin: Acoustic guitar
Paco de Lucia: Acoustic guitar
Al Di Meola: Acoustic guitar
Recorded May–July 1996 at Real World Studios, England
Produced by John McLaughlin, Paco de Lucia, and Al Di Meola
Released on October 15, 1996 (September 11, 1996, in Japan)

After the reunion of kindred spirits that produced *The Promise*, John took another journey into his past by reforming the fabled *Friday Night In San Francisco* acoustic guitar trio with Di Meola and de Lucia. They had gathered briefly on *The Promise* but hadn't recorded a complete album for thirteen years.

According to Di Meola, the record was the idea of Verve executive Jean-Philippe Allard. All three players initially agreed it was a good one. But despite the best intentions, it became a bit of a trial. It seems no one could even decide on a decent name for the album—it's variously described on streaming platforms as *The Guitar Trio* and simply *Paco de Lucia, Al Di Meola, John McLaughlin*.

They recorded in the so-called Big Room at Peter Gabriel's Real World Studios near Bath. This was a state-of-the-art, residential complex in the English countryside, away from the buzz of the big city but possibly resulting in a sense of cabin fever. *The Guitar Trio* was a completely digital recording, utilizing both Pro-Tools and Logic Audio computer interfaces, but musically kept as organic as possible—all three played mostly nylon-string acoustic guitars, and they move around the stereo spectrum from tune to tune, possibly a hint at the power games that occurred during the recording. Di Meola remembered: "There were just a lot of differences of opinion on so many different issues, mostly from a managerial side, and some musical things, too."[57] There was little or no reverb added, real or digital, though a tiny bit of chorusing is audible on Di Meola's guitar. The trio even utilized the sundry percussion instruments hanging around the studio on a few overdubs.

De Lucia's "La Estiba" makes for a terrific introduction to the album though, with marvelous solos from all three players. John provides three new compositions: the cheerful "Midsummer Night" starts with some vocal clowning, including another Miles impression from John—"You can do it!"—and borrows some chords from "Mattinale." The underwhelming "Letter From India" sounds more Spanish than Indian, and is reminiscent of "Guardian Angels." Paco says, "Nice, eh?" at the end. "Le Monastère dans les Montagnes," inspired by John's stay in a Trappist monastery, is also curiously unmemorable despite his excellent solo.

Also less effective is John and Di Meola's duet on "Manhã de Carnaval" composed by Luiz Bonfá and Antônio Maria, a very literal reading inexplicably shorn of the aspects that made it a crowd-pleaser when played live during 1979 and 1980. De Lucia's absence is marked. Of Di Meola's trio of tunes (all of which are, at the time of writing, by far the album's most listened to on Spotify), the through-composed "Azzura" is the standout. "Perhaps the best thing on the whole album, a rich soundscape that inspires a wonderful opening solo from McLaughlin," was Cook and Morton's verdict in *The Penguin Guide To Jazz On CD.*

The US market was treated to a gatefold vinyl version of *The Guitar Trio*, and the album was another good seller there, getting to #1 on the *Billboard* Jazz chart. But it pales in comparison to the previous two trio albums. The players embarked on a world tour lasting from September to November 1996. The rumours of a rift between Di Meola and the other two were not helped when, at London's Royal Festival Hall on October 24, Al is said to have proclaimed: "Nice to be back someplace where they speak English." Not surprisingly, this attempt at banter did not go down well with de Lucia. A famous photo was printed in the *Guardian* newspaper that emphasized the distance between the performers onstage. Compare that to the picture of camaraderie that emerged from the early 1980s tours.

But somewhere along the way, a *rapprochement* seems to have been brokered—de Lucia later struck a more conciliatory tone: "We are OK, but we're not like three monks. We have strong personalities and sometimes it's difficult. But we can live with it." Di Meola: "It wasn't going great this summer; it was so hard to get used to one another again. I can't begin to tell you the differences in the personalities and the clashes, compromises. It got so bad, it was almost a cancellation, but we returned to our senses and realized we're here to play." John was characteristically philosophical about the inter-band tensions, seeing them as an enriching experience: "As soon as you put human beings together you get some conflict, but what's wrong with it? Existence is chaotic and we're looking to find order. Chaos and conflict are synonymous; personalities clash, but isn't this necessary? In my opinion it's essential to finding something, and maybe the greater the conflict, the greater the creation."[58] (Di Meola could also possibly plead accentuating circumstances—his mother had passed away over the summer, but it isn't known if his bandmates were informed.)

Meanwhile John ended 1996 being pipped by Bill Frisell, John Scofield, and Kenny Burrell in the *Down Beat* Best Guitarist critics' poll. His response was to take off the acoustic guitar for a while and make another excursion into electric jazz/rock.

## THE HEART OF THINGS (1997)

Gary Thomas: Tenor and soprano saxophones, flute
Jim Beard: Synthesizers, acoustic piano
Matthew Garrison: Bass guitar

Dennis Chambers: Drums
John McLaughlin: Electric guitar, acoustic guitar and MIDI guitar
Victor Williams: Percussion
Jean-Paul Celea: Acoustic bass
Recorded at Studio Officine Mechanich, Milan, Italy
Produced by John McLaughlin

As John's thoughts returned to classic jazz/rock, one of the genre's progenitors and John's good friend/onetime boss, Tony Williams, tragically passed away in February 1997 after complications resulting from gall bladder surgery. He was just fifty-four years old. It was a crushing blow that would impact John's life and music over the next few years.

But for now, his album *The Heart Of Things* showcased a new ensemble of the same name and presented five original compositions and one reversion. There were elements of *Electric Dreams* from almost twenty years before, but the main inspiration for the album came via Gary Thomas's saxophone playing. Thomas was yet another Miles connection, playing live with the trumpeter during 1986 and 1987 after a recommendation from Chambers. John also added a storming new bass player: Matthew Garrison. Thomas, Chambers, and Garrison were all a link to M-Base, but John's music on this album was extremely polite in comparison to that genre. *The Heart Of Things* came nearer to the sound of The Zawinul Syndicate, with lots of percussion and distinct "World" and Latin influences.

Garrison, whom John had met while performing with The Syndicate during the summer of 1995, was born in New York City on June 2, 1970. His father was John Coltrane's bassist Jimmy Garrison, his mother, Roberta, a respected dancer and choreographer. Garrison enjoyed a bohemian SoHo upbringing among modern dance shows, concerts, and poetry readings. He moved to Italy after his father's death and started playing bass at fifteen. He was offered Italian citizenship at eighteen but was told he would have to do a year of National Service, so he moved back to the United States to live with his godfather, Jack DeJohnette, in Woodstock for a year. DeJohnette encouraged Matthew to pursue a career in music. The bassist got a scholarship to the Berklee School in Boston for two years beginning in 1989, studying at the same time as future Tribal Tech keyboardist Scott Kinsey. During this time he also became very close to saxophonist Ravi Coltrane, DeJohnette becoming almost like a father to both. Garrison played with The Zawinul Syndicate regularly in the mid-1990s appearing on the 1996 album *My People*. He was also a regular in Steve Coleman's bands, playing on *The Tao of Mad Phat* and *Def Trance Beat*.

Gary Thomas was also a frequent collaborator with Coleman. Born June 10, 1961, in Baltimore, Thomas had established himself in DeJohnette's band Special Edition alongside Greg Osby, Lonnie Plaxico, and Mick Goodrick, while touring with Miles and recording several critically acclaimed solo albums for the JMT label. John was a huge fan of Thomas's *The Kold Kage*, and he found much to admire about his playing: "This guy is really unique. He's taken the Sonny Rollins school up to the nth degree. He's an amazing musician," he told *Jazzwise* in February 2004.

Jim Beard, last to play with John on the 1985 and 1986 Mahavishnu tours, returned on keyboards. He had enjoyed a long, fruitful collaboration with guitarist Mike Stern in the meantime, and had also recorded and toured with Wayne Shorter, Bob Berg, Michael Brecker, and Steely Dan, as well as releasing several solo albums, his 1991 debut *Song Of The Sun* featuring guest spots from both Shorter and Brecker.

*The Heart Of Things* gets off to a promising start with "Acid Jazz"—surely pun intended—with an intro touching on John's composition "Girls With Red Shoes" from the Katia/Marielle Labeque album *Love Of Colours*. It's very noticeable that John doesn't solo until the seven-minute mark, and then only very briefly—Thomas's unclichéd soprano is the main feature. The other outstanding composition from the album is "Fallen Angels," harmonically hinting at both Zawinul's "A Remark You Made" and John's own "Shin Jin Rui."

But the album is weighed down by three overcomplicated, strangely unmemorable pieces, which again nod to John's past. "Seven Sisters" opens with arpeggios that hint at "The Sunlit Path" section from "Trilogy," John tuning his low E string down to a C. Then John and Thomas solo over the chords from the long middle section of "Reincarnation." "Mr. D.C."—not to be confused with Coltrane's "Mr. P.C."—was John's tribute to his drummer, initially with a groove similar to "Jazz" and a nod to Weather Report's "Teen Town." Also thrown in were a weird reference to "The Dance Of Maya" and equally odd Hermeto Pascoal–style flute/piano breakdown. "Healing Hands" was pure Zawinul, mainly courtesy of Beard's synth sounds and the alternating/interchanging 6/8 and 4/4 time signatures. A new version of "When Love is Far Away" closed *The Heart Of Things*, recorded during John's solo spot on the Guitar Trio tour of 1996. It was a delightful, if confusing, closer to an extremely inconsistent album.

*The Heart Of Things* also came with a very underwhelming cover—possibly an ill-conceived pastiche of the Quentin Tarantino film *Reservoir Dogs*—but John's return to jazz/rock was generally well-received, peaking at #4 on the *Billboard* Jazz chart. Despite that, it now seems a very light, underproduced record, short of memorable compositions and with a curious lack of bottom-end, despite the formidable Garrison/Chambers engine room. It's a pleasant, undemanding listen, rather than a vital and challenging project.

It was a very different story in concert, though. The Heart Of Things band was on the road pretty much from September 1997 through May 1998, and they developed and improved John's new material almost beyond recognition. Garrison and Chambers became one of the greatest rhythm section teams of his career, while Thomas proved an able soloist and instrumental foil, also contributing excellent compositions. They keyboard chair on the tour was shared between Beard and Venezuela-born Otmaro Ruiz, of which much more later. The former sometimes caused some scheduling headaches for John, though, despite introducing interesting tune "Social Climate" to the live repertoire.

## *REMEMBER SHAKTI* **(1999)**

John McLaughlin: Guitars, synthesizer
Zakir Hussain: Tabla
Vikku Vinayakram: Ghatam
Hariprasad Chaurasia: Bansuri
Una Metha: Tambura
Produced by John McLaughlin
Recorded on Wednesday, September 24, 1997, at Queen Elizabeth Hall, Oldham; Thursday, September 25, 1997, at Royal Festival Hall, London; Friday, September 26, 1997, at Symphony Hall, Birmingham; and Saturday, September 27, 1997 at Turner Sims Concert Hall, Southampton

A very busy decade for John ended with another trip down memory lane, a rethinking of the Shakti concept. During the summer of 1997 he returned to his concept of fusing North Indian, South Indian, and jazz/rock styles, this time utilizing the electric guitar—with MIDI-assisted "drones"—rather than a steel-string acoustic. (He reported loaning his original Shakti guitar to an acquaintance, and it had got "really destroyed, to my eternal regret.")[59]

Once the idea had formed in John's head, his first port of call was getting in touch with L. Shankar. The violinist had enjoyed a varied career since Shakti's dissolution in the late 1970s, recording with pop artists such as Echo & The Bunnymen, Phil Collins, and Peter Gabriel, and releasing several solo albums in varying styles, from rock to classical. There were rumors he had relocated to Africa. Emails and phone calls went unanswered. Finally, Shankar called John back, but he was in the middle of a press conference in Paris. And it was one day before the beginning of the tour.

So, for the British sojourn (for which the group reportedly had only one three-hour rehearsal), John, Vikku, and Zakir were joined by flautist Hariprasad Chaurasia, who had appeared on the 1984 *Mahavishnu* album and also on Zakir's *Making Music*. John decided to record the concerts, regardless of any label interest: "I spoke about the idea of taping the shows with Zakir during rehearsals. 'We may never play in this formation again, so wouldn't it be nice to have a souvenir for ourselves?' He thought it was a great idea too. It's a nice idea to have memories because as time goes by, you don't know if things will come together in this way again. So, we rented an (eight-track) recorder and taped the shows. Upon listening to the playback, we thought that this was really amazing music."[60] The tour also gained significance by taking place during the fiftieth anniversary of Partition, when the British Raj was dissolved, and India and Pakistan became independent dominions.

Universal expressed an interest to release the tapes and also suggested a new name for the group: the band and album became the rather oddly titled *Remember Shakti*. And it's a good thing John had the foresight to record these concerts because *Remember Shakti* is an excellent album, despite its excessive length. The absence of Shankar and John's decision to play electric guitar—necessitating more chordal/textural work—removes some kinetic energy from the original Shakti but ensures the music is both more meditative and harmonically interesting. The recording quality is excellent, aided by the natural ambience of the relatively large concert halls. John delivers nothing less than a masterclass of creative improvisation and empathetic accompaniment. The addition of Chaurasia on bansuri (wooden flute) also gives the music an epic, otherworldly quality.

His composition "Chandrakauns" kicks off the album, delivering over half an hour of exquisite music (despite the fact that John is completely absent), suspending time, going way beyond words. Chaurasia's other composition, "Mukti," is almost twice as long and based on a Hindustani raga leaning heavily on the whole-tone scale, but not a single note is wasted.

John decided to include three older works for the album and tour: "The Wish" starts with his superb unaccompanied five-minute solo, connecting the blues with Eastern modalities and drawing on rhythmic patterns similar to "Florianapolis" and "Guardian Angels." "Lotus Feet" is exquisite; John's guitar is rich and full of body, and there are a few fascinating moments—Chaurasia seems to enter a few beats too late with his main melody at 1:54, and John apparently adds a few to compensate. On the delightful "Zakir," another duet with Chaurasia, John's ingenious comping hints at "When Love Is Far Away."

The officially released *Way Of Beauty* DVD was an essential companion piece for this special album. Meanwhile John's decade of prolific musicmaking ended in surreal fashion when his most famous band received a surprising namecheck from one of the biggest pop stars on the planet. During her television interview on *Larry King Live* in 1999, Madonna was asked about the sort of role her older brothers had played during her formative years. She explained: "They were into the whole LSD drug culture and The Mahavishnu Orchestra." (In *Power, Passion & Beauty*, Koloksy mocks her for saying "The *Maharishi* Orchestra," which she clearly does *not* say.)

John looked back on a decade of intensive touring and a small but stellar pool of classic compositions—"Hijacked," "Mother Tongues," "Mila Repa," "Fallen Angels," "Qué Alegría," "No Return," "Shin Jin Rui," "The Wish"—as well as some memorable cover versions. He had also reconvened with two of the original Shakti line-up, and he would return to that fusion of East and West in the opening years of the 2000s.

**7**

# THE 2000s

From *The Heart Of Things Live*
to *Five Peace Band Live*

## THE HEART OF THINGS: LIVE IN PARIS (2000)

John McLaughlin: Electric guitar
Dennis Chambers: Drums
Gary Thomas: Saxophones and flute
Matthew Garrison: Bass
Otmaro Ruiz: Keyboards
Victor Williams: Percussion
Produced by John McLaughlin
Recorded at La Cigale, Paris, France, on November 4–5, 1998
Released in Europe on March 3, 2000
Released in the United States on July 11, 2000

As John entered the new millennium, he seemed to have more and more in common with his friend and colleague Joe Zawinul; he would never again return to "acoustic jazz," and he would increasingly gear his music and career toward Europe. While he continued to enjoy a sizeable, loyal following in Britain and America, his chances of healthy radio play or substantial sales in those two territories were becoming ever slimmer since he played neither "smooth" nor "mainstream" jazz.

But he was anything but disheartened. John's first release of the 2000s was arguably the greatest live album of his career, a seriously underrated collection ripe for reappraisal, a situation not helped by its absence on streaming platforms at the time of writing. The Heart Of Things band had been hotting up throughout 1998, and by the last few months of the year, it was a juggernaut of a live unit. The Garrison/Chambers rhythm section was a classic and new keyboard player Otmaro Ruiz was bringing new colors and an effervescent soloing style to the table. Thankfully Verve Records were onside, too, and recorded two consecutive nights at Paris's La Cigale during November 1998.

There are a few reasons why *The Heart Of Things: Live In Paris* is so special—first, the heartfelt tribute to Tony Williams, essentially a once-in-a-generation drum solo from Chambers, bookended by a beguiling ballad. Then its sumptuous mix—it flies out of the speakers, leaving the studio material in the dust. The call/response sections are thrilling, and John digs in with some brilliant solos, frequently adding a ring modulator for added spice.

Then there was the addition of Venezuelan keyboardist Ruiz. Born June 27, 1964, in Caracas, he briefly set his sights on becoming a biologist before turning to music full-time, moving to Los Angeles and playing with Frank Gambale, Gino Vannelli, Dianne Reeves, Arturo Sandoval, Alain Caron, Herb Alpert, Yes's Jon Anderson, and Alex Acuna. He was a much more vibrant soloist than Beard, favoring the acoustic piano and Mini Moog, and he brought more subtlety to his comping. John remembered the band's reaction to first playing with Ruiz: "We were rehearsing in Nice, France, and after we ran down the very first tune, Dennis (Chambers) walked over and said, 'Jim who?' Otmaro Ruiz—killer, wonderful."[1]

Strangely, the least-successful track, "Seven Sisters," opens the album, John and Thomas's solos sounding unusually restrained. "Fallen Angels" is a wonderful update, though, featuring Ruiz's panoramic synths and ingenious dynamics from Chambers. On "Acid Jazz," Thomas demonstrates his unique approach to rhythm while Williams's percussion flies across the stereo spectrum and John plays his most raucous solo since the mid-1980s, even quoting Hendrix's "Foxy Lady." The latest version of "Mother Tongues," with Chambers's blockbusting beats and some remarkable solos, is a fairly astonishing band performance and surely the match of anything John released during the 1970s.

But the really stunning selections of the album are the new tunes. Thomas's composition "The Divide," originally appearing on *The Kold Kage*, is arguably the highlight. (In *Follow Your Heart*, Kolosky describes it as "ugly"—dark and complex, yes, but majestic and beguiling too.) Chambers delivers the goods with an epochal solo on "Tony" in tribute to the drummer he saw playing with Miles in Baltimore when he was just eight years old: "That was brutal, man. That stuff was so far over my head that I didn't know what I was listening to! But I knew it was something great."[2] Chambers's solo begins and closes with a press roll, another tribute to Williams: "He would always open his shows with both a press and open roll to warm up his hands." (Chambers also reports that he generally prefers to play yellow drums due to Williams's famous yellow Gretsch USA Custom kit.)[3]

Hampered by a lack of promotion outside Europe, *Live In Paris* reached just #25 on the *Billboard* Jazz chart, a disappointing performance for arguably John's most consistent work since *Electric Dreams*. He was very fond of the Heart Of Things period, though he wasn't sure which album he loved more, studio or concert: "They're two paintings from the same epoch. They are both meaningful to me. The fact that this event happened and Otmaro (Ruiz) came in almost makes the second more attractive to me. It's live and it's very spontaneous. It was a very special night," he told *JazzTimes* in its July/August 2016 issue.

However, he characteristically refused to rest on his laurels—John disbanded The Heart Of Things band at the end of 1998 and subsequently turned his back on electric jazz/rock for a few years.

## *REMEMBER SHAKTI: THE BELIEVER* (2001)

John McLaughlin: Guitar
Zakir Hussain: Tabla
U Srinivas: Mandolin
V Selvaganesh: Kanjira and ghatam
Produced by John McLaughlin
Recorded live during the 1999 European Tour
Released on June 9, 2001

John's Remember Shakti project had been a hit with live audiences around the world, and as a result the group toured every summer between 1999 and 2001. This time, they didn't leave anything to chance: the 1999 European trip was recorded in its entirety, and selected tracks were released a few years later as *The Believer* (a response to John's 1984 composition "The Unbeliever"?).

The album benefited from its injection of younger players and three substantial new compositions from John. A major find was U. Srinivas, who came in on electric mandolin. Born Uppalapu Srinivas in Palakollu, Andhra Pradesh, India, on February 28, 1969, he was a child prodigy of Carnatic (South Indian) music, picking up the mandolin at the age of five. His family moved to Chennai, and he graduated to an electric five-string mandolin (tuned C-G-C-G-C, unlike the usual acoustic eight-strings tuned GG-DD-AA-EE) to better facilitate the sustained notes so intrinsic to South Indian classical music. But Srinivas also became a student and fan of Western pop, rock, and jazz, bringing these influences to the table when collaborating with artists as varied as ambient guitarist/producer Michael Brook and composer Michael Nyman.

V. Selvaganesh (the son of Shakti's Vikku Vinayakram) came in on *kanjira*, a South-Indian steel frame drum, and *ghatam*. He was born in Chennai on December 28, 1966. Another child prodigy, he became a star student at his grandfather's music school before making his performing debut at the age of ten. As he began to participate in fusion, jazz, blues, Flamenco, folk, and Latin sessions, he augmented his setup with various cymbals and a bass drum.

John's three compositions are the standouts on *The Believer*: "5 In The Morning, 6 In The Afternoon" sets out the band's stall very well, a deceptively simple melody line over a C pedal point in 11/4, but with many rhythmic surprises and some bluesy soloing from John. Srinivas's solo is less inspired and seriously outstays its welcome, also hampered by a strange slapback-echo effect.

"Anna" is a traditional raga in a nine-beat cycle, with various modes superimposed over a C tonality. John finds endless ways to ramp up the interest, from palm harmonics to ingeniously voiced chords. It's a masterclass in playing over one chord, one of his greatest recorded solos. The funky "Finding The Way" has echoes of "Are You The One?," "Get Down And Sruti," and "Honky Tonk Haven." Zakir's "Ma No Pa," a tribute to his father, Ustad Alla Rakha, sees John add R'n'B and jazz comping and even a quote from "Layla." On Srinivas's "Maya," the composer's mandolin sounds uncannily like a fretless bass guitar at times, but the composition fails to create much interest despite some lightning-fast soloing.

*The Believer*'s excessive length and sometimes less-than-essential musicianship make it a difficult listen. Srinivas's tone is rather weak and badly recorded, and there's an undercooked, insubstantial feel to the album, despite some of John's finest playing of the 2000s. But the ecstatic audience reaction is a testament to the importance and relevance of this project.

Meanwhile, in the late fall of 2000, John made a rare onscreen appearance as a talking head in Mike Dibb's documentary *The Miles Davis Story*. He was persuaded to appear by his old friend Ian Carr, who also served as music consultant and chief interviewer on the film. John spoke candidly and with great humor about Miles's modus operandi in the studio, clearly reveling in reminiscing about his friend and mentor. Dibb's documentary was shown on Channel 4 in the UK during 2001 and later released on DVD, earning a Royal Television Society award and an International Emmy.

# REMEMBER SHAKTI: SATURDAY NIGHT IN BOMBAY (2001)

John McLaughlin: Guitar
Zakir Hussain: Tabla
U Srinivas: Mandolin
V Selvaganesh: Kanjira, ghatam, mridangam
Shankar Mahadevan: Vocal
Debashish Bhattacharya: Hindustani slide guitar
Sivamani: Drums and percussion
Bhavani Shankar: Dholak and pakhawaj
Roshan Ali: Dholak
Aziz: Dholak
Taufiq Qureshi: Def, dafli, and percussion
Shiv Kumar Sharma: Santur
A.K Pallanivel: Tavil
Recorded on December 8 and 9, 2000
Released on June 19, 2001

They say strike while the iron is hot—*Remember Shakti* and *The Believer* had sold very well outside the UK and America, and there was demand for another live album. The opportunity arose to record two special concerts in Bombay (now Mumbai) on December 8 and 9, 2000, and they were combined to create *Saturday Night In Bombay* (the title, of course, a reference to *Friday Night In San Francisco*, the revolutionary 1981 John/de Lucia/Di Meola guitar trio album).

John took a more supportive role than he had in recent years, content to lay the groundwork for other soloists, the core four-piece band now augmented by various guest musicians. The formidable Shankar Mahadevan was the first vocalist to be used by Remember Shakti, soon to become a very important collaborator for John. A singer with huge range and presence, he was born in Mumbai on March 3, 1967. He learned both Hindustani and Carnatic music at a very young age, studying the *vina* under Shri Lalitha Venkataraman and also developing a taste for jazz. Mahadevan gained early fame as a pop star when his 1998 album, *Breathless*, topped the charts. He had also composed music for Bollywood films and appeared as an actor before getting the call from John about guesting with Remember Shakti in Mumbai.

John's irresistible "Luki," named for his son Luke, was reminiscent of "1 Nite Stand" and "Florianapolis," a superb fusion of Indian, jazz, and world sounds. "Shringar" was a spellbinding vehicle for its composer and santur player Shiv Kumar Sharma, a raga in D. John plays some uncharacteristically muted lead lines at 24:53, reminiscent of Di Meola. The album was rounded off with Srinivas's "Giriraj Sudha" and Zakir's "Bell'Alla," uplifting pieces heavily featuring Mahadevan's vocals and Hindustani slide guitarist Debashish Bhattacharya. Selvaganesh even added some drum kit on the latter.

*Saturday Night In Bombay* was better recorded than its predecessor and also benefited greatly from his guests, particularly Mahadevan. Zakir was particularly excited about the group's future, claiming that there was a lot more to come. John also expressed a hope that the band would continue beyond his demise, predicting—tongue firmly in cheek—that another Westerner might take his place once he popped his clogs!

## THIEVES AND POETS (2003)

John McLaughlin: Acoustic guitar
Pommeriggi Musicali di Milano, conducted by Renato Rivolta with featured soloists:
- Paul Meyer: Clarinet
- Viktoria Mullova: Violin
- Matt Haimovitz: Cello
- Philippe Loli: Guitar
- Bruno Frumento: Timpani

The Aighetta Quartet:
- Olivier Fautrat: Acoustic guitar
- Francois Szonyi: Acoustic guitar
- Alexandre Del Fa: Acoustic guitar
- Philippe Loli: Acoustic guitar
- Helmut Schartlmueller: Acoustic bass guitar

Produced by John McLaughlin

During the summer of 2002, John was invited by the French Cultural Association to play a few concerts on La Réunion, an island in the Indian Ocean near Madagascar. He took the opportunity to form a four-piece fusion band (essentially a forerunner to The 4th Dimension). Mark Mondesir, last to work with John in 1996, took the drum chair, and his brother Michael came in on bass. An experienced, versatile player, Michael had toured and recorded with Jason Rebello, Billy Cobham, Django Bates, and Lewis Taylor. John recruited fellow

Yorkshireman Gary Husband to play keyboards and occasional drums, a musician who would soon become a very crucial collaborator.

Born June 14, 1960, Husband was a prodigious talent, equally proficient on piano and drums. In his formative years, he played concertos and also big-band drums with The Syd Lawrence Orchestra, before becoming a key jazz/rock player for artists such as Billy Cobham, Jack Bruce, Gary Moore, and Barbara Thompson. He enjoyed a fruitful collaboration with Allan Holdsworth, touring regularly with the guitarist and appearing on the classic albums *Metal Fatigue*, *Secrets*, *Hard Hat Area*, and *Wardenclyffe Tower*. Between 1988 and 1993, he had also been a full-time member of jazz/funk/pop band Level 42. John spoke about tracking Husband's career with Holdsworth:

> I met Gary, it must have been '91 or '92—and of course I'd been to see him and Allan whenever they were in town or when I was in their town. Allan, he's just an amazing guitarist, he's special. So I'd been listening to Gary on drums for some time, and then we started to hang here and there when I was with Dennis [Chambers], because they've been tight for a while. We were hanging out one day and Gary said, 'I want to send you a CD,' and he sent me a piano CD which was the one of Allan Holdsworth music, which is wonderful. (*The Things I See: Interpretations Of The Music Of Allan Holdsworth*). He's really an outstanding player.[4]

Later in the summer of 2002, John was invited by his old friend Jeff Beck to guest during his three-night Royal Festival Hall residency in London, celebrating forty years in the music business. John summarily appeared on September 14, playing on "Django" and the *Blow By Blow* classic "Scatterbrain." "My hero," Beck said to the audience as John left the stage after a memorable fifteen minutes of music.

After an intensive period of touring with Remember Shakti and the two attendant live albums, John slowly found himself returning to the acoustic guitar. His main pursuit of late 2002 was putting together a new concerto. Originally titled *Europa* and commissioned in the late 1980s, the Deutsche Kammerphilharmonie Bremen chamber ensemble toured the work briefly in the early 1990s. John reworked *Europa* for symphony orchestra, adding Paco de Lucia on guitar and performing it for five nights with the Orchestra d'Paris during the Gulf War: "There was also a war going on between the orchestra and conductor! Paco and I really suffered those nights, when you go to rehearsals and hear things not quite right—the brass section is out, the percussion, the flute. . . . 'Maestro, stop, please,' we have to say. 'Later, later, later. . . .' We had to go and speak to the musicians ourselves, it was such a shame."[5]

The piece was then put on the shelf for a while. But in 2001, John received an invitation from Jean-Christophe Maillot, choreographer of the Ballets de Monte-Carlo, to present it again. John decided to add five soloists and compose some new music: "It's a very big work. It's basically a piece for guitar and symphony orchestra but there are five soloists—two guitars, violin, cello and clarinet. It's maybe three days' work for Mozart but three years' work for me, just so much work!"[6]

This three-part piece became the centrepiece of the *Thieves And Poets* album, but John decided to add four tribute pieces (for Bill Evans, Herbie Hancock, Gonzalo Rubalcaba, and Chick Corea) to flesh out the CD, performed with the Aighetta Quartet, returning from *Time Remembered* and "The Peacocks."

### Thieves and Poets, Pt. 1    12:32

The first movement of the concerto is a sort of requiem for wartime Europe, with a trumpeter playing The Last Post at 0:32, echoed by the orchestra. There are hints of *The Mediterranean Concerto* at 2:28, and violinist Viktoria Mullova solos effectively at 4:12 and then intermittently throughout the movement.

### Thieves and Poets, Pt. 2    8:15

The opening revisits "Blues For L.W.," with hints of Maurice Ravel's *Rhapsodie Espagnol Pt. 1* in its use of oboes and clarinets. At 1:33, John inserts a few "shock" chords with voicings similar to Gil Evans's work. The piece then nods toward Stravinsky's "The Rite Of Spring," "Giant Steps," and especially "Goodbye Pork Pie Hat" at 4:49. This wonderful section is the album's standout and one of John's greatest compositional achievements.

### Thieves and Poets, Pt. 3    5:38

The most progressive, combustive section of the concerto, part three contains elements of Stravinsky, Leonard Bernstein's "West Side Story," and "Mercury" from Gustav Holst's *The Planets*. The brass section also channels John Williams's *Star Wars* soundtrack and jazzy film-noir thrillers of the 1940s.

### My Foolish Heart (Ned Washington, Victor Young)    5:03

Dedicated to Chick Corea, this has a very different mood to the version on *Johnny McLaughlin Electric Guitarist*. It's in "straight" 4/4, but John can't resist taking some chances during his reading of the melody, including a strikingly "out" note at 1:26.

## The Dolphin (Luiz Eça) 4:16

This piece, dedicated to pianist Gonzalo Rubalcaba and given a gentle bossanova treatment, was first played by John in duet with Jonas Hellborg in 1987. "The Dolphin" was a signature piece for saxophonist Stan Getz. Composer Luiz Eça was a Rio de Janeiro–born pianist who died in 1992.

## Stella By Starlight (Washington, Young) 4:27

Dedicated to Herbie Hancock, this sticks very closely to Miles Davis's 1964 arrangement of the Washington/Young classic, as heard on the famous *Complete Concert* double album alongside Hancock, George Coleman, Tony Williams, and Ron Carter.

## My Romance (Lorenz Hart, Richard Rodgers) 4:09

The album ends with a romantic, uplifting tribute to Bill Evans. John's short solo is transcribed in his book *Improvisations*, along with three other solos from *Thieves And Poets*.

*Thieves And Poets* is a rewarding, enriching forty-five minutes of music, and yet another interesting career detour for John. It's also a subtle progression from both *The Mediterranean Concerto* and *Time Remembered*. The album benefits from John's relatively "dry" acoustic guitar and the general lack of reverb throughout. It was a reasonable success, hitting #20 on the *Billboard* Jazz chart but not receiving the same kind of media attention *The Mediterranean Concerto* had enjoyed. One reason for that might have been the sudden interest in John's 1970s work. During October 2003, Columbia/Legacy released Miles's *The Complete Jack Johnson Sessions*, overseen by Bob Belden and Michael Cuscuna. It was a chance to hear John tearing it up on those fabled sessions, unedited and unadorned. He burned brightly on "Johnny Stratton" and alternate takes of "Right Off" and "Honky Tonk."

But not everybody was happy with this monumental release, particularly original producer Teo Macero: "It's a piece of shit. I'm so discouraged by these greedy guys at Sony putting out all these alternate takes and all this crap. Miles would never have allowed this stuff to be released. He didn't want any shit out that wasn't representative of him. I swear to God, if Miles were alive today, he'd kill every fuckin' one of 'em!"[7] Macero apparently saw the project as an "undoing" of all his careful editing work with Miles on the original albums: "It was all a process of searching for something . . . and Miles didn't even know what it was he was looking for—so it took a while to get there."[8]

Meanwhile, in March 2004, John's music also got the box-set treatment—*The Montreux Concerts* contained seventeen complete performances recorded between 1974 and 1999, taking in The Mahavishnu Orchestra mark 2, Shakti, One Truth Band, the John/Chick Corea duet, Mahavishnu mark 4, John/de Lucia duo, Free Spirits, Heart Of Things, and Remember Shakti. John was thrilled to be asked by Montreux Festival MD Claude Nobs to select the material: "The first set he did was Miles (*The Complete Miles Davis At Montreux 1973–1991*, released in 2002), and he's doing me second! I am honoured, truly honoured."[9]

John also issued his first guitar instruction DVD in 2004. *This Is The Way I Do It* was a fascinating, informative roundup of his improvisational techniques and thought processes. Later that same year, Jeff Beck embarked on a UK tour featuring not one but three frequent John collaborators, including Jan Hammer on keyboards. And they opened every concert with "Resolution." Hammer loved these gigs—"Mark and Mike Mondesir were complete Mahavishnu freaks. They knew every note of Mahavishnu or what I had done."[10] Beck loved them, too: "Just to stand there and play that song to 3,500 people in the Royal Albert Hall was great. It was over in a flash."[11]

Meanwhile, interest in the original Mahavishnu Orchestra was growing. In February 2005, the all-acoustic Los Angeles Guitar Quartet won a Classical Crossover Grammy for their album *Guitar Heroes*, featuring a tribute to John called "We Know You Know (Reverie For Mahavishnu)." Later that year, a tribute CD called *Visions Of A Mounting Apocalypse* was released on Tone Center Records. It featured a rhythm section of Vinnie Colaiuta, Kei Eckhardt, and Mitch Forman, a myriad of guest guitarists and Jerry Goodman on violin. Then, a month later, an event called "Vishnu-Fest" ran between July 12–14 at New York City's Cutting Room with a house band including drummer Gregg Bendian and keyboard player Steve Hunt, plus guest guitarists. Then, on January 27, 2006, in Darmstadt, Germany, Billy Cobham joined the HR Big Band, conducted and arranged by Colin Towns, for a night of Mahavishnu covers. The concert was later released on the IN+OUT label.

It seemed the resurgence of interest in John's electric jazz/rock work of the 1970s was only increasing from month to month. He did the decent thing and returned to the genre for his next—and final—Verve album.

## *INDUSTRIAL ZEN* (2006)

Dennis Chambers: Drums
Vinnie Colaiuta: Drums
Mark Mondesir: Drums
Marcus Wippersberg: Drums
Hadrien Feraud: Bass guitar
Matthew Garrison: Bass guitar
Tony Grey: Bass guitar
Gary Husband: Drums, keyboards
Zakir Hussain: Tabla
Eric Johnson: Guitar
Shankar Mahadevan: Vocals
John McLaughlin: Chant, drum programming, guitar, synthesizer
  programming
Bill Evans: Saxophone
Ada Rovatti: Saxophone
Otmaro Ruíz: Synthesizer, synthesizer programming
Recorded at The Cutting Room Studios, Under the Bed Studios, Tony Grey
  Studio, and Winsome Farm Studio, New York City; Metropolis Studios,
  London; Mediastarz Studio, Monaco, Monte Carlo; Saucer Sound Stu-
  dio, Austin, Texas; Otmatic Sound and Beatnik Studio, California
Produced by John McLaughlin
Released on May 22, 2006

John had hinted to *Jazzwise* magazine in February 2004 about his plans for a return to challenging jazz/rock on *Industrial Zen*: "I'm hoping to have Jan Garbarek on it—we'll see if it can be worked out. This one will really annoy the critics, it's going to be wild!" Garbarek didn't show (but Bill Evans did, reuniting with John for the first time since 1986), but it was certainly wild and woolly, ten years on from *The Promise* and returning to that album's mixture of high-profile guest appearances and an unashamedly eclectic blend of styles.

There was also a pressing context for John. The album was his response to an article that appeared in *The New Yorker* in early 2000s about jazz/rock and its related styles, which contained the memorable line: "Thank God this pestilence is dead"! John defended his endless pursuit of "fusion," come hell or high water: "This way of playing is part of me. I feel I'm going forward but my past is there too. . . . *Industrial Zen* is very much part of my history, part of my future too, and part of my present."[12]

John was again railing against conservatism in jazz, and had the radio-friendly sounds of Larry Carlton, Lee Ritenour, Mark Whitfield, and Russell Malone in his sights: "There has been this huge retrospective look back to those warm '60s sounds of Wes Montgomery. Guitar records . . . are all going the same way."[13] Meanwhile, John had hit upon his own latest signature electric guitar sound as he approached his mid-sixties, and it was anything but "conservative"—a relatively "angry" tone, with fuzz, a little delay, and lots of whammy bar, possibly influenced by Jeff Beck and Scott Henderson.

John was developing his composing chops, too, and entering a very prolific period. *Industrial Zen* was entirely "mapped out" on computer, with John laying down dummy guitar synthesizer and programmed drum parts (some of which would survive on the final master) before being presented to the musicians for their input, a process akin to drawing over tracing paper. Hard-disk recording was a new way for John to organize sounds: "What you can call the art of noise is, I think, an aspect of music that I began to explore with *Industrial Zen*, but I would like to continue looking at. Certain sounds that you would not normally call musical sounds, when used in a particular way, evoke a reaction that can only be called musical. A kind of emotive reaction."[14]

There was also an electrifying new bassist in tow, the latest "new Jaco" in a long line of wunderkinds running from Hellborg to Di Piazza: Frenchman Hadrien Feraud. He had sent John a demo CD via his friend Christian Pegand, and John was thrilled, contacting him only three days after receiving the disc. John then sent Feraud two mp3 tracks to learn, "For Jaco" and "Senor C.S.," the latter, of course, John's tribute to Carlos Santana. John was stunned by Feraud: "We played and we recorded and, for me, he's the new Jaco. He's twenty-two now, it's terrible! And he doesn't even read music, but he's got amazing ears. Harmonically, I say, 'Do you know this chord?' and he says, 'Yeah, yeah, yeah,' or 'Let me hear it,' and boom! He's got it. Amazing, like Wes Montgomery. Incredible."[15]

*Industrial Zen* was John's sixth and last album for Verve/Universal. It was also the beginning of his instantly recognizable modern jazz/rock sound, with airtight production; driving, ever-exploratory drums; sundry percussion; lots of "straight" sixteenth notes; and keyboard stabs. But sadly, there is very little light and shade here, few memorable compositions, and the album on the whole has not dated well. There's a fidgety, hyperactive quality to this music—themes appear and disappear without taking root, and *Industrial Zen* is the first record of John's career that needs an arranger. One wonders if his new composition methods were too rigid. In addition, too many of the musicians are interchangeable, with the exception of John, Evans, and Eric Johnson. The drummers are hard to identify, with similar kit tunings and styles—a strange state of affairs considering the calibre of players. Most worryingly, there are few memorable guitar moments from John during this period.

Still, Feraud makes an auspicious debut on "For Jaco," showcasing a superb tone and even closing with a little tribute to "Continuum." "New Blues Old Bruise" comes with a disappointingly humdrum Eric Johnson guitar solo and some richly chorded vocal samples inspired by Take 6: "I've been a fan since they began but my budget didn't extend to hiring them. So I did a tremendous amount of work in programming to get the sound of voices with some feeling."[16] Elsewhere, Chambers, Zakir, and John generate some heat on "Dear Dalai Lama"—John claimed he was trying to re-create the rapport between the three musicians during their gig at the Crossroads Festival in 2004. And "Senor C.S." at least has a pleasant melody and a relatively nuanced arrangement. But it's a long time coming.

Buoyed by a concerted media assault from John, though, *Industrial Zen* was a critical and commercial success, reaching #14 on the *Billboard* US Jazz Albums chart. In his five-star *Down Beat* review, Ken Micallef commented that "this brilliant collective plays as a single unit. . . . This is a case of Indian musicians using their extraordinary skills to explore US fusion, giving the now 70-year-old guitarist an amazing platform for compositional/improvisational development. This is a landmark recording, marked by detail, subtlety and extraordinarily moving performances." John Fordham also awarded the album five stars out of five in his *Guardian* review: "This boiling new set sounds as if it's driven at least as much by cutting-edge Indian crossover musicians as by McLaughlin himself. . . . This is 99% an absolute cracker, and not just for guitar nuts either."

John also received a celebrity endorsement from one of his best friends: "*Industrial Zen* came out and the next week Chick [Corea] called me and he said, 'Damn, this record is beautiful. . . . Can I borrow this bassist (Feraud)?'"[17] Feraud did indeed tour with Corea soon after *Industrial Zen*'s release.

Meanwhile, there were more echoes from John's past when Jack DeJohnette, organist Larry Goldings, and John Scofield revisited the Lifetime songbook on the Trio Beyond's *Saudades* album for ECM Records and subsequent tour. John: "I ran into Scofield . . . and he told me, 'Man I've been learning your tunes, they're so hard!'"[18]

# *FLOATING POINT* (2008)

John McLaughlin: Guitar synthesizer, guitar
Hadrien Feraud: Bass guitar
Louis Banks: Keyboards
Ranjit Barot: Drums
Sivamani: Percussion, konnakol
George Brooks: Soprano saxophone
Debashish Bhattacharya: Hindustani slide guitar
Shashank Subramanyam: Bamboo flute
Shankar Mahadevan: Voice
U. Rajesh: Electric mandolin
Naveen Kumar: Bamboo flute
Niladri Kumar: Sitar
Produced by John McLaughlin
Recorded in April 2007 at AM Studios, Chennai, India
Released on May 20, 2008

John was once again without a major label in February 2007 when his contract with Universal expired. With hindsight, it's easy to see his reaction to this as being incredibly prescient, a harbinger of the music industry's forthcoming travails, attacked from both sides by free downloads and the streaming revolution: "I'm very happy not to be with (Universal) anymore, and it's a shame, because I'm going to have to put records out my own way, but I'd much rather do it, because the labels are like my 360 guitar synthesizer system in the '70s, with six Mini Moogs, one for each string—they're like an unwieldy elephant. It's like we're back to E.F. Schumacher's *Small Is Beautiful*. You have to be fluid and spontaneous."[19]

John's solution was Abstract Logix. Led by founder/president Souvik Dutta, they were a small but ambitious jazz/rock record label who had released two of 2006's best fusion discs—guitarist Alex Machacek's *(Sic)* and keyboardist Scott Kinsey's *Kinesthetics*—to excellent sales and good media take-up. Most importantly, the label seemed to understand John's aesthetic and his commitment to producing progressive jazz/rock more.

John had stockpiled a lot of new material and didn't waste time planning his new album. He invited collaborations from young Indian musicians on *Floating Point*, as he had become aware of a new wave of players who were influenced as much by modern rock music as they were by Shakti and The Mahavishnu Orchestra: "These guys are like the Young Lions of India. They buy all the records and they go on YouTube and MySpace and they're really checking out everybody all the time. They're part of this global culture that exists now through the internet. And if I can bring people's attention to these wonderful players, then so much the better."[20]

Drummer Ranjit Barot would become a key collaborator for John over the next fifteen years. Born in Mumbai in 1959, Barot grew up steeped in Indian classical music, his mother being the renowned Kathak dancer, Sitara Devi. At twelve years old, he moved over to the Western drum set, inspired by American jazz and rock, and by 1980 he was performing in jazz and fusion bands alongside some of the world's biggest names. He moved into soundtrack composition and also joined Ravi Shankar's ensemble, during which time John first heard his playing.

*Floating Point* was recorded at AM Studios in Chennai, southeast India, a world-class facility owned by John's close friend and Bollywood music magnate A. R. Rahman. John marveled at its 380-square-foot control room and a 1,300-square-foot live room: "It's a fabulous environment with a beautiful Neve 88R mixing board, a perfect sound system and PowerMac G5s all over the place, as well as engineers that know Logic inside and out."[21]

John used guitar synthesis a lot on the album, as much as he had since the mid-1980s. "I spent seven months in India, and due to baggage restrictions, I opted to take only the Godin Freeway (guitar synth). I like its neck and fingerboard; as well as the fact that it's lighter than other guitars, without sacrificing the sustain." He connected his Freeway's MIDI out to a Roland GI-20 USB interface and linked it to an Apple Power Mac G5 running Apple Logic Pro 7 with Emagic's ES2 synthesizer plug-in and AmpliTube 2 for amp modeling. "I used one synth-guitar patch from the ES2 that I tweaked for the whole album, simply because I liked the contrast it provided to my electric guitar sound. Synth guitar puts completely different demands on me. It forces me to use my fingers in different ways and makes me go places I wouldn't normally go when I play regular electric guitar. There's also a lyrical side that synth guitar allows me to explore that's becoming more important to me."[22]

The title of the album alluded to the near-telepathic feeling that musicians occasionally experience: "Every now and then a group of musicians will gel together in such an incredible way, and at that point it's like you lose normal gravity. You're kind of floating with the other guys. It doesn't happen every day, sometimes it doesn't happen every month, but you gotta be ready when it happens. It's not a Western thing, it's not an Eastern thing. It's a global thing."[23]

Sadly, the same problems that assailed *Industrial Zen* also blight *Floating Point*. John's themes are generally unmemorable and overcomplicated, and the album has dated rather badly. The most arresting moments come from the Indian guest musicians—U Rajesh's (the younger brother of Shrinivas) electric mandolin on "Inside Out," Naveen Kumar's bamboo flute on "14U" and his brother Niladri's zitar (electric sitar) on "Five Peace Band." The latter piece and "Raju" became key compositions for John, played in concert frequently over the next few years.

The album in the can, July 2007 saw an invitation from Eric Clapton for John to perform at the Crossroads Festival in Chicago. This was a series of occasional concerts throughout the United States that aided Clapton's Crossroads Center in Antigua, a drug and alcohol treatment facility. Festival MC Bill Murray memorably introduced John's set, while Jeff Beck played later on the bill, featuring "Resolution" and "Eternity's Breath" during his performance.

John then moved his attention to a coast-to-coast North American tour. Feraud took the bass chair, Husband played keyboards and Mark Mondesir drums (with Husband occasionally manning a small subsidiary kit, too). John named this new band The 4th Dimension. The tour began in Durham, North Carolina, on September 13, 2007, after just two days of rehearsal. Joe Zawinul had sadly died just before the tour's opening night, and Feraud played Weather Report's "A Remark You Made" and Jaco's "Continuum" in tribute during the Canadian leg.

For Mondesir, working so intensively with John this time round brought its own pressures, but also potential for development: "The biggest challenge for me on this tour is adapting the Indian *konnakol* rhythmic system into my own playing. The system involves counting, which is something I never do when I play. I see rhythms and song forms as shapes, rather than bar lines or numbers, so as soon as I learn something, I never get lost. *Konnakol* is a very different way of thinking for me, so making that work will be a very interesting and educational experience."[24]

For his part, Husband was very much made aware by John of his role as a "disruptor" in The 4th Dimension: "He demands interaction, he doesn't want to hear the same solo every night, he wants to be kicked in the ass, and he wants some friction."[25] John was generally thrilled with his new group, and also heralded his technical team on the last night of the tour at Massey Hall in Toronto on October 5, saying from the stage: "I would like to thank our sound engineer Sven Hoffman and our tour manager Christophe Deghelt. You do not see them, but we really need them."[26]

Meanwhile, at the tail end of 2007, John couldn't fail to notice the ongoing interest in the original Mahavishnu Orchestra that was building among younger musicians and fans:

And it's not just The Mahavishnu Project, which itself is very moving. I saw them in New York, it must have been four or five years ago, and I had to go onstage and say something. They played with such a passion, that was wonderful. And that string quartet (the radio.string.quartet.vienna's album *Celebrating The Mahavishnu Orchestra* was released in July 2007), how about that? When they sent me the demo and I said, 'Yes, I'll do your liner notes,' then they went through terrible traumas, lost two of the quartet, and everything was put on the back burner for about eighteen months. But they got back to me, the two who stayed faithful, and they brought another couple of people in and went ahead with the record. I was just so impressed when I listened to it.[27]

Toward the end of 2007, John wrote and produced the title track of the tribute album *Miles From India*, overseen and arranged by Bob Belden. Many Miles alumni also appeared on the CD including Michael Henderson, Dave Liebman, Jimmy Cobb, Ron Carter, Mike Stern, Pete Cosey, Ndugu Chancler, and Lenny White. Once invited by Belden to appear on the album, John couldn't resist: "I started thinking about Miles and how much he had given to me over the years. Wherever I am, Miles is there."[28]

Meanwhile, John and The 4th Dimension began their European tour in spring 2008 just as *Floating Point* was finally released, reaching #14 on the *Billboard* Top Jazz Albums chart and nominated for a Best Contemporary Jazz Album Grammy, losing out to Randy Brecker's *Randy In Brasil*.

A busy year for John came to an end when he contributed to the second and third episodes of a BBC documentary called *Jazz Britannia*, which aired during December 2008 (other contributors included John Surman, Courtney Pine, Jack Bruce, Georgie Fame, and Jon Hiseman). John spoke passionately about recording *In A Silent Way* with Miles, in the 1960s London jazz scene, and how America had been a crucial escape route for many British musicians during the rock era.

## FIVE PEACE BAND LIVE (W/CHICK COREA) (2009)

Chick Corea: Acoustic piano, electric piano, synthesizer
John McLaughlin: Electric guitar
Kenny Garrett: Alto saxophone
Christian McBride: Acoustic and electric bass
Vinnie Colaiuta: Drums, percussion
Herbie Hancock: Piano

Recorded live on the European tour between October 22 and November
23, 2008
Produced by Chick Corea and John McLaughlin
Released on April 28, 2009

John's headlining collaboration with Chick Corea for the Five Peace Band was
another long-overdue and almost inevitable musical matchup. They had been
close friends and admirers of each other's work since John's very first arrival in
New York City in February 1969, and of course had both worked extensively
with Miles between 1969 and 1972. They were also neighbors during the
1970s, John living on West 22nd Street and Corea on West 21st Street. But
their close friendship was not based exclusively on music, but also on philosophy, religion, and spiritual matters. Corea became a Scientologist a few years
before John entered the Sri Chinmoy cult, and they would regularly expound
on the nature of the universe long into the night, always with a smile.

The Five Peace Band was Corea's idea (though John chose the name), and
he already had Colaiuta, alto saxophonist Kenny Garrett, and bassist Christian
McBride in mind. Garrett was yet another connection to Miles, a gifted improviser who had played with the trumpeter from 1987 until his death in 1991,
and recorded nine solo albums in the 1990s and 2000s. McBride was one of
the most respected jazz bassists of the modern era, a double threat on electric
and acoustic who had recorded seven solo albums before hooking up with John
and Corea. Colaiuta was, on paper, the perfect drummer for this band, equally
comfortable with complex metric perambulations as per his playing with Frank
Zappa as he was with hard grooving, courtesy of gigs with Joni Mitchell, Sting,
and Jeff Beck (and he had recorded an excellent tribute to John, "John's Blues,"
on his 1994 self-titled album for Corea's Stretch Records).

Understandably, Miles was an unseen presence throughout the whole project. The band's set was littered with allusions to the trumpeter, with two signature pieces ("Dr Jackle" and "Someday My Prince Will Come"), plus a lengthy
exploration of the "In A Silent Way/It's About That Time" medley. The album
was recorded during a sold-out European tour during the fall of 2009 (the
second leg of the tour took place in the United States and Far East during early
2010, and featured Brian Blade on drums instead of Colaiuta).

Corea wrote about the album and tour on his website: "I decline to attempt
to describe this music or give it a name. But I will say that it's a music that is
made by five musicians who don't care about what it's called or where it comes
from or what are its 'influences'. I will also say that we've just scratched the
surface of what more might be done with this collaboration. So, humbly offered

(but not so humbly played) is a selection of the performances from our first outing—22 concerts throughout Europe, fall of 2008."

It is not surprising that most of the photographs taken of the Five Peace Band show John and Corea smiling. Very little was off-limits during this joyful collaboration—jazz, blues, funk, classic fusion, Indian, and even modern classical influences courtesy of Corea's solo piano excursions. However, it's a very long album, and John struggles to produce many memorable or telling guitar moments—he generally plays so many notes that they seem to flow into one, and he declines to modify his sound for the acoustic piano pieces. He is happy to let his bandmates shine, and shine they do.

The album kicks off in very promising fashion, though: "Raju" is transformed from John's original 2006 studio version. Notice is served by Corea's zany comping from the first few seconds of the tune. There's a great moment at 4:33, when Colaiuta digs into a swing section, demystifying the complexity of the cross rhythms, and at 9:58, he almost drags the band into a hard-rocking 4/4. There's also a pleasing blast from the past with John referring to "Radio-Activity" during his tags between solos.

"Senor C.S." is reborn with the kind of high-speed Latin groove found on *Love Devotion Surrender*, and McBride plays a fluid, Jaco-like fretless bass solo. "New Blues, Old Bruise," originally from *Industrial Zen*, was apparently a great challenge for Corea. According to John, the keyboardist called it "the hardest tune I ever played in my life," and he would frequently come off-stage saying, "I'm getting it, I'm getting it!"[29] That is quite something coming from him, composer of some of the most complex jazz/rock pieces in history. (John claims that "New Blues, Old Bruise" is best understood as centering around three cycles of a very slow 5/4.)

Corea's two compositions are more successful: "The Disguise" is an ingeniously arranged piece with phenomenal solos from Garrett and McBride, while "Hymn To Andromeda," written specially for this band, sees Corea reaches inside the piano for some striking *musique concrète* "events" during his unaccompanied, Ligeti-esque opening.

Then there are three tracks that explicitly honor Miles. Jackie McLean's blues "Dr Jackle," famously kicking off Miles's 1958 album *Milestones*, offers lots of surprises. Corea's piano intro, with audible encouragement from McBride, channels Bud Powell and Monk. At 2:50, John and Corea almost lay into "Blue Monk," before the piece bursts into life with an unexpected second-line New Orleans groove.

Herbie Hancock guests on "In a Silent Way/It's About That Time" and finds some fascinating spaces in which to play, intertwining around Corea's

Rhodes textures, and both come close to matching the mood of the original. But the piece becomes somewhat of a formless jam, despite McBride's spicy Jaco-isms. "Someday My Prince Will Come," the title track of Miles's 1961 album, is a John/Corea duet, but John's tone doesn't sit comfortably with Corea's piano; though performed with a lot of love, the track is crying out for acoustic guitar.

*Five Peace Band Live* was a big critical success, winning the 2010 Grammy Award for Best Jazz Instrumental Album (Corea's sixteenth Grammy). The general consensus was that John was leaving the 2000s on a high—and he would stick to his fusion guns for the first album of the new decade.

# 8

# THE 2010s

## From *To The One* to *Is That So?*

### *TO THE ONE* (2010)

John McLaughlin: Guitar
Gary Husband: Drums, keyboards, percussion
Etienne Mbappé: Bass
Mark Mondesir: Drums, percussion
Recorded at Solid Sound Studio, Nice, France, and Mediastarz, Monaco,
    November–December 2009
Produced by John McLaughlin
Released on April 20, 2010

Approaching seventy years old and seldom busier, John was a very fit man as he entered the 2010s: "I bike, I swim, I play Ping-Pong, I play tennis, I do meditation, I do yoga. If I didn't, I would probably be dead by now."[1] He was also fully dedicated to his new 4th Dimension group, and it was rapidly becoming a highly effective vehicle for his compositions. Gary Husband came onboard as full-time keyboardist and occasional drummer/percussionist. He was thrilled to join the pantheon of jazz/rock greats: "John is the most inspirational leader I've ever had the opportunity to work for. He is the ideal leader, and he embodies the Miles Davis greatness: the intuition, the wisdom and that whole kind of genius."[2]

The new man on bass was Étienne Mbappé. Born in Cameroon, he had moved to France in the 1990s, joining the Parisienne scene and hooking up with The Zawinul Syndicate in the process. John clocked him playing with

Zawinul—"He was killing in his little black gloves"[3]—and was desperate to work with him. But, upon leaving the Syndicate, Mbappé formed his own band and became busy with touring and recording. John was happy to wait awhile—he was a once-in-a-generation player, a master of both Jaco-style single lines and deep grooves.

John wasted no time getting into the studio with his new rhythm section. *To The One* came with a long liner message outlining the inspiration for his current compositions: John Coltrane's *A Love Supreme*, and also his "own endeavours towards 'the one' throughout the past 40 years." John claimed that Coltrane "integrated the spiritual dimension into jazz music," and that *A Love Supreme* "could not have come at a better moment for me—the musical and spiritual encouragement I obtained from this record was a determining factor in my life." He went on to outline his own spiritual quest "to feel the blessings of the infinite one."

John's spiritual animus certainly had a positive effect on his first album of the new decade—*To The One* was his best solo release since 2003. There was a lot more space in the music than there had been for a long while, and Mondesir brought a breezy, open, expressive kit sound and lots of dynamics, the "jazziest" drumming on a John project since the 1990s. The album also benefited from its relatively short length, focusing on just six compositions.

The blues-flavored "Discovery" kicked things off with a flavor of "Pursuance" from *A Love Supreme* and a clever co-opting of drum parts between Mondesir and Husband (the latter takes over for the first half of John's solo, and then reappears intermittently on kit and percussion). There's an engaging, spontaneous flavour to this music. "Special Beings" is a return to waltz time for John, an ecstatic composition with a touch of both "Someday My Prince Will Come" and "My Favorite Things" and some excellent Husband comping.

"The Fine Line" is an altered blues built around a memorable bass vamp, intriguing melody and some chord architecture similar to "The Dark Prince." Also check out the subtle tempo change at 1:00; this band was getting an almost telepathic understanding. "Lost And Found," in a very slow 11/4, nods to Shakti's "Bridge Of Sighs," with John soloing engagingly on guitar synth before Husband's uncharacteristically spare acoustic piano solo.

But *To The One* almost comes unstuck with its final two tracks. "Recovery" sounds like a leftover from *Floating Point* with its skittish rhythm and underwhelming melody. Not even Mbappé's solo can save this one. Ditto the title track. Its groove is inert, the harmonic structure very familiar, and a reference to "Lila's Dance" at 2:40 seems a little superfluous. Husband's drumming performance was an overdub after all the other parts had been laid down—he reports that John decided to stand in front of his kit and "conduct" him: "We only did it once. I wandered into the control room, not convinced I'd done anything coherent that would add much value to the piece. When the playback started, I felt a shock as I slowly realized what a journey the piece suddenly was and how it was transformed by this approach on the drums. I flippantly commented, 'John, you did a Miles on me!'"[4] The track ended with a vocal variation on the "A Love Supreme" motif, this time with John intoning: "Infinite One/ The Supreme Infinite One."

*To The One* was well received on both sides of the Atlantic, reaching #27 on the *Billboard* Jazz Albums chart and nominated for a Best Contemporary Jazz Album Grammy. John celebrated with an extensive European tour, including a memorable date at London's Barbican on May 11, 2010, which showed that The 4th Dimension was gelling effectively. The new compositions worked well, and there were memorable airings of "The Unknown Dissident" and "Nostalgia."

As the summer progressed, there were to be other echoes from John's past. As usual, he spent July in Montreux, hanging out and getting to as many jazz festival gigs as possible. But then he received a call from Claude Nobs on the morning of July 2, while cycling with his wife, Ina, and son Luke alongside Lake Geneva. Roxy Music's support act Melissa auf der Maur had pulled out—would he consider jamming with Billy Cobham (who lived just an hour's drive away in Bern)? John was keen: "Me and Billy got together, did the fastest soundcheck you ever heard and played for about 40 minutes, just guitar and drums. It was terrific."[5] They played "You Know, You Know," "Meeting Of The Spirits," and "The Fine Line." John used a Fender Stratocaster lent to him by Nobs and utilized a far less refined, much rawer guitar tone than of recent years. He was pleased with the results, and it was a burying of the hatchet after their falling-out during the summer of 1984. It also possibly signaled a softening from John in terms of addressing his 1970s Mahavishnu days.

John also guested with the David Sanborn Trio at the Antibes Jazz Festival on July 15, playing "I've Got News For You" with Steve Gadd and Joey DeFrancesco, a superb performance available to watch on YouTube. Sadly, it was his last-ever concert appearance with DeFrancesco, who died in 2022.

## NOW HERE THIS (2012)

Ranjit Barot: Drums
Gary Husband: Drums, piano, synthesizer
Étienne Mbappé: Electric bass

John McLaughlin: Electric guitar, guitar synthesizer
Produced by John McLaughlin
Recorded at Studio 26, Antibes, France, summer 2012
Released on October 16, 2012

Through the winter of 2010 and the first six months of 2011, John was in a rich seam of writing form, new compositions coming thick and fast. There was no contractual obligation to make a new album, but he felt a calling again: "I never intend at any point to make a record, but the music comes and then it's time to record."[6] But he did make a change in the drum department, Ranjit Barot coming in for Mark Mondesir. The Mumbai native had previously played on *Floating Point* and was now a full-fledged 4th Dimension member: "Since he came in, the band just took off. Ranjit was like the top stone of the pyramid."[7]

In the meantime, the rest of 2011 and early 2012 saw some high-profile guest appearances from John. On July 1, he got together at the Montreux Jazz Festival with Carlos Santana and band (including Dennis Chambers on drums and former Miles bassist Benny Rietveld). Kicking off with a long devotional intro and then "The Life Divine" from *Love Devotion Surrender*, there were other tributes to John Coltrane ("Peace On Earth," "Naima," and "Acknowledgement"), plus references to Bob Dylan ("A Hard Rain's A-Gonna Fall"), Hendrix ("Voodoo Child [Slight Return]"), Sonny Sharrock ("Venus/Upper Egypt"), and Led Zeppelin ("Stairway To Heaven"). However, the most effective selections of the concert were those celebrating Miles ("Right Off" and "Black Satin") and Lifetime ("Vuelta Abajo" and "Vashkar"), which provided some much-needed respite from the hysterical soloing and double-drum onslaught. The entire concert would be released in 2015 on a joint album/DVD.

In November 2011, John was delighted to accept an invitation to celebrate Chick Corea's seventieth birthday at New York's Blue Note club. There was almost a whole month of concerts in all, many of which were recorded. Corea and John reunited the Five Peace Band with John Patitucci and Brian Blade taking the bass and drum chairs. Gayle Moran—the former Mahavishnu keyboard/vocalist, now married to Corea—also joined John and Chick for a memorable version of "Smile Of The Beyond."

Meanwhile John revealed that he had had quite a few "financially interesting" offers to reform the original line-up. But he had to turn them down: "The sight of these old fogeys going onstage and playing that music? I just couldn't see it. I don't want to go out there just for money. It's gotta be a musical thing."[8]

John turned seventy on January 4, 2012, and then it was time to record a new album. He chose Studio 26 in Antibes, only about half an hour's drive along the coast from his home. *Now Here This* was essentially a document of the band playing live. Though featuring more guitar from John than in recent years, sadly it was an inferior record to *To The One*. The production was exceptionally dry, and it featured only one really outstanding composition, "Echoes From Then": "That is right up Mahavishnu's street. That's why I gave it that title, because when it came out of my mind, I said, 'Wait a minute, this is Mahavishnu Deluxe!'"[9]

Elsewhere, John's compositions were somewhat formulaic, not a quality you usually associate with his work. "Trancefusion," "Riff Raff," and "Call And Answer" radiated a frantic, fidgety energy but not enough harmonic intrigue. "Wonderfall" and "Not Here Not There" provided some relief, but they lacked the surprise element of John's best ballads. Still, *Now Here This* reached #25 on the *Billboard* Jazz Album chart and garnered some good reviews.

Meanwhile, John guested with the band Spectrum Road at the Montreux Jazz Festival on July 7, 2012. He joined Jack Bruce, Vernon Reid, John Medeski, and Cindy Blackman-Santana in the Miles Davis Hall for a celebration of Tony Williams's Lifetime, playing "Vuelta Abajo," "There Comes A Time," "One Word," "Emergency," and Cream's "Politician."

## *THE BOSTON RECORD* (2014)

John McLaughlin: Guitar
Gary Husband: Keyboards and drums
Etienne Mbappé: Bass
Ranjit Barot: Drums and vocals
Recorded live on June 22, 2013, at the Berklee Performance Center, Boston
Produced by John McLaughlin
Released on March 31, 2014

John was getting used to reunions with ex-Mahavishnu Orchestra members during the 2010s, but even he probably couldn't have predicted one with Jean-Luc Ponty, the violinist who had jumped ship from the band in early 1975. There were joined onstage by Zakir Hussain to play "Lotus Feet" at the International Jazz Day Global Concert in Istanbul, Turkey, on April 30, 2013. An annual event since 2011, the United Nations Educational, Scientific and Cultural Organization (UNESCO) had officially designated April 30 as International Jazz Day to highlight jazz and its diplomatic role of uniting people in all corners of the globe.

As John continued to fly the flag for "jazz" guitar, he also acknowledged that the 1990s, 2000s, and 2010s had not been a particularly fecund period for those players who dared to stray onto the path less traveled:

> Over the past 20 years, there has been a kind of dissipation in jazz which troubles me somewhat. The movements of 'smooth' jazz and 'funky' jazz is jazz music riddled with clichés and does not conform to my conception of jazz, which is a music of liberation and passion. The guitar has been heavily featured in these forms of jazz, and reveal a similar surfeit of clichés.[10]

His continuing devotion to The 4th Dimension was a deliberate affront to that conservative attitude, a relentless pursuit of true "fusion" music (one recalls a great band name of the 1980s—Desperately Seeking Fusion). John ploughed on, touring America throughout the summer of 2013 and very keen to document the band with a live album, as he felt this was one of the most potent units of his musical life. The Berklee College in Boston was deemed a very appropriate venue, especially since so many alumni of John's bands had attended the college over the years, from Stu Goldberg to Kai Eckhardt. John expressed absolute pride in capturing the music played on June 22 in the *Boston Record*'s liner notes:

> From time to time, a live record is made that has everything: great collective playing, a terrific audience, fantastic recorded sound, and a wonderful atmosphere. In the new recording of our concert, you'll find all of the above. I'm really happy about this recording.

Sadly, despite the album's excellent psychedelic cover design by Arkyaduti Basu, it's hard to agree with John. While the *Boston Record* features excellent sound with a lot of punch and presence, it's another very difficult album to get through. John's playing is superb, with a little more "fizz" than usual, but memorable guitar moments are again hard to come by—notes fly by at enormous speed apparently without much in the way of organization. And one yearns for another instrumental foil for John, despite Husband's sterling efforts. But Mbappé enlivens the half-time-shuffle take on "Little Miss Valley" with some terrific funk playing, and his vocal cameo on "Love And Understanding"/"Abbaji" also works. "Señor C.S." benefits from its reimagining as an acoustic piano/guitar duet.

As John's schedule wound down during late 2013 and early 2014, he had a few personal and professional setbacks. Firstly, he began to experience a health problem that was seriously affecting his ability to play; he had developed arthritis in both hands. In the July/August 2021 issue of *Jazz Times* magazine, he looked back on that time:

> I thought maybe that's it for me. But I started seeing doctors and having steroid injections every three months and it was very helpful. But I got to a point where I thought I should be able to heal myself. So before my morning meditation I began to talk to my hands. I told them how beautiful they are and how grateful I am to have them. I know that sounds loony but I don't care. Within about six months, I told my doctor I feel so good I don't have to have a needle in my hand. To this day I don't have any pain. What the human mind is capable of is phenomenal!

Then John's dear friend and collaborator Paco de Lucia died on February 26, 2014. John penned a tribute for *Jazz Times*' March 2015 issue: "Paco was a deep, funny, spontaneous human being. . . . He would speak to me about the unspoken traditions in flamenco and the world of the Gypsy in Andalucía. . . . Paco was a radical. He never broke the rules of musical traditions but he definitely bent them to accommodate his new perception of harmony and rhythm. He was the first guitarist to to integrate improvisation into the mainstream of flamenco."

The year 2014 continued to bring forth ever more references to John's most famous band: also in that March issue of *Jazz Times*, editor Evan Haga asked readers to send in their "Mahavishnu Moments," fond memories of the original band. Haga set out his stall: "*Birds Of Fire* hit me like an alien transmission when I heard it at 15. . . . I became infatuated with Mahavishnu-era McLaughlin. . . . He didn't seem to want to think about anything except music and the guitar, and neither did I."

Meanwhile, Billy Cobham turned seventy in May 2014, and he reminisced about his time in the Orchestra via a far-reaching cover story in the UK-based *Drummer* magazine. Later that year, John bid farewell to Remember Shakti's electric mandolin player U. Srinivas, who died on September 14, 2014. It had been a very mixed year for John, both personally and professionally.

## BLACK LIGHT (2015)

John McLaughlin: Electric and acoustic guitar, guitar programming, synthesizer
Gary Husband: Synthesizer, piano, drums, percussion
Étienne M'Bappé: Electric bass
Ranjit Barot: Drums, vocals

Produced by John McLaughlin
Recorded at Eastcote Studios, London, and Mediastarz, Monaco
Released on October 9, 2015

As 2014 became 2015, The Mahavishnu Orchestra just wouldn't die—the original 1971–1973 band was voted nineteenth-greatest small group in jazz history in the September edition of *JazzTimes*. But, characteristically, John wasn't looking back—he believed his current band was the equal of The Mahavishnu:

> This particular band never ceases to amaze me with what they do. I'm standing there in the studio with them and they're blowing my mind. It's as good as it gets! In a way, I'm writing to provoke them to get something extra or unexpected out of them. It's one thing to structure a tune with an arrangement but when it comes to the playing then we need to push and provoke each other in order to get to those places where we've never been before. That sounds like Captain Kirk, doesn't it?[11]

John was particularly enjoying the camaraderie with his bandmates: "Playing and working with the same musicians in a band is a living process which unfolds as time goes by. I am always excited to play with these musicians. Not only are they marvelous players, but they are great human beings, and as such we have developed, over the years, a deep complicity that comes through in the music."[12]

With *Black Light*, John was also returning to the kinds of musical avenues explored on mid-2000s albums such as *Industrial Zen*, namely the world of computer-based, hard-disk composition and sequencing:

> I worked a long time with what is called 'sound designs,' which are either soundscapes or rhythmic elements that have the capacity to evoke feelings and visions in my imagination that would not come otherwise. I became involved in synthesis as far back as 1975, and I'm still attracted to the possibilities of expression. It actually is a fascinating world, but can be quite easily abused in an artistic sense. To me, this is the seductive side of sound design.[13]

Sadly, the album shares many problems with *Industrial Zen* and *Now Here This*, despite more explicitly referring to much of John's previous work. "Here Come the Jiis" was a tribute to U. Srinivas: "Since we lost Srinivas last year I haven't had the heart to replace him (in Remember Shakti). I really don't know what to do about it. Fourteen years we were playing together and he was so dear to me. There are plenty of great players in India but right now I don't have the heart. Maybe later . . . I don't know."[14]

The strangely titled "Clap Your Hand" was the album's one classic, an intriguing modal blowout in the tradition of "Honky Tonk Haven" and "Radio-Activity," with superimposed *konnakol* polyrhythms. "Being You Being Me" referenced both "Lotus Feet" and "Lila's Dance" but lacked the strong melody lines of both and was hampered by an overbearing Barot groove. John discussed the animus behind the track "El Hombre Que Sabia (The Man Who Knew)":

> It was one of a number of pieces that Paco de Lucia and I already had been working on. We'd been exchanging music because we planned to record in 2014—a new album, just acoustic. We had about four pieces ready. He was travelling to Cuba first, then to Mexico, which was where he died, playing football with his kids on the beach. He had a heart attack; too many cigarettes. The day before he left for Cuba, he called . . . and he said how much he loved it. I took this particular tune and said I have to do something, just as a goodbye. The passion and tenderness they (the 4th Dimension) bring to this piece is wonderful. I think Paco would be very happy with that."[15]

## *LIVE AT RONNIE SCOTT'S (2017)*

John McLaughlin: Guitar
Ranjit Barot: Drums, konnakol
Gary Husband: Keyboards, drums
Etienne MBappé: Bass
Recorded live at Ronnie Scott's, London, March 13–14, 2017
Produced by John McLaughlin
Released on September 15, 2017

John revisited one of his key collaborations with Miles on April 30, 2016, when he played "Spanish Key" during International Jazz Day at the White House, Washington, DC, alongside Marcus Miller, Chick Corea, Terence Blanchard, Kendrick Scott, John Beasley, Wayne Shorter, and Zakir Hussain. Introduced by President Barack Obama, the entire concert was filmed and later broadcast. John laid down a frantic, snarling solo on the *Bitches Brew* classic, pushing the boundaries again. His vision of jazz was fluid and ever challenging.

John and The 4th Dimension then played a number of concerts during the summer of 2016. After a short break, John guested with Chick Corea at the Blue Note in New York City to celebrate the keyboard player's seventy-fifth birthday. On December 11, alongside Victor Wooten on bass and Lenny White on drums, they played three Return To Forever tracks ("Captain Senor Mouse,"

"Hymn Of The Seventh Galaxy," and "The Romantic Warrior") and "Smile Of The Beyond" with Gayle Moran Corea on vocals. John reported they'd had just one four-hour rehearsal on the afternoon of the gig. There were certainly a few hiccups—they had to replay the ending of "You Know, You Know" three times before they got it right—but it was all done with humor.

The 4th Dimension then reconvened for several more European dates in March 2017, including two notable concerts at London's Ronnie Scott's club. This was John's nostalgic return to the scene of many early career triumphs. It was difficult not to compare these concerts to Jeff Beck's famous "reunion" gigs in the same venue ten years earlier, and both events shared a dazzling mixture of genres and completely sold-out houses.

John's setlist included four compositions written for the original Mahavishnu Orchestra, including "Meeting Of The Spirits," the set-opener to nix all set-openers. Husband kicked off "Miles Beyond" with some very strange, atonal Rhodes chords, inexplicably staying completely away from the blues, and his Moog tone almost swamped "Sanctuary." "Vital Transformation," however, was superb, and "Here Come The Jiis" and "Gaza City" were big improvements over the album versions.

Buoyed by a lot of media interest and despite a rather humdrum album cover, *Live At Ronnie Scott's* sold well and further reignited interest in John's Mahavishnu Orchestra work of the 1970s.

## LIVE IN SAN FRANCISCO (2018)

John McLaughlin: Twelve-string double neck and six-string guitars
Jimmy Herring: Guitar
Gary Husband: Keyboards
Matt Slocum: Keyboards
Jason Crosby: Violin, keyboards, vocals
Etienne Mbappé: Bass, vocals
Kevin Scott: Bass
Ranjit Barot: Drums, konnakol, vocals
Jeff Sipe: Drums, gong
Recorded live at the Warfield Theatre in San Francisco on December 8, 2017
Produced by John McLaughlin
Released on September 21, 2018

John had been a fan of Jimmy Herring for a while before their collaboration, even going on record as saying that he and Jeff Beck were his favorite guitarists. He also revealed that he had once recommended Herring to Chick Corea (perhaps Herring's raunchy, searching guitar style reminded John of Bill Connors, the original electric guitarist in Corea's Return To Forever). For his part, Herring had loved John's music from a young age: "I first heard John's playing when I was 17. Right from the first few seconds of *The Inner Mounting Flame* I felt like I'd stuck my finger in an electric socket."[16]

Born January 22, 1962, in Fayetteville, North Carolina, Herring began his musical career playing saxophone in his high school band, but he then took up the guitar at age thirteen. He attended the Berklee School for one summer session and was then a graduate from the Guitar Institute of Technology in Hollywood, California. He went on to play with Jazz Is Dead, The Allman Brothers Band, and Derek Trucks, and he recorded two solo albums in the 2000s and 2010s. Herring covered John's "Hope" for 2013's *Subject To Change Without Notice*—a version the composer was particularly struck by: "I'm still knocked out by what he did. He plays it like he wrote it, and I'd have given my back teeth to play his solo on the album."[17] Just prior to hooking up with John, Herring had also played in the excellent twin-guitar band of drummer Lenny White.

John and Herring finally met at a concert celebrating the thirtieth anniversary of Paul Reed Smith guitars in June 2015. They discussed each other's bands and hatched a plan to collaborate. John announced that their twenty-five-date double-header—subtitled The Meeting Of The Spirits Tour—would be his final US sojourn. Herring's band, alongside drummer Jeff Sipe, bassist Kevin Scott, and keyboardists Jason Crosby and Matt Slocum, played the first set, then The 4th Dimension played, and finally the two bands combined for some Mahavishnu classics.

The tour touched down at the Warfield in San Francisco on December 8, 2017. This was a special concert, at the scene of the famous *Friday Night In San Francisco* gig in December 1980, and aptly it featured a very vocal, excited crowd. The music generally lived up to the occasion: Herring was a much-needed instrumental foil to John's recent music, and the former's band also brought other options to bear, most notably keyboardists Crosby and Slocum (the former also doubling up on violin, another key flavor). John also took a lot more time over his solos, apparently relishing the increased division of labor. (Husband also benefits from this.) The net result, recorded at the third and final night of the Warfield concerts, was John's most consistent and listenable release since 2010's *To The One*.

"Meeting Of The Spirits" is the jolting, highly effective opener. John showcases a cleaner attack than for a while, eschewing any chorus effects, and there's a great moment during his solo at 3:32 when he nearly drags Barot into a 4/4 rock feel. Herring's relatively bluesy solo makes for a fascinating contrast of styles, and the violin/guitar unison lines are brilliantly played. "Birds Of Fire" inspires some of John's finest electric soloing since his 1970s heyday, particularly during the duel with violinist Slocum.

Sipe and Barot's double drums enliven an uplifting, almost anthemic "Lotus On Irish Streams," superbly arranged for this big band. "Eternity's Breath" and "Be Happy" repeat the trick, the latter with a superb, apparently Ornette Coleman–inspired solo from Mbappé, while "Trilogy" almost brings the house down with Barot's *konnakol*/drum solo followed by a brilliant Husband/Crosby keyboard duel. "The Dance Of Maya" is, predictably, a highlight, benefiting hugely from Mbappé's low B string and taken at a deliciously slow pace, ramming home the majestic riff. At 4:01, Herring quotes from John's original 1971 solo.

John was thrilled with the music on *Live In San Francisco*, saying in his liner notes: "The musicians in both band played the music like they had written it, and the way they brought the music back to life was an unforgettable experience for me personally." Herring concurred: "Playing these timeless compositions with John and The 4th Dimension was a life-changing experience! We are forever grateful to our mentor John McLaughlin for this gift of enduring inspiration."

The album was also graced by a tremendous, psychedelic-era cover, courtesy of California-based Marq Spusta, and it benefited from an excellent mixing job by George Murphy at London's Eastcote Studios in London; every instrument is well-defined and beautifully recorded, no easy feat with nine musicians all playing at a very high volume.

## *IS THAT SO?* WITH SHANKAR MAHADEVAN/ ZAKIR HUSSAIN (2020)

John McLaughlin: Guitar synthesizer
Shankar Mahadevan: Vocals
Ustad Zakir Hussain: Tabla
Recorded at Mediastarz Studio, Monaco; Purple Haze Studio; Airship
   Laboratories, 2015 to 2019
Produced by John McLaughlin
Released on January 2020

It's hardly surprising that John was generally taking it a little easier as the decade drew to a close. But The 4th Dimension embarked on a smattering of European gigs during spring 2019, including a trip to London's Barbican on April 23. This was his first London concert since the Brexit vote of July 2016, which had severed the UK from the European Union, and near the beginning of the evening's uplifting music, he couldn't resist drawing attention to the fact: "It's nice to be back in Great Brexit, Great Britain, whatever it is . . ." The subtext was clear. The setlist also featured a double bill of spiritual jazz courtesy of Pharoah Sanders's "Light At The Edge Of The World" and "The Creator Has A Master Plan." John signed off the concert with a plaintive: "You are all one. Thank you."

But the Barbican gig had offered few hints of the music John had been working on for the last five years with vocalist Shankar Mahadevan. The possibilities of fusing Western harmony with Eastern rhythmic theory/song forms were revealing ever new compositional ideas for John. But it was Shankar who laid down the first sketches for *Is That So*—he would record a *tanpura* (drone) on one track, then improvise his remarkable vocals on another track utilizing different ragas (keys). He then sent the mp3 file to John, who would create his own accompaniment for the vocal, only initially referring to the *tanpura*'s key: "Once I knew the tonality, my harmonic progression would depart from the *tanpura* and refer only to the way Shankar was singing."[18] The roots of this approach can be found in some of John and Shankar's improvised duets during Remember Shakti concerts, notably at the start of a filmed 2004 Vienna Jazz Festival performance.

Shankar was excited by the process after he heard the first fruits of John's and his labors: "The whole texture of the music really excited me since harmonic content does not exist in Indian classical music. We started by recording one piece as an experiment and after listening to the outcome we were so thrilled that both of us wanted to record an entire album. It took a few years to complete because of our geographical locations and travelling, but we did it!"[19]

John's accompaniment was also inspired by a few modes of guitar synthesis he had been working on since 2014. His lush, orchestral backings, creating a rich chordal palette to underpin Shankar's vocals, were achieved using a Fishman Triple Play MIDI pickup system. Then there was his new lead sound, getting ever closer to his beloved legato, horn-like attack. This came initially via a Logic Pro ES-2 synth plugin, but a lot of work had to be done with it: "It was a long time coming . . . Oh brother! I was tweaking aspects of the inside of the tone," John told *JazzTimes*.[20]

He also added aspects of a program called MiGiC, processing audio from the guitar's output to generate MIDI messages: "It took some experimenting with pickups. But the amount of gain you put into it can give you different 'inside' tonal effects, which become much more personal. You need your playing to be pretty accurate. It can handle whatever you can give it. It has that singing tone you only get from a guitar string."[21] John was also inspired by the playing of Michael Brecker: "One of the greatest tenor players, but he was also playing the Akai EWI. He did fabulous things with it, and I understand absolutely why he would pick up an electronic instrument like that because it made him think outside the box, and this was exactly the same for me. I cannot play this software like I play guitar. I am playing very differently on this instrument because I have to."[22]

Still, John's rationale was all well and good, and his artistic intentions noble, but the proof is in the listening; fortunately, all the hard work paid off—his lead lines are original and sympathetic, never sounding like an average synthesizer player. (John might also have been influenced by some of the keyboard/vocal duets played by Joe Zawinul during the 1990s, "Sunday Morning/Sunday Evening" from the *World Tour* album a particular case in point.)

The result was an album of six long, meditative pieces, all but one a variation of the Indian *Bhajan* form, vaguely translating as "a song with a spiritual theme." Almost by stealth, *Is That So?* became John's most affecting/effective project for years, and his most consistent since 2010's *To The One*. It screams "classic" pretty much from the first bar, but obviously foregrounds a vastly different soundworld to John's classic jazz/rock work. He integrates elements of electronica far more successfully than on his solo albums of the 2000s and 2010s via very unobtrusive rhythm loops, always embellished by Zakir Hussain's tablas. Shankar's vocals are consistently enthralling, frequently offering the sound of surprise.

John's harmonic mastery emerges particularly on "The Search," a beautiful fusion of Western "jazz" chords and Shankar's microtonal excursions, before John duets expressively with Zakir in 10/4 time. The piece ends with John craftily inserting some chords from his 1981 piece "Aspan." "Tara" features elements of Shakti's "Bridge Of Sighs" while "The Guru" is the only track wherein Zakir, John, and Shankar play together throughout, improvising a beguiling raga in G.

"Sakhi," co-written by all three collaborators and regularly played live by Remember Shakti since 2004, is the only track that initially seems a little pat, with an unsubtle string-synth sound, but it changes gear halfway through to become a fascinating exploration of *konnakol*. "The Beloved" makes for a wonderful finale to *Is That So?*, Shankar's vocals enhanced by some very shrewd use of delay and stereo panning.

Despite its wonderful music and striking cover art by Marq Spusta, the album rather fell through the cracks upon its January 2020 release, possibly due to its departure from big-name jazz/rock, and it is yet to find the audience it deserves. But who could have known that, two months after its release, *Is That So?* would suddenly become a soundtrack to the COVID era of lockdowns and medical emergencies, offering hope and despair in equal measures. Nowadays, it is difficult to listen to *Is That So?* without that perspective—for better or worse. But if the album is anything, it is a celebration of life.

# EPILOGUE

## COVID, *LIBERATION TIME*, AND JOHN'S GOALS BEYOND

At the outset of 2020, John pondered a tour to support the release of *Is That So?* and he played with Shakti at Calcutta's Saturday Club on January 14. His career was still geared toward concerts rather than studio albums. So, the COVID-19 era—when the live music industry atrophied and musicians were locked down along with the rest of the global population—was a huge professional setback (though, of course, he was relatively fortunate to live in a comfortable house in the south of France). He gradually managed to engage with his 4th Dimension bandmates via Zoom, performed some live "lockdown" music, including a new version of "You Know, You Know," and was also very busy being interviewed, including lengthy appearances on the podcasts of Vinnie Colaiuta and Narada Michael Walden (see References section).

But John confessed to a gnawing feeling of unease as 2020 came to a close. Things weren't helped by the sudden death of Chick Corea the following February. Then he heard that his old Mahavishnu friend Rick Laird was terminally ill in a New York hospice—thankfully they managed to speak before the bassist passed away in July 2021. There were brief, happier moments for sidemen past: Zakir Hussain was voted number-one percussionist in *Jazz Times*' 2021 Readers' Poll, and Joey DeFrancesco was number-one organist (he, too, sadly passed away in 2022).

But a musician as industrious and disciplined as John couldn't allow himself to succumb to negativity. By early 2021, he had written a new set of material, and the album *Liberation Time*, released in July, was the result. It featured five new compositions performed with various line-ups, including Colaiuta, Husband, and MBappe, and—intriguingly—two solo piano pieces, "Mila Repa" and "Shade Of Blue" (AKA "3 Willows").

John celebrated his eightieth birthday in January 2022 and released *The Montreux Years*, showcasing more live material from his 1978–2016 performances at that famous festival, from The One Truth Band to The 4th Dimension. Later that year, *Saturday Night In San Francisco* was issued, the long-awaited concert from the second night at the Warfield Theatre on December 6, 1980, also featuring Paco de Lucia and Al Di Meola. John then toured Europe during the summer of 2022 with his new 4th Dimension line-up featuring Nicholas Viccaro on drums. He also announced that Shakti would return in 2023 to celebrate their fiftieth anniversary, with concerts in Bangalore, Mumbai, Kolkata, and New Delhi throughout January followed by further gigs in Europe and America in the summer and fall.

Early 2023 then brought more sad news and a seismic shock throughout the guitar community when Jeff Beck passed away at the age of seventy-eight. "You are the greatest! I love you forever," John tweeted in tribute.

It had been a trying period. But despite the earthly setbacks of 2020–2023, we can rest assured that John will focus on higher goals and take the long view. The future is unwritten, but music is a constant companion. As he once said: "What I really feel in my heart is that music is higher than any religion. We don't know if there's a God, but if there *is* a God I think music is the face of God."[1] He reiterated this sense of wonder in February 2022 during his fascinating, wide-ranging interview with Walden: "I live every day as if it's my last day. I'm in perpetual wonder of existence in this amazing, unfathomable, majestic universe."

And though his reputation as one of the all-time greats is assured, John's attitude toward his formidable back catalog is not as rigorous as some. He generally takes an egalitarian attitude to past works. There are many "bootleg" concerts on YouTube and at *Wolfgang's Vault*, though Harper reports John told Jon Hiseman over lunch in 1990 that he'd been "totally ripped off with all the Mahavishnu albums" and that he "got so upset about this that halfway through the meal he actually stood up and walked off."[2]

But mainly John has ploughed ahead with gratitude and a positive mind-set. He told *The Irish Times* in 2022:

When I look back on my life as musician, I can only say 'Hey, thank you God!', not just God, 'Thank you people, thank you music!', because what a fantastic life I've had. How fortunate I am, to have played with the best in the West, the best in the East. I mean, Jesus, come on! I can't ask for more than that. And I'm still here. I just need a gig, man.[3]

And he remains the eternal student, never resting on his laurels, never assuming his formidable musical knowledge is finite:

> However much you put into music, you get paid back manifold, but only if you go the extra mile. You sleep less, work harder. Otherwise it stays superficial. But life is too deep and too mysterious not to want to explore it further. That initially requires some dedication, and after that, you're hooked - you don't need nothin'. I'm too curious to need a push, I know less about life now than I thought I did when I was 25. I know almost absolutely nothing about absolutely very little. But that's great, because this feeling of wonder, it's the greatest sensation in the world. It keeps me alive.[4]

Still, John foresees very difficult times ahead for improvising musicians in the 2020s and beyond, lamenting the era when there was plenty of live work and "blood on the stage." One thinks of the Elvin Jones's quote, appropriated by Branford Marsalis in Ken Burns's *Jazz* film, when asked how the drummer retained his formidable intensity for so long when accompanying John Coltrane: "You gotta be willing to *die* with the motherfucker . . ."[5] John has certainly never short-changed his audience, nor his collaborators.

He also remains a very potent symbol of freedom and independence in a world—at the time of this writing—blighted by division. He's a hero to many and a link to the 1960s ideals of peace, love, and understanding—not to mention multiculturalism—who retains a remarkably youthful, Zen-like outlook. Miles would surely be proud.

# NOTES

## INTRODUCTION

1. Applebaum, interview.
2. Ewing, interview.
3. Milkowski, interview, 2013.
4. Fripp, interview.
5. Rosen, interview.
6. Kolosky, *Power, Passion and Beauty.*

## CHAPTER 1

1. Walden, podcast.
2. Berendt, *The Jazz Book.*
3. Harper, *Bathed,* 19.
4. Harper, *Bathed,* 20.
5. Reed Smith, interview.
6. Ibid.
7. Randall, interview.
8. Rosen, interview.
9. Resnicoff, interview, 1996.
10. Balliett, *Collected Works.*
11. Harper, *Bathed In Lightning,* 35.
12. *Jazz Britannia*, BBC, episode 2.
13. Williams interview, 1972.
14. Penzer, interview.

15. Williams, interview, 1972.
16. Jeske, interview.
17. Menn, *Secrets From The Masters*, 179.
18. Hultin, *Born Under*, 158.
19. Harper, *Bathed*, 118.
20. Milkowski, interview, 2004.
21. Ibid.
22. Harper, *Bathed*, 156.
23. Robson, interview.
24. Walden, podcast, 2022.
25. Harper, *Bathed*, 239.
26. Milkowski, interview, 2004.
27. Berendt, *The Jazz Book*, 131.
28. Ibid.

## CHAPTER 2

1. Harper, *Bathed*, 318.
2. Welch, interview.
3. Parillo, interview.
4. Shoemaker, interview.
5. Fripp, interview.
6. "John McLaughlin and Bob Cornford—Jamming in London, UK (early 1968)(3 hours!)," YouTube.
7. Spicer, interview.
8. *Jazz Britannia*, episode 2.
9. Larkin, interview.
10. Randall, interview.
11. Berendt, *The Jazz Book*, 132.
12. Milkowski, interview, 2013.
13. Jarrett, *Pressed For All Time*, 131.
14. "Electric Miles: A Conversation."
15. Tingen, *Miles Beyond*, 58–59.
16. Berendt, *The Jazz Book*, 133.
17. Appelbaum, interview.
18. Fripp, interview.
19. Giddins, *Weather Bird*, 476.
20. Stern/Menn, interview, 1978.
21. Harper, *Bathed*, 347.
22. Parillo, interview.
23. Milkowski, interview, 2013.

## CHAPTER 3

1. Harper, *Bathed*, 356.
2. Berendt, *The Jazz Book*, 134.
3. Fripp, interview.
4. Harper, *Bathed*, 375.
5. Trigger, interview.
6. Ibid.
7. Milkowski, interview, 1992.
8. Tingen, *Miles Beyond*, 105.
9. "Electric Miles: A Conversation."
10. Larkin, *All What Jazz*, 285.
11. Berg, interview.
12. Carr, *Keith Jarrett*, 51.
13. Kusnur, interview.
14. Milkowski, interview, 2004.
15. Resnicoff, interview, 1994.
16. Coleman, interview.
17. Tamarkin, interview.
18. Parillo, interview.
19. Rosen, interview.
20. Keefe, interview.
21. Ibid.
22. Ibid.
23. Parillo, interview.
24. Bourne, interview.
25. Parillo, interview.
26. Kolosky, *Power, Passion and Beauty*.
27. Ibid.
28. Ibid.
29. Harper, *Bathed*, 392.
30. *Rolling Stone Presents Twenty Years of Rock & Roll*, VHS, 1987.
31. Bianchi, *Elegant People*, 143.
32. Khan, interview.
33. Kent/Hamilton, interview.
34. Schaffer, interview, 1973.
35. Kolosky, *Power, Passion and Beauty*.
36. Ibid.
37. Ibid.
38. Ibid.
39. Ibid.
40. Keddie, interview.

41. Kolosky, *Follow Your Heart.*
42. Berg, interview.
43. https://www.mixcloud.com/sonos/radio-hour-with-dangelo/.
44. Nicholson, interview, 2020.
45. Kolosky, *Power, Passion and Beauty.*
46. Milkowski, interview, 1992.
47. Whittet, interview.
48. Farber, interview.
49. Kolosky, *Power, Passion and Beauty*
50. Milkowski, *Rockers, Jazzbos & Visionaries*, 175.
51. Cavanagh, interview
52. Dannen, *Hit Men*, 86.
53. Kolosky, *Power, Passion and Beauty.*
54. Mercer, *Footprints*, 223.
55. Walden, podcast, 2022.
56. Ross, interview.
57. Kahn, *A Love Supreme*, 204.
58. Ibid.
59. Kolosky, *Power, Passion and Beauty.*
60. Walden, podcast, 2022.
61. Kolosky, *Power, Passion and Beauty.*
62. Walden, podcast, 2022.
63. Toshio Sudo, *Zen Guitar*, 79.
64. Kolosky, *Power, Passion & Beauty.*
65. Fripp, interview.
66. Kolosky, *Power, Passion and Beauty.*
67. Ibid.
68. Schaffer, interview, 1974.
69. Farber, interview.
70. Prasad, interview.
71. Kolosky, *Power, Passion and Beauty.*
72. Ferris, interview.
73. Kolosky, *Power, Passion and Beauty.*
74. Keefe, interview.
75. Berendt, *The Jazz Book*, 137.
76. Tamarkin, interview.
77. Berendt, *The Jazz Book*, 137.
78. Glasser, interview.
79. Kolosky, *Power, Passion & Beauty.*
80. Ibid.
81. Ibid.
82. Milkowski, interview, 2013.

## CHAPTER 4

1. Walden, podcast, 2019.
2. Ibid.
3. Ibid.
4. Ibid.
5. Ibid.
6. Flans, interview.
7. Liebman, interview, 2010.
8. Kolosky, *Power, Passion and Beauty*.
9. Williams, *Long Distance Call*.
10. Walden, podcast, 2019.
11. Massey, *Behind The Glass*, 98.
12. Kolosky, *Power, Passion and Beauty*.
13. Ibid.
14. Charlesworth, interview.
15. Harper, *Bathed*, 431.
16. Kolosky, *Power, Passion & Beauty*.
17. Walden, podcast, 2019.
18. Berendt, *The Jazz Book*, 137.
19. Schaffer, interview, 1974.
20. Power, *Hot Wired Guitar*.
21. Isler, interview.
22. Kolosky, *Passion, Power and Beauty*.
23. Walden, podcast, 2022.
24. Berg interview.
25. Nicholson, Jazzwise, 2022.
26. Carr, *Miles Davis*, 330.
27. Bendian, podcast.
28. Kolosky, *Power, Passion and Beauty*.
29. Bendian, podcast.
30. Bianchi, *Elegant People*, 214.
31. Kolosky, *Power, Passion and Beauty*.
32. Steve Khan, email to author, August 23, 2021.
33. Stern, interview.
34. *The South Bank Show*.
35. Berg, interview.
36. Prasad, interview.
37. Underwood, interview.
38. Smith, interview.
39. Stern, interview.
40. Ibid.

41. Prasad, interview.
42. Menn, *Secrets From The Masters*, 274.
43. Aledort, interview.
44. Berg, interview.
45. Ibid.
46. Ibid.
47. Ibid.
48. Bendian, podcast.
49. Ibid.
50. Ibid.
51. Stu Goldberg, email to author, December 30, 2022.
52. Stephen, interview.
53. Stu Goldberg, email to author, December 30, 2022.
54. Haga, interview.
55. Milkowski, *Jaco*, 88.
56. Bianchi, *Elegant People*, 289.
57. Milkowski, *Jaco*, 88.
58. Bianchi, *Elegant People*, 289.
59. Haga, interview.
60. Milkowski, Jaco, 89.
61. Haga, interview.
62. Milkowski, *Jaco*, 89.
63. Haga, interview.
64. Parillo, interview.

## CHAPTER 5

1. Nicholson, interview, 2022.
2. Ferguson, interview.
3. Coryell, *Improvisation*, 115.
4. Ibid.
5. Nicholson, interview, 2022.
6. Ibid.
7. Wheeler, interview.
8. Ibid.
9. Milkowski, "Caught Live."
10. Nicholson, interview, 2022.
11. Williamson, interview.
12. Nicholson, interview, 2022.
13. Haga, interview.
14. Wheeler, interview.

15. Aledort, interview.

16. Carr, *Music Outside*, 173.

17. Keepnews, interview.

18. Kolosky, *Follow Your Dreams*.

19. Fripp, interview.

20. Berendt, *The Jazz Book*, 140.

21. Fripp, interview.

22. Nicholson interview, 2022.

23. Milkowski, interview, 1984.

24. Milkowski, interview, 1993.

25. Ibid.

26. Ferguson, interview.

27. https://jazztimes.com/archives/mahavishnu-orchestra-live-at-montreux -19841974/.

28. Calvin Smith, *The Wire*, March 1985.

29. Milkowski, interview, 1987.

30. Danny Gottlieb, email to author, November 9, 2022.

31. Ibid.

32. Ibid.

33. Ibid.

34. Ibid.

35. Ibid.

36. Ibid.

37. Ina McLaughlin, email to author, December 20, 2022.

38. Ibid.

39. Kalbacher, interview.

40. Cole, *The Last Miles*, 188.

41. *Round Midnight*, soundtrack liner notes.

42. Hultin, *Born Under The Sign Of Jazz*, 227.

43. Ferguson, interview.

44. Danny Gottlieb, email to author, November 9, 2022.

45. Ibid.

46. Steve Khan, email to author, March 3, 2022.

47. Milkowski, "Caught," 1986.

48. Danny Gottlieb, email to author, November 9, 2022.

49. Milkowski, interview, 1993.

50. Danny Gottlieb, email to author, November 9, 2022.

51. Ibid.

52. Aledort, interview.

53. Stump, interview.

54. Milkowski, interview, 1993.

55. Milkowski, interview, 1992.

56. Mattingly, interview.
57. Ibid.
58. Ibid.

## CHAPTER 6

1. Cook, interview.
2. Ibid.
3. Shulgold, interview.
4. Ferguson, interview.
5. Cook, interview.
6. Prasad, interview.
7. Ibid.
8. Prasad, interview.
9. Ibid.
10. Birnbaum, interview.
11. Mattingly, interview.
12. Resnicoff, interview, 1990.
13. Devine, interview.
14. Ibid.
15. Ibid.
16. Liebman, interview.
17. Milkowski, interview, 1992.
18. Appelbaum, interview.
19. Rotondi, interview.
20. Ibid.
21. Nicholson, interview, 2006.
22. Liebman, interview.
23. Milkowski, interview, 1992.
24. Rotondi, interview.
25. Mattingly, interview.
26. Resnicoff, interview, 1994.
27. Diliberto, interview.
28. Ibid.
29. West, interview.
30. Beato, interview.
31. Kolosky, *Power, Passion and Beauty.*
32. Tolleson, interview.
33. Ibid.
34. Ibid.
35. Ibid.

36. Ibid.
37. Dennis Chambers, email to author, January 24, 2023.
38. Ibid.
39. Gilbert, interview.
40. Resnicoff, interview, 1996.
41. Ibid.
42. Stump, interview.
43. Prasad, interview.
44. Resnicoff, interview, 1996.
45. Mandel, interview.
46. Stump, interview.
47. Resnicoff, interview, 1996.
48. Mondesir, *Abstract Logix* interview.
49. Resnicoff, interview, 1996.
50. Chappell, interview.
51. Stump, interview.
52. Parillo, interview.
53. Resnicoff, interview, 1996.
54. Ibid.
55. Stump, interview.
56. Resnicoff, interview, 1996.
57. Chappell, interview.
58. Resnicoff, interview, 1996.
59. *The Way Of Beauty*, DVD.
60. Ibid.

## CHAPTER 7

1. Haga, interview.
2. West, interview.
3. Dennis Chambers, email to author, January 18, 2023.
4. Kelman, interview.
5. Nicholson, interview, 2006.
6. Ibid.
7. Milkowski, interview, 2004.
8. Ibid.
9. Nicholson, interview, 2006.
10. Kolosky, *Power, Passion and Beauty*.
11. Power, *Hot Wired Guitar*.
12. Nicholson, interview, 2006.
13. Ibid.

14. Kelman, interview.
15. Ibid.
16. Nicholson, interview, 2006.
17. Kelman, interview, 2007.
18. Nicholson, interview, 2006.
19. Prasad, interview.
20. Ibid.
21. Ibid.
22. Milkowski, interview, 2008.
23. Ibid.
24. Mondesir, interview, *Abstract Logix.*
25. Kelman, interview, 2007.
26. Ibid.
27. Ibid.
28. Prasad, interview.
29. Colauita, podcast.

## CHAPTER 8

1. Milkowski, interview, 2013.
2. Ibid.
3. Ibid.
4. Ibid.
5. Ibid.
6. Ibid.
7. Ibid.
8. Ibid.
9. Ibid.
10. Kusnur, interview.
11. Smith, interview.
12. Proper Music press release, *Black Light.*
13. Ibid.
14. Smith, interview.
15. Haga, interview.
16. Randall, interview.
17. Ibid.
18. Nicholson, interview, 2020.
19. Ibid.
20. Menasche, interview.
21. Ibid.
22. Nicholson, interview, 2020.

# EPILOGUE

1. Mandel, *Future Jazz*, 83.
2. Harper, *Bathed*, 173.
3. Larkin, interview.
4. Resnicoff, interview, 1996.
5. Ken Burns, *Jazz*, episode 10, *A Masterpiece At Midnight*, 2001.

# BIBLIOGRAPHY

## BOOKS

Balliett, Whitney. *Collected Works: A Journal of Jazz 1954–2000*. London: Granta, 2001.

Balliett, Whitney. *New York Notes: A Journal of Jazz In The Seventies*. New York: Da Capo Press, 1977

Batty, Mark. *About Pinter: The Playwright and the Work*. London: Faber & Faber, 2005.

Benson, George. *The Autobiography*. London: De Capo Press, 2014.

Berendt, Joachim E. *The Jazz Book*. London: Granada, 1983.

Bianchi, Curt. *Elegant People: A History of the Band Weather Report*. Guilford: Backbeat Books, 2021.

Breithaupt, Don. *Aja*. New York: Continuum, 2007.

Bruford, Bill. *The Autobiography*. London: Jawbone Press, 2009.

Carner, Gary. *The Miles Davis Companion*. London: Omnibus Press, 2001.

Carr, Ian. *Keith Jarrett: The Man and His Music*. London: Da Capo Press, 1991.

Carr, Ian. *Miles Davis: The Definitive Biography*. London: Harper Collins, 1999.

Carr, Ian. *Music Outside*. London: Northway Publications, 2000.

Carver, Reginald, and Lenny Bernstein: *Jazz Profiles: The Spirit of the Nineties*. New York: Billboard, 1998.

Cole, George. *The Last Miles, The Music of Miles Davis 1980–1991*. London: Equinox Publishing, 2005.

Cook, Richard, and Brian Morton. *The Penguin Guide to Jazz On CD*. London: Penguin, 2002.

Coryell, Julia, and Laura Friedman. *Jazz-Rock Fusion: The People, The Music*. Milwaukee: Hal Leonard, 2000.

Coryell, Larry. *Improvising: My Life in Music*. New York: Hal Leonard, 2007.

Dannen, Fredric. *Hit Men: Power Brokers and Fast Money Inside the Music Business*. London: Helter Skelter Publishing, 2003.

Davis, Miles, and Quincy Troupe. *The Autobiography*. London: Picador, 1990.

DeCurtis, Anthony. *In Other Words: Artists Talk About Their Life and Work*. Milwaukee: Hal Leonard, 2005.

Doggett, Peter. *You Never Give Me Your Money: The Battle for the Soul of The Beatles*. London: Vintage Books, 2010.

Feather, Leonard, and Ira Gitler. *Encyclopaedia of Jazz in the Seventies*. London: Quartet Books, 1976.

Gambaccini, Paul, with Tim Rice, Jonathan Rice. *British Hit Albums*. London: Guinness Publishing, 1990.

Giddins, Gary. *Weather Bird: Jazz at the Dawn of Its Second Century*. Oxford: Oxford University Press, 2006.

Glasser, Brian. *In a Silent Way, A Portrait of Joe Zawinul*. London: Sanctuary Publishing, 2001.

Harper, Colin. *Bathed In Lightning: John McLaughlin, the 60s and the Emerald Beyond*. London: Jawbone Press, 2014.

Heckstall-Smith, Dick. *The Safest Place in the World*. London: Quartet Books, 1984.

Hepworth, David. *A Fabulous Creation: How the LP Saved Our Lives*. London: Bantam Press, 2019.

Hultin, Randi. *Born Under the Sign of Jazz*. London: Sanctuary Publishing, 2003.

Jarrett, Michael. *Pressed for All Time: Producing the Great Jazz Albums*. University Of North Carolina Press, 2016.

Kahn, Ashley. *A Love Supreme: The Creation of John Coltrane's Classic Album*. London: Granta, 2002.

Kahn, Ashley. *Kind of Blue: The Making of the Miles Davis Masterpiece*. London: Granta, 2001.

Kastin, David. *Nica's Dream: The Life and Legend of the Jazz Baroness*. New York: W.W. Norton, 2011.

Kolosky, Walter. *Follow Your Dreams: John McLaughlin song by song*. Kindle, 2010.

Kolosky, Walter. *Power, Passion and Beauty: The Story of the Legendary Mahavishnu Orchestra*. Kindle, 2013.

Larkin, Philip. *All What Jazz*. London: Faber & Faber, 1985.

Mandel, Howard. *Future Jazz*. Oxford: Oxford University Press, 1999.

Massey, Howard. *Behind the Glass, Top Record Producers Tell How They Craft the Hits*. San Francisco: Backbeat Books, 2000.

Mercer, Michelle. *Footprints: The Life and Work of Wayne Shorter*. London: Penguin, 2007.

Menn, Don: *Guitar Player Presents Secrets from the Masters*. San Francisco: GPI, 1992.

Milkowski, Bill. *The Extraordinary and Tragic Life of Jaco Pastorius*. San Francisco: Miller Freeman Books, 1995.

Milkowski, Bill. *Ode to a Tenor Titan: The Life and Times and Music of Michael Brecker*. New York: Backbeat Books, 2021.

Milkowski, Bill. *Rockers, Jazzbos and Visionaries*. New York: Billboard Books, 1998.

Mongan, Norman. *The History of the Guitar in Jazz*. New York: Oak Publications, 1983.

Murphy, Chris. *Miles to Go*. London: Da Capo Press, 2002.

Needs, Kris. *George Clinton and the Cosmic Odyssey of the P-Funk Empire*. London: Omnibus Press, 2014.

Pegg, Nicholas. *The Complete David Bowie*. London: Reynolds & Hearn Ltd, 2009.

Perry, John. *Electric Ladyland*. New York: Continuum, 2004.

Pinter, Harold. *Various Voices: Poetry, Prose, Politics, 1948–98*. London: Faber & Faber, 1998.

Power, Martin. *Hot Wired Guitar: The Life of Jeff Beck*. London: Omnibus Press, 2012.

Robustelli, Anthony. *Steely Dan FAQ*. New York: Backbeat, 2017.

Sandford, Christopher. *Sting: Demolition Man*. London: Warner Books, 1998.

Scott, Ken, with Bobby Owsinski. *Abbey Road to Ziggy Stardust*. New York: Alfred Publishing, 2012.

Stein, Seymour. *Siren Song: My Life in Music*. London: St Martin's Press, 2018.

Stump, Paul. *Go Ahead John: The Music of John McLaughlin*. London: SAF Publishing, 2000.

Szwed, John. *So What: The Life of Miles Davis*. London: Arrow, 2003.

Taylor, Arthur. *Notes and Tones*. London: Da Capo Press, 1993.

Terkel, Studs. *And They All Sang*. London: Granta, 2006.

Thomas, J. C. *Chasin' the Trane: The Music and Mystique of John Coltrane*. London: Da Capo Press, 1976.

Tingen, Paul. *Miles Beyond: The Electric Explorations of Miles Davis 1967–1991*. New York: Billboard Books, 2001.

Toshio Sudo, Philip. *Zen Guitar*. New York: Simon & Schuster, 1998.

Watson, Ben. *The Complete Guide to the Music of Frank Zappa*. London: Omnibus Press, 1998.

Watson, Philip. *Bill Frisell: Beautiful Dreamer*. London: Faber & Faber, 2022.

Weinberg, Max. *The Big Beat*. New York: Watson-Guptill Publications, 1993.

Williams, Richard. *Long Distance Call: Writings on Music*. London: Aurum, 2000.

Zappa, Frank, with Peter Ochogrossio. *The Real Frank Zappa Book*. London: Pan Books, 1989.

## SELECTED ONLINE INTERVIEW REFERENCES (FEATURING JOHN AS THE SUBJECT UNLESS OTHERWISE STATED)

Jaco Pastorius, "Bass Legend," interview by Clive Williamson, *Sound Archives*, October 1978. http://www.soundarchives.co.uk/jaco-pastorius-interview/.

"Sounds: Donnie interviewing John McLaughlin and Paco De Lucia," interview by Donnie Sutherland, *Countdown*, 1982, https://www.youtube.com/watch?v=EL18xRpwUoI.

*The Tonight Show Starring Johnny Carson*, interview by Johnny Carson, November 1985, https://www.youtube.com/watch?v=CCO6ZPtxa9k.

"McLaughlin Steps into a New Arena," interview by Marc Shulgold, *Los Angeles Times*, November 27, 1985, https://www.latimes.com/archives/la-xpm-1985-11-27-ca-4698-story.html.

"From the Symphonic Stage to the Frontiers of Technology," interview by Jim Ferguson, *Guitar Player*, September 1985, https://www.joness.com/gr300/John_McLaughlin_Guitar_Player_September_1985_Roland_G-303_NED_Synclavier.htm.

"John McLaughlin, Remembering Shakti," interview by Anil Prasad, Innerviews, 1999, https://www.innerviews.org/inner/john-mclaughlin.html.

"Zakir Hussain, In The Moment," interview by Anil Prasad, *Innerviews*, 1999, https://www.innerviews.org/inner/zakir-hussain.html.

*The Miles Davis Story*, interview by Ian Carr, 2000, https://www.youtube.com/watch?v=YOK1Ox9hbsM.

"Kai Eckhardt, Unknown Zones," interview by Anil Prasad, *Innerviews*, 2001, https://www.innerviews.org/inner/eckhardt.html.

"Jeff Berlin, Vision Quest," interview by Anil Prasad, *Innerviews*, 2002, https://www.innerviews.org/inner/berlin.html.

"John McLaughlin Interview," interview by Bill Milkowski, *Abstract Logix*, April 16, 2004, https://www.abstractlogix.com/john-mclaughlin-interview/.

"Jonas Hellborg Interview," interview by Bill Milkowski, *Abstract Logix*, 2005, https://www.abstractlogix.com/jonas-hellborg-interview/.

"On The Road," interview by John Kelman, *All About Jazz*, September 3, 2007, https://www.allaboutjazz.com/john-mclaughlin-on-the-road-part-1-the-interview-john-mclaughlin-by-john-kelman.

"Mark Mondesir Interview," *Abstract Logix*, 2007, https://www.abstractlogix.com/drummer-mark-mondesir-interview/.

"Defying Gravity," interview by Anil Prasad, Innerviews, 2008, https://www.innerviews.org/inner/mclaughlin2.html.

"Bill Milkowski Talks About Floating Point," interview by Bill Milkowski, April 3, 2008, https://www.johnmclaughlin.com/2008/04/bill-milkowski-talks-about-floating-point/.

John Surman, "Interview With Bill Shoemaker," johnsurman.com, July 2009, https://johnsurman.com/interview-with-bill-shoemaker/.

Frederica Randrianome, "Interview with Mark Mondesir," *Riviera Jazz Club*, April 2010, https://www.youtube.com/watch?v=mmnYnnBEmzQ.

"Ralphe Armstrong Interview," interview by Jon Liebman, *For Bass Players Only*, August 9, 2010, https://forbassplayersonly.com/interview-ralphe-armstrong/.

Dominique Di Piazza, "For Bass Players Only," interview by Jon Liebman, June 28, 2010, https://forbassplayersonly.com/interview-dominique-dipiazza/.

"One on One," interview by Riz Khan, *Al Jazeera English*, December 25, 2010, https://www.youtube.com/watch?v=VZTKYhxrLis.

"Interview With Kai Eckhardt," interview by Jon Liebman, *For Bass Players Only*, April 25, 2011, https://forbassplayersonly.com/interview-kai-eckhardt/.

"Interview with John McLaughlin (conclusion)," interview by Larry Appelbaum, *Let's Cool One (Musings About Music)*, April 12, 2013, https://larryappelbaum.wordpress.com/2013/04/12/interview-with-john-mclaughlin-conclusion/.

"The Rolling Stone Interview," interview by Narendra Kusnur, *Rolling Stone India*, April 2, 2014, https://rollingstoneindia.com/rolling-stone-interview-john-mclaughlin/.

"It's As Good As It Gets!" interview by Sid Smith, *PROG*, November 13, 2015, https://www.loudersound.com/features/it-s-as-good-as-it-gets-john-mclaughlin-celebrates-black-light.

"John McLaughlin Chooses His Favourite Prog Artist . . . ." interview by Jerry Ewing, *PROG*, December 16, 2015, https://www.loudersound.com/features/john-mclaughlin-chooses-his-favourite-prog-artist.

Kai Eckhardt, "Playing with John McLaughlin," interview by Scott Devine, *Scott's Bass Lessons*, December 5, 2016, https://www.youtube.com/watch?v=qRfUmnJMYrM.

"Jan Hammer Talks Mahavishnu, Emerson, Hendrix, Jaco...and Getting the JuJu Happening!" interview by Paul Kent and Dave Hamilton, *Gig Gab Podcast*, August 9, 2021, https://www.youtube.com/watch?v=5zFH0Rk4WFI.

Dennis Chambers, "Sounding Off with Rick Beato," interview by Rick Beato, April 20, 2017, https://www.youtube.com/watch?v=L7qf5wKOv90.

Narada Michael Walden, "Jimi Hendrix, Santana, John McLaughlin, Aretha and more!" July 1, 2019, https://www.youtube.com/watch?v=7qCSFBCl-D0.

Dennis MacKay, "Legendary Producer Talks Rock History!" interview by Ray Shasho, *Interviewing the Legends*, January 31, 2020, https://www.youtube.com/watch?v=zymOvugWrwM.

Tommy Campbell, "In Conversation with Tommy Campbell—Who's That Drummer?" interview by Aubrey Dayle, *Aubrey Drum Lessons*, August 6, 2020, https://www.youtube.com/watch?v=mDH_wfu4t3c.

Stu Goldberg, "The ProgCast with Gregg Bendian," interview by Gregg Bendian, January 15, 2021, https://www.youtube.com/watch?v=9zZTW7DRQao.

"John McLaughlin Struggled on Violin, but When He First Played Guitar? 'Skyrockets Went Off'," interview by Marc Myers, *Wall Street Journal*, August 10, 2021, https://www.wsj.com/articles/john-mclaughlin-guitarist-11628611105.

"Long Distance: Paul Calls John McLaughlin," interview by Paul Reed Smith, PRS Guitars, August 20, 2021, https://www.youtube.com/watch?v=9EN_2mLpIXk.

"I tell my hands how beautiful they are. Now I have no pain at all," interview by Cormac Larkin, *Irish Times*, April 23, 2022, https://www.irishtimes.com/culture/music/john-mclaughlin-i-tell-my-hands-how-beautiful-they-are-now-i-have-no-pain-at-all-1.4857319.

Narada Michael Walden, "NMW ALL IN Podcast Episode 009—Interview with Mahavishnu John McLaughlin," February 11, 2022, https://www.youtube.com/watch?v=p55eCOjWmX4.

Narada Michael Walden, "NMW ALL IN Podcast Episode 010—Interview with Carlos Santana," February 25, 2022, https://www.youtube.com/watch?v=DMqjZ971FOk.

"Breakfast with Vinnie," interview by Vinnie Colaiuta, *Breakfast With Vinnie*, June 2021, https://open.spotify.com/episode/6Cdc9xtauhpgtpV5z4dUmU?si=7c73f8a85ac44e18.

"Rockonteurs with Nitin Sawhney," interview by Gary Kemp and Guy Pratt, *Rockonteurs*, July 2022, https://open.spotify.com/episode/0UmIFNJrvJ2rZmLK5PhZYj?si=fd39d541a59a4.

"Rockonteurs with Ken Scott," interview by Gary Kemp and Guy Pratt, *Rockonteurs*, June 2022, https://open.spotify.com/episode/1KvVAfdscyZaV3Jbwxp033?si=2e6127aa39a54773.

"Rockonteurs with Bill Bruford," interview by Gary Kemp and Guy Pratt, *Rockonteurs*, May 2022, https://open.spotify.com/episode/32qUnLtTILHvJtEefSXPbG?si=b5b371b8e6bd423d.

"The Monterey Pop Festival: 40 Years Ago," https://www.youtube.com/watch?v=OnV34yEby44.

"Shakti/John McLaughlin documentary (1977)," https://www.youtube.com/watch?v=usWGn0JUCEM.

"1978—John McLaughlin—South Bank Show (w. L Shankar)," https://www.youtube.com/watch?v=SUYQzYDcVJA.

*Jazz Britannia* Episode 2, "Strange Brew," https://www.youtube.com/watch?v=vGrQz3mpRRw.

*Jazz Britannia* Episode 3, "The Rebirth Of Cool," https://www.youtube.com/watch?v=Uz2eFjvvel8.

# SELECT PRINT INTERVIEW REFERENCES (FEATURING JOHN AS THE SUBJECT UNLESS OTHERWISE STATED)

"Alan Skidmore," interview by Daniel Spicer, *The Wire*, August 2022.

Robert Fripp, interview by David Cavanagh, *Uncut*, December 2013.

"The Inner Flame," interview by Richard Williams, *Melody Maker*, January 15, 1972.

"'A Different View: John McLaughlin,' interview by Michael Parillo," *Modern Drummer*, July 2008.

"The Cultural Improvisation of John McLaughlin," interview by Bill Stephen, *International Musician and Recording World*, March 1979.

"Billy Cobham: The Pulse Behind the Horace Silver 5," interview by Chris Welch, *Melody Maker*, December 14, 1968.

"Coffee and Chocolate for Two Guitars," interview by Robert Fripp, *Musician*, July 1982.

"Echoes From Then," interview by Bill Milkowski, *Down Beat*, January 2013.

"John McLaughlin Past, Present & Future," interview by Bill Milkowski, *JazzTimes*, August 1992.

"Bright Moments: John McLaughlin," interview by Evan Haga, *JazzTimes*, July/August 2016.

"Jonas Hellborg: More Than an Elegant Punk," interview by Bill Milkowski, *Bass Player*, June 1993.

"Johnny McLaughlin: Acoustic Guitarist," interview by Lee Jeske, *Down Beat*, April 1982.

"An Interview with Guitarist John McLaughlin," interview by Jonathan Penzer, *Hit Parader*, May 1971.

Billy Cobham, "On the Attack," interview by Bill Beuttler, *Down Beat*, April 1987.

"Trilok Gurtu: Funk from the East," interview by Larry Birnbaum, *Down Beat*, January 1, 1994.

Billy Cobham, "Have Drums, Will Travel," interview by Bill Milkowski, *Down Beat*, April 1984.

"My Life and Guitar: Mahavishnu John McLaughlin," interview by Steve Rosen, *Guitar Player*, February 1975.

"Electric Miles: A Conversation," *JazzTimes*, April 2019.

"Dennis Chambers: Leading the Way," interview by Robin Tolleson, *Modern Drummer*, September 1994.

"Yngwie Malmsteen Meets John McLaughlin," interview by Matt Resnicoff, *Musician*, September 1990.

"John McLaughlin: A Continual Process of Discovery," interview by James Rotondi, *Guitar Player*, July 1992.

"After Mahavishnu and Shakti, A Return to Electric Guitar," interview by Don Menn and Chip Stern, *Guitar Player*, August 1978.

"Evolution of a Master," interview by Chuck Berg, *Down Beat*, June 15, 1978.

"John McLaughlin," by Matt Resnicoff, *Guitar Player*, May 1994.

"To the Power of Zen," interview by Stuart Nicholson, *Jazzwise*, July 2006.

Billy Cobham, "The Sonic Art of Thwap," interview by Nick Coleman, *The Wire*, July 1986.

Billy Cobham, Blowin' in the Crosswinds," interview by Jeff Tamarkin, *JazzTimes*, October 22, 2019.

Billy Cobham, "Covering the Spectrum," interview by Brent Keefe, *Drummer*, May 2014.

Billy Cobham, interview by Mike Bourne, *Down Beat*, October 12, 1972.

"Turning Point: Blue Moods," interview by Brian Glasser, *Jazzwise*, December 2018/January 2019.

"Mahavishnu John McLaughlin," interview by Vic Trigger, *Guitar Player*, December 19, 1972.

"John McLaughlin," interview by Mark Gilbert, *Jazz Journal*, November 1996.

Jan Hammer, "A Different View," *Modern Drummer*, August 1992.

"Rick Laird: An Innermost Vision," interview by James P. Schaffer, *Down Beat*, April 26, 1973.

Mark King, "Level Crossing," interview by Gibson Keddie, *Guitarist*, September 1991.

"Who Said Spiritual Music Should Be Quiet?" interview by Jim Farber, *JazzTimes*, July/August 2021.

"The Journey Continues," interview by Stuart Nicholson, *Jazzwise*, March 2020.

Teo Macero, "Jack Johnson Revisited," interview by Bill Milkowski, *Jazziz*, February 2004.

"Lenny White Returns to Forever," interview by T. Bruce Wittet, *Modern Drummer*, July 2008.

Miles Davis, "Miles Special," interviews by Gene Kalbacher, *Miles Special*, May 1985.

"Love Devotion and Surrender—McLaughlin Tosses Santana to the Lord," interview by Penelope Ross, *Circus*, August 1973.

"Mahavishnu's Apocalypse," interview by Jim Schaffer, *Down Beat*, June 6, 1974.

"John McLaughlin & Rex Bogue, 'Creating the Double Rainbow," interview by Leonard Ferris, *Guitar Player*, May 1974.

Allan Holdsworth, "A Different View," interview by Robyn Flans, *Modern Drummer*, August 1996.

"Spirit Road—John McLaughlin & Jimmy Herring," interview by Mac Randall, *JazzTimes*, September 2017.

"John McLaughlin Makes MiGic," interview by Emile Menasche, *JazzTimes*, January/February 2020.

"John McLaughlin," interview by Chris Charlesworth, *Melody Maker*, May 4, 1974.

"Jeff Beck's Chop Shop," interview by Scott Isler, *Musician*, September 1989.

"Smoke on the Water," interview by Stuart Nicholson, *Jazzwise*, June 2022.

"Profile: L. Shankar," interview by Lee Underwood, *Down Beat*, November 2, 1978.

"Translating the Language of the Spirit," interview by Andy Aledort, *Guitar*, December 1987.

Trilok Gurtu: The Language of Rhythm," interview by Rick Mattingly, *Modern Drummer*, November 1992.

"The Cultural Improvisation of John McLaughlin," interview by Bill Stephen, *International Musician and Recording World*, March 1979.

"Tour 1980: A Victory for the Acoustic Guitar: John McLaughlin, Al Di Meola, Paco de Lucía Super Trio," interview by Tom Wheeler, *Guitar Player*, March 1981.

"Caught: Acoustic Guitar Masters—New York City," interview by Bill Milkowski, *Down Beat*, April 1981.

"Caught: Mahavishnu/Weather Update at the Ritz," interview by Bill Milkowski, *Down Beat*, December 1986.

"Devout Madness," interview by Howard Mandel, *Down Beat*, June 1996.

"John McLaughlin's Discipline: Ultimate Devotion to the Instrument," interview by Peter Keepnews, *Guitar World*, July 1981.

"Muso in the Promised Land," interview by Paul Stump, *The Wire*, March 1996.

"Still Fretting After All These Years," interview by Richard Cook, *The Wire*, July 1988.

"Dennis Chambers: The Return of Rhythm," interview by Michael J. West, *JazzTimes*, November 2015.

"Waltz for Bill Evans," interview by John Diliberto, *Down Beat*, December 1993.

"John McLaughlin: A Promise Delivered," interview by Jon Chappell, *Guitar*, May 1996.

"Guitar's Triumvirate Returns: The Trio," interview by Jon Chappell, *Guitar*, February 1997.

"Paco de Lucia, Al Di Meola and John McLaughlin: The Guitar Trio Returns," interview by Matt Resnicoff, *Guitar Player*, February 1997.

# ACKNOWLEDGMENTS

Guitarist and composer Allan Holdsworth once described his experience of musical development as a bit like climbing a hill, getting down the other side, and then finding an even bigger hill . . . and so on. At the risk of an appearance in Pseuds Corner, writing this book has been a similar experience, enormously rewarding if somewhat hampered by some very strange personal/political times during the COVID era and its aftermath. So thanks to the following guides who aided me in my climb:

George Cole went way beyond the call of duty to offer whatever was needed. During the rotten era of 2020–2022, it was good to make a new friend. Thank you, George, and thanks for writing *The Last Miles* too;

To the editors of/contributors to music magazines—past and present—that were invaluable during the writing of this book and have given enormous pleasure since my teenage years and, in some cases, still do: *Musician*, *Melody Maker*, *NME*, *Q*, *Modern Drummer*, *Guitar World*, *Guitarist*, *Guitar Player*, *Bassist*, *Rhythm*, *The Wire*, *JazzTimes*, *Down Beat*

Steve Harnell at *Classic Pop*;

My valued movingtheriver.com readers Richard Seabrook, Oh Regine, Heavy Metal Overload, Ashley Groombridge, Winston Murphy, Paul Kelly, Simon Hopkins, David Gray, Alvaro Almeida, 1537, Nikola, Vinyl Connection, David Goodall, and Jose Luis Carvalho for feedback and support;

Iain Murray at Propernote for invaluable resources and advice;

Peter Kramer at UEA for advice and encouragement;

William Ellis for friendship, support, and great photos;

Don Breithaupt, Michelle Mercer, Paul Tingen, Bill Milkowski, Jason Miles, and Curt Bianchi for generosity, contacts, and essential books (see Bibliography);

Steve Khan for advice, contacts, friendship, and muso gossip;

Scott Henderson for musical inspiration and the Blindfold Tests;

Adam Freeman at Universal Music for friendship and number-crunching;

My tennis partner Mike Dibb for advice, encouragement, and *The Miles Davis Story;*

Marisa Sheehan for friendship and her knowledge of Dante and Lorca;

John McLaughlin, of course, for constant musical inspiration and for answering my questions, and Ina McLaughlin for advice;

Paul Stump, Walter Kolosky, and Colin Harper for their invaluable work on John's life and music (see Bibliography);

Danny Gottlieb, Dennis Chambers, and Stu Goldberg for answering my questions with such grace and in such detail, and for kindly donating photographs;

Peter Erskine for his terrific photos and generosity;

Billy Cobham;

Mark King;

Gary Husband;

James Canton;

Jan-Mikael Erakere;

Cem Kurosman at Blue Note;

Jamie Krents and Ken Druker at Verve Records;

Michael Tan and Meaghan Menzel for coaxing this book out of me with patience and understanding;

RIP Wayne Shorter, Jeff Beck, and Allan Holdsworth, huge musical inspirations/teenage heroes who played a big part in the writing of this book;

My uncle Jim, who always passed on his Mahavishnu and McLaughlin vinyl to me;

Much-missed Dad, who first played me *Electric Dreams*, *Star People*, and *Heavy Weather*, and took me to John's 1984 gig at the Hammersmith Odeon.

This book is dedicated to my mother Viviane for her constant support and for insisting that I do that touch-typing course.

# INDEX

# ABOUT THE AUTHOR

**Matt Phillips** is the founder of the websites movingtheriver.com and sounds ofsurprise.com and has contributed to various magazines, including *Jazzwise*, *Classic Pop*, and *Record Collector*. He won the inaugural Write Stuff award for new jazz writing in 2003 and has been Universal Music's jazz catalog manager and Jazz FM's web editor. Matt wrote the liner notes for the Emmy award-winning *Miles Davis: Birth of the Cool* DVD/Blu-ray and was a music advisor on the 2004 documentary *Keith Jarrett: The Art Of Improvisation*. As a multi-instrumentalist, he has performed extensively in London and Europe and records under the name mattjoplin. Matt's first book, *Level 42: Every Album, Every Song*, was a number-one Amazon Music bestseller. He lives in London.